A Cumberer of the Ground

No. 752   *Constance Smith*   60 Cents

Entered at the Post-Office at New York, as Second-class Mail Matter.   Issued Monthly.   Subscription Price per Year, 12 Nos., $7.50.

A CUMBERER OF THE GROUND

𝔄 Novel

BY

CONSTANCE SMITH

NEW YORK

HARPER & BROTHERS PUBLISHERS

August, 1894

HARPER'S FRANKLIN SQUARE LIBRARY.—LATEST ISSUE

PUBLISHED BY HARPER & BROTHERS, NEW YORK.

☞ HARPER & BROTHERS will send any of the above works by mail, postage prepaid, to any part of the United States, Canada, or Mexico, on receipt of the price.

A CUMBERER OF THE GROUND

A Novel

BY

CONSTANCE SMITH

*" There are some whose destiny it is to finish nothing ; to
leave the feast on the table, and all the edges of life ragged"*

NEW YORK
HARPER & BROTHERS PUBLISHERS
1894

F

CONTENTS

A CUMBERER OF THE GROUND

A PROLOGUE

> "Roses in the flush of youth,
> And laurel for the perfect prime;
> But pluck an ivy branch for me,
> Grown old before my time."

> "Much ado there was, God wot—
> He wold love, and she wold not."

"THAT fellow on the chestnut cob—over there by the railings
—is nodding to you, Charlie."

"Which fellow? Where?" Mr. Charles Crosse looked round
him a trifle wildly, adjusting his eyeglass. (He was painfully
short-sighted, and the crowd in the Row this fine June morning
was unusually thick.) "I really don't—oh, yes,·I see—young
Travers!" Here the rider of the chestnut received an answering
nod, civil, if not cordial, in acknowledgment of his reported
salutation; and, having received it, rode on.

Lord Osborne turned in his saddle and honored the vanishing
figure with a pretty long stare through *his* eyeglass—he invariably
wore and used one, not, indeed, as an aid to defective vision, but
because he considered a glass a tasteful adjunct to a gentleman's
personal appearance—remarking laconically, on the completion of
his survey, "Good-looking chap, eh?"

"What! Travers? The man who nodded to me just now?
H'm! I hardly know. Swarthy as a Spaniard, and rather reedy,
don't you think?" responded Mr. Crosse, who boasted a small
yellow mustache and light blue eyes, while his figure inclined to
rotundity.

"Well, he might be a bit broader in the chest with advantage,
certainly. Probably he'll fill out, though. He looks as if he had
only just done growing. Who is he? Where does he come
from?"

"Oh, he's nobody in particular. A parson's son, I believe.
Father has a living in Hillshire or Loamshire, I really forget

which. This youth was for a few months in my brother's regiment, the 50th Lancers. That's how I come to know something of him."

" I shouldn't have taken him for a soldier."

" Well, he isn't one, now. His military career was singularly brief. He ran up debts at such a rate that he had to resign his commission at the end of two or three years. Of course, with his private means, or want of them, it was utter folly his attempting to live the life of any cavalry regiment, much less of a regiment like the 50th."

" What is he doing now ? "

" For the moment, nothing, I believe. But I heard something the other day from Tom about his being on the point of leaving England—for one of the colonies, I presume, the usual refuge of the destitute."

" Poor beggar ! " commented Lord Osborne good-naturedly ; " I'm sorry for him. Doesn't strike one that he'd enjoy roughing it. Now the man who was riding with him looks much better fitted for that kind of existence. Do you know who he is ? I've begun to see him about lately."

" You'd be likely to. He came into a biggish property some-where in Yorkshire a little while ago, and people are beginning to take him up. His name's Lyon. I believe he's a good sort of fellow in his way, but a trifle heavy. No enterprise in him, I'm told ; doesn't know how to spend his money now he's got it."

" Lyon ? Never heard of any Lyons in Yorkshire," Lord Osborne remarked doubtfully.

" I dare say not. This man's inheritance came to him from some very distant relatives on the mother's side—I forget their name for the moment. I hear Lyon himself was abjectly poor to begin with. People tell a story of his having gone out to Australia as a lad, a mere penniless emigrant; and certainly he was recalled from Queensland to take up his estates. He looks rather like that kind of thing, you know."

" He does. In contrast to his young friend, who looks emi-nently *un*like that kind of thing," Lord Osborne responded. " But the two are pretty strongly contrasted altogether, I should say. There's clearly stuff in the one which one would be a fool to dream of finding in the other."

" You take a man's measure hastily," Crosse observed, with a smile that faintly suggested a sneer behind it. " Instantaneous photography this, with a vengeance ! "

"Random sketching, rather, I'm afraid," Osborne returned, with an embarrassed laugh. Making no pretension to cleverness himself, he was always easily embarrassed by Crosse, whose pretensions on that point were lofty, and pretty generally acknowledged sound. "Nevertheless, do you know, I can't help putting faith in those first hasty impressions. I've seen so much reason to believe in them, at one time and another."

Whether all Lord Osborne's impressions in the present case were correct or no, he was undoubtedly right in one of them; the two men he had been discussing—and who, all unconscious of the discussion to which their momentary appearance had given rise, were now riding leisurely in the direction of Hyde Park Corner—certainly presented the most marked possible contrast to one another, as far as their outward seeming was concerned. Travers, the younger of the two by six or seven years, was brilliantly, almost aggressively, handsome. With his tall, slender figure (a little over-slender maybe, for its height, but otherwise admirably proportioned), his finely modelled head well set on, his clear-cut features and rich olive complexion (that complexion which Lord Osborne's captious friend had libellously dubbed swarthy), the young man was a personage whom, even in the midst of a crowd, it would have been impossible to overlook. His good looks took the most careless eye by storm at once, asserting themselves in what some people—Crosse to wit—felt to be too startling, too knock-me-down a fashion. Yet, as there was nothing singular in Mr. Travers' appearance, so there was no hint of insolence or swagger in his bearing; and no more of self-consciousness than seemed natural, and even graceful, in a young fellow of five-and-twenty, fairly well born and bred, and so exceedingly pleasing to the view. Indeed, goodly specimen of manhood though Travers was, it is doubtful whether in the case of most persons an idea of beauty would have been the principal idea produced by a first sight of him; whether such new acquaintances would not rather, and chiefly, have carried away an impression of young vigor, of sanguine spirits, of eagerness and freshness, almost boyish in their rare and delightful intensity. This charming suggestion of youthfulness, these hints of exuberant vitality, made Travers, at the age of five-and-twenty, seem considerably younger than he was, even to the point of causing Lord Osborne to set him down as a lad whose growing days were barely over. His laugh was still the laugh of a schoolboy. He was at his handsomest when he laughed,

tossing back the dark head that would have been curly but for
remorseless cropping, and showing a gleam of white teeth under
his heavy dragoon's mustache (the only memorial left him of his
short military service), and the lights and shadows chased each
other across his face as constantly and swiftly as one may see them
fly over the face of a seven-year-old child.

His companion might have been chosen to play the part of foil
to this piece of glowing youth. Mr. Lyon was really little more
than thirty ; but he looked as much older as Travers looked
younger than his actual age. He was, indeed, a singularly
*un*youthful-looking young man; there was already much of the
heaviness, the rigidity, the unresponsive calm one is apt to asso-
ciate with middle life about him. His figure, while excellently
built from an athletic point of view, and giving an impression of
immense muscular strength, was too massive for grace ; and his
unusually deep chest and broad shoulders detracted from a height
which in a slighter man would have been accounted stately, making it, in his case, scarcely even satisfying to the eye. His face
was massive like his figure, square-browed and square-jawed, with
strongly marked features emphasized by scrupulously close shav-
ing ; the lips somewhat thin, with a faint tendency to curl in the
upper one (a tendency which must have been the result of an
indulged habit rather than of natural formation, since it was an
upper lip having no pretensions to classical shortness) ; the complexion olive, but a *pale* olive—a variety of the hue possessing
none of the dusky warmth of Travers' skin. It was a face full of
sense and power, and therefore not wholly without attractive
qualities, but a plain face nevertheless, and one that might have
been accounted unpleasantly hard but for the lucky circumstance
that Mr. Lyon's maternal grandmother, having been the happy
possessor of the most beautiful dark eyelashes in England (some
affirm in Europe), had had the kindness to bequeath them, scarce
shortened by the thousandth part of an inch, to her grandson.
Lying on weather-beaten masculine cheeks, those long curling
lashes looked, indeed, almost ludicrously out of place; still, their
good effect in softening the general expression of a countenance
otherwise somewhat grim was undeniable ; while in the eyes of
certain persons, interested in sounding the depths of Mr. Lyon's
character, they possessed, besides, a distinct symbolic value. One
or two benevolent physiognomists, who should have known better,
had argued from them to unknown soft spots in Lyon's disposi-

tion ; and women forgave him his most cynical speeches when, as not infrequently happened, he chanced to deliver himself of them with downcast eyes. He had a bad habit of keeping his eyelids lowered when talking ; not, certainly, with any view to the advantageous display of his grandmother's legacy, but simply, as it seemed, because more often than not he felt no great interest in his interlocutor. Neither, when he was not talking, did his surroundings—whatever they might be—appear to engage his attention much. His ordinary air was that of a man half preoccupied, faintly bored, slightly but unmistakably tired—an air that sat rather singularly on so young a man, who appeared, moreover, to be in such superexcellent physical condition.

Thus, he scarcely glanced once to right or left of him as he rode by Travers' side through the crowded park ; and suffered his companion, a fluent and eager talker, to monopolize the conversation entirely, barely encouraging him, now and then, by a slight nod or murmured monosyllable, to proceed in his verbal outpouring. Perhaps he did not attend very closely to the matter of this outpouring ; for it was with a touch of compunction that, at Hyde Park Corner, he responded to Travers' rather hesitating "Good-morning, then. Shall I see you again before I sail, I wonder?" —with an abrupt but friendly,

"Oh, we haven't had half a chat as yet ! Come on and lunch with me, if you've nothing better to do."

"I've nothing at all to do—certainly nothing better."

"All right, then. This way ; I've pitched my tent in Half-Moon Street. Things alter quickly in a new country like Queensland," continued Mr. Lyon, as the two men turned their horses' heads Piccadilly-ward. "Still, in a couple of years the change can hardly be great ; and I may be able to put you up to a thing or two. Then there are some people in Brisbane I think you'd find it useful to know ; I could give you some letters to them."

"Thanks awfully. It's uncommonly good of you to trouble yourself."

"No trouble at all, my dear fellow. I've grown shamefully lazy of late, but I can still rise to the stupendous exertion of scrawling half a dozen lines on occasion." Lyon smiled as he spoke, showing just such a set of teeth, strong, square, and hardily white, as befitted a man of his physique.

"I sha'n't have much to do with Brisbane, I'm afraid," the younger man went on reflectively.

"And acquaintances several hundred miles away seem scarcely worth having, eh ? But in Queensland they don't think much of a few hundred miles. And when once you've put the breadth of the globe between yourself and every friend you ever had, I can assure you you'll find the value of a mere acquaintance rising enormously in your estimation ; even though he should be a dull fellow living a week's journey distant. You'd better take the letters."

"I will, thanks. I suppose the loneliness of one's life out there is about the worst part of the business ?" Travers added tentatively after a moment ; tentatively and almost timidly. It was easy to see that he felt himself bound to be on his best behavior with Lyon. The truth was, he could never quite forget that he had been Lyon's fag at Eton ; and, in addressing his former master, fell every now and then into the old mental attitude of the "lower boy" in the august presence of a "fellow in the sixth."

"Did you find it—trying yourself ?"

"Trying ?" repeated Lyon. "Well, since you ask me, I should say it was about the nicest slow torture invented of the devil for the benefit of civilized man. As an incentive to speedy going to the dogs, and staying there, I don't know its equal. I speak from experience. I had five years of the thing, in its undiluted form."

Lyon uttered these strong words in a perfectly level, passionless tone. His voice, a deep and fairly agreeable baritone, had one grave defect—that of monotony. It knew no change of key, and appeared incapable of anything like cadence. If it had ever possessed any tendency to vary under pressure of emotion, the tendency had been carefully, and successfully, suppressed.

"No need to argue from my experience to yours, though," he continued in response to Travers' muttered comment of "Cheerful lookout for me !" "The two cases are not on all-fours. You go out under totally different circumstances, with a fixed object in view, work ready and waiting for you, and you don't start alone."

"No, thank Heaven ! My father himself"— Travers spoke in a slightly injured tone, as of a man conceiving himself to have a legitimate grievance against his parent—"my father himself would hardly think it necessary to condemn me to absolutely solitary banishment, I suppose. That's rather too heavy a sentence, even for an eminently disappointing son. Besides, there could be but one result in such a case. One would have to take to drinking in self-defence. That's what most lonely exiles do, I fancy."

" A pretty large proportion of them."

" And you ? How did you——"

" Escape ? I'm sure I don't know. Not through any heroic efforts at self-restraint certainly, for I tried my best to console myself in the usual way for a time. But, somehow, the prescription didn't work in my case. It wasn't only that I had a headache the next morning ; I couldn't even manage to enjoy myself overnight. Perhaps I didn't take enough to begin with. How many do you go out together ? "

" Three. Two besides myself."

" All of you concerned in the making of the Waiapu Railway ? "

" Yes. I go as surveyor ; a man called Holcroft as engineer ; and the third fellow—his name's Milman—as superintendent. It's to be hoped he'll turn out decent. Holcroft I know already; *he's* a very good sort."

" You ought to do, then."

" Oh, I dare say I shall do—well enough. I suppose I ought to be thankful, as my father says, that I learned some surveying in the old Woolwich days ; and overjoyed that this ' advantageous opening in a young and rising colony ' should have offered itself at this particular juncture." Travers spoke with considerable bitterness.

" I'm afraid you're not as grateful to Providence, or your good luck, as you ought to be."

" Perhaps not. Why on earth did my father encourage me to go into the army, if he hadn't means to keep me there ? And, failing the army, why must I be sentenced without alternative to ' the colonies ' ? Delightful expression that ! such a convenient cloak for the brutal fact that you've sent your son across seas to pick up his living as a day-laborer ! There are other ways of earning one's bread."

" You've tried some of them, haven't you ? "

Travers turned sharply in his saddle, glancing suspiciously at his companion. But there lingered not the ghost of a smile on Lyon's lips. He was looking straight between his horse's ears, his face as grave as the tone in which he had just put his question.

" Oh, you mean that unlucky three months in my uncle's office ? " the younger man said sulkily, after a moment. " He is the most impossible old curmudgeon. No man who respected himself could work under him."

" I dare say. As it happens, I hadn't heard of your essay in that direction. No ; I was thinking of the private secretaryship to Lord Hatherop, and that foreign correspondence work you undertook for Messrs. What's-their-names, the publishers in Southampton Street."

"Who led one the life of a slave, and treated one no better than a beggarly copying-clerk to boot! No, that was out of the question. I'll be hanged if any gentleman could have put up with such an existence a twelvemonth!"

"Well, in Queensland at least you'll have independence, and fresh air. To say nothing of very fair sport, when you've time for that sort of thing."

"True. But one values sport less when it has to be purchased at the price of exile."

"You speak as a sentimental German speaketh, my dear boy. Whence this sudden blazing up of the patriotic flame?"

"Well, a man may be allowed to feel some regret on leaving his native country, for three years at least," retorted the ex-lancer. "After all's said, expatriation isn't a pleasant thing. One leaves one's home and friends behind one."

"With a view to doing better elsewhere. Travers, you must drop the patriot. It isn't in your line, believe me. You're far too modern and cosmopolitan."

"Oh, it's all very well to make a joke of the thing," returned the other, with a flash of boyish indignation. "Possibly it may not have cost you anything to banish yourself from England for a term of years." Lyon's bridle-hand closed a little more sharply on the reins it held, but he made no rejoinder. "It costs me— or will cost me, in all probability—everything I care for in the world."

There was absolute sincerity in the young man's tone; evidently he spoke out of a full heart. A faint shade of surprise crossed Lyon's features.

"I'm sorry I mistook you," he said, curtly apologetic. "Of course, when a man has special reasons for wishing to stay at home——"

"And I have them, if ever man had," Travers interposed. "Do we stop here?" seeing that Lyon drew rein at a Gothic portico on the left-hand side of the street into which they had turned a moment before. "I'll tell you all about it presently—if you have time, and would care to hear," he added hurriedly, as he dismounted, and the door was thrown open by Lyon's servant.

"Of course I care," returned Lyon, dismounting in his turn.

"We'll talk the matter out after luncheon, if you will. I've the whole afternoon free. Turn to your right; I'm on the ground floor. I found stairs a nuisance after a long course of log huts," he added in explanation, as he followed his guest into the first of the set of chambers.

Travers, not too deeply immersed in his own affairs to take stock of his friend's quarters, was conscious of a shock of disappointment as he surveyed these apartments. He had looked for something at once more imposing and more luxurious; above all, for something more clearly stamped with the impress of the tenant's individuality. The rooms he saw were large, lofty, suitably and sufficiently furnished; they contained everything necessary for comfort, but they were perfectly commonplace rooms; nothing magnificent, nothing exquisite was to be found in them, and they certainly conveyed not a single hint of artistic feeling or independent taste on the part of their owner and occupant.

In the luncheon served in Lyon's uninteresting dining-room Travers suffered a second disappointment. Here, too, he found nothing *recherché*. The meal was one calling for no remark whatever; and the same might be said of the wine served with it. Travers, lighting one of his friend's cigars when it was ended (and remarking incidentally that the brand was inferior to that he usually smoked himself), came to the conclusion that old Lyon was not getting very much out of his ten thousand a year.

He pursued these reflections for a minute or two in silence after the cigar was well alight, and he had seated himself in a big arm-chair near the open window to enjoy it. Lyon, with an unfilled meerschaum in one hand, and a tobacco-pouch in the other, leaned against the window-shutter, and surveyed his companion attentively through the wreaths of smoke that curled about his handsome head.

"Well," he observed at length, abandoning his contemplative attitude, and beginning to fill the bowl of his pipe with great care and deliberation, "how about the story you were to tell me—the true cause of your reluctance to go over-seas?"

Travers started slightly. He had been engaged, when Lyon spoke, in a curious speculation concerning that gentleman's disposal of his annual income; so the question took him by surprise.

"It's not much of a story," he said apologetically, recovering himself. "Simply this: that I've got a chance within my reach

—the best chance I shall ever have in life. And if I go to Australia next week, I—I chuck it up for good and all. Do you see ?"

"Not very clearly. What's the nature of the chance ?"

"I dare say you'll call it unsubstantial. There's a girl——" Travers stopped suddenly short.

"Oh !" rejoined Lyon somewhat dryly. "There's a girl, is there ? Well ?"

Travers' dark face flushed. "I don't understand what you mean by taking that tone," he remarked hotly.

"Well, you know," replied the other, without looking up from his occupation, "there generally *is* a girl, isn't there ?"

"Of course "—impatiently—"I know I've been a fool in my time. But all those affairs meant nothing. You never imagined they meant anything, did you ?"

"No ; to be honest, I can't say I ever did. History repeated itself so often in your case, you see."

"Yes, yes ; I acknowledge all that ! But this is a different matter. Those mock businesses are over forever with me ; I've lighted on the real thing now, it seems. And a terrible thing it is when you do light upon it," Travers added huskily.

This time, the meerschaum being now completely filled, Mr. Lyon did look up, and stared straight at his young friend for the space of thirty seconds or so. His direct gaze was surprisingly keen and penetrating. I say surprisingly so, because such a searching glance, coming from under those heavy eyelids and feminine eyelashes, had something of a startling and even disconcerting effect. But Lyon's eyes played your reasonable expectations false in every respect. Whereas, in accordance with all the laws of probability, they should have been black, dark brown, or sombre gray, their actual color was a brilliant deep blue, of that rare shade which nearly approaches violet, and is invariably found associated with singularly vivid whites. At your first discovery of their quality you felt taken aback, for they upset all your preconceived notions of the man to whom they belonged. The tolerably symmetrical theory of his character which you had hastily constructed at first sight of him, fell incontinently to pieces as soon as he looked you full in the face, leaving you in presence of a new and puzzling element in his composition which you found yourself helpless to name or classify. At the same time, your probable sense of irritation was not soothed by an irresistible conviction that the eyes in question were coolly reading in your ingenuous countenance all the most cherished secrets of your soul.

The object of Lyon's scrutiny on the present occasion did not, however, suffer this last inconvenience—for the simple reason that he sat looking out of the window, and hence remained unconscious of his friend's observation. His brief study completed, Lyon enquired:

"Has this been going on long?"

"A year or two. Don't ask me how it began; I don't know myself. I don't know how or when, why or wherefore. There's no particular reason for it that any other man would see—none that I can see myself, for the matter of that."

"Is she—excuse me if I go too far, Travers; remember, you have encouraged me to ask questions—is she a woman in your own rank of life, one who would be welcomed by your people?"

"Good Heavens, yes! My people would be only too delighted. She is rather better born than we are. She has a little money, too; not much, but still something."

"Young?"

"Twenty. She's not beautiful—nor accomplished. She has lived all her life in the country, and knows nothing of the world."

"And you've made up your mind that you're in love with her?"

"Made up my mind? Lyon, you'll bear me witness I never affected the melodramatic style. In sober, honest truth, I'd give my life for her to-morrow, if that would do her any good. I tell you, I *worship* her! What for, Heaven knows!—unless it's her goodness. She *is* good."

"All girls are good—or supposed to be."

"This one has goodness enough to furnish forth half a dozen ordinary girls. If ever there was a woman capable of making a man go straight, and keeping him straight, it's—it's the girl I speak of."

"If ever!" echoed Lyon. "Confiding traveller, do you, then, still keep your belief in female stars as the wayfarer's guides to straight paths? Because, as far as my limited experience goes, their work is quite of another order; consisting chiefly in acting as pointers to quicksands."

"You're a cynic."

"No; I'm simply six or seven years your senior. But I've

knocked about the world a bit, as you know ; and all I've seen has led me to the conclusion that you can't well have a less trustworthy moral guide than a woman—any kind of woman. A so-called 'good' woman won't commit crimes ; it's not likely that she'll run away from her husband, for instance. But she'll make that man's life a burden to him ; she'll deceive him every day and hour of his life in a hundred petty matters ; she'll stultify his ambitions, ride rough-shod over his tenderest feelings—and never know a moment's remorse for her deeds. As to trusting any member of the sisterhood—— Take my word for it, Travers, women are without a sense of honor. Truth is a virtue they can't understand. They look upon regard for their word as a sort of scrupulous weakness." Lyon broke off suddenly in his tirade to take two or three protracted pulls at his pipe. "Well, of course there's no use my talking to you in this strain. It's simply so much wasted breath. Your opinions are already fixed——"

Travers interposed. "Even if your rule were sound, and in accordance with facts, which I don't admit, mind, you would have to grant the existence of possible exceptions."

"Oh, of course! And I am quite prepared to grant also that the young lady we have been glancing at belongs to the ranks of those exceptions. Well, since you are so firmly convinced that she would act as a kind of moral walking-stick to your weaker nature, I suppose you intend taking steps to obtain her valuable support ? "

Lyon's bantering tone had no unkindness in it.

"I have tried already; that's the trouble.   Tried without success."

"What's the difficulty ? Means ? or want of means ? Prudent parents intervening ? "

"No. She doesn't care for me."

"That *is* a difficulty."

"When I say ' doesn't care,' " the rejected suitor hastened to add, "I mean, *enough*. At least, that's how she put it herself in —in——"

"In refusing you." Lyon completed the sentence with unsparing brutality. Then he fell into thought for a moment. "I think I see. She is ' not indifferent to you,' as they say, or used to say, in novels. At the same time, she doesn't like you well enough to marry you—at present. It's something like that, isn't it ? "

" You put the situation in a nutshell. What do you think of it ? "

" I think," replied Lyon with deliberation—" at least, I am strongly inclined to believe—that she wants you to ask her again."

" No, she doesn't. There isn't a grain of coquetry in her." .

" You know her best, no doubt." Had Lyon been a Frenchman, he would have shrugged his shoulders here. Being Anglo-Saxon, he denied himself the gesture ; he merely looked it.

Travers was too excited to heed either his friend's looks or his words. " Nevertheless, if only I could stay in England, stay near her, and see her constantly," he resumed, leaving his chair, and crossing the room to the mantel-piece, where he suddenly faced round again, " I believe I could get her to care enough in the end. *Now* you see why I don't hail the prospect of sailing for Queensland next week."

Lyon nodded.

" Three years out there ! why, it simply cuts every ground of chance from under my feet."

" Three years pass. You say she is very young. When you come back——"

" To find her married, six months before, to some beggarly parson in a neighboring village," Travers interrupted with bitterness. " Don't try to quiet me with soothing syrups of that kind, Lyon; I can't swallow them. No, this is the end, no doubt, the end ! "

Lyon did not attempt to controvert his friend's gloomy prognostications. He thought it only too likely that they would find fulfilment.

" The end of everything—for me," the young man went on, with savage insistence. " *She* might have made something of me, if she had chosen. As she doesn't choose—— Doubtless I'm a bad lot—not worse than others, perhaps——"

" Which is not saying much, seeing we're most of us pretty bad lots, if you come to that," the elder man put in quietly.

" But for her sake I believe I could have been different. In that case, there would have been something to work for, something to go on living for. Now, what is there—I put it to you, Lyon, frankly—*what is there* to make life worth living for a poor wretch like me ? My career at an end ; hustled out of the country like a criminal; left to choose between downright beggary and keeping myself barely alive by a drudgery I detest—truly, the prospect's a lively one ! "

"It's not quite so black as you have just painted it, at any rate. You're disappointed, man, and out of sorts; consequently, you view things, for the moment, in an exaggerated light. If your position were really so desperate as you make it out, I take it you would hardly have had the effrontery to ask a young lady to share it. Besides——"

Travers was not listening. He had been pursuing a fresh train of thought while Lyon spoke, and now cut his friend's scarcely, commenced sentence ruthlessly short.

"I wouldn't even insist on a formal engagement. Something to look forward to, something to live for—that's what I want. That's what I must have, if I'm ever to be worth anything from her point of view. She thinks pure love of virtue should be incentive enough. That's where we differ."

"Naturally."

"A man who's asked to sacrifice everything ought to have some sort of hope given him in return. If she would give me any, the smallest shred——"

"Have you tried putting things to her in that way?"

"No, I haven't. The truth is, her—her attitude took me rather by surprise——"

Lyon turned aside, and made a feint of knocking non-existent ashes out of his pipe. It was almost impossible not to smile at the young fellow's *naïve* self-betrayal.

"Well"—he took up his parable again, turning back as soon as he had succeeded in reducing the corners of his mouth to something like order—"why not try that plan now? Women, especially very young women, like to be approached humbly, you know. It flatters their vanity to have a man metaphorically, if not literally, on his knees before them. Well, well, she may not be vain; say she's tender-hearted. No tender-hearted girl of twenty would be likely to deny a man, for whom she had some sort of liking already, mere permission to hope that in the future she would like him better still. And if that sort of thing will content you——"

"Of course it won't *content* me. But it would be better than nothing at all. It would save me from going straight to the dogs at once. It would be something to hold her by." This last sentence Travers half muttered to himself. But Lyon caught the murmur.

"Will it?" was his mental aside in rejoinder. "If the lady,

grown weary of the idea, and perhaps with a more promising suitor on the spot, consents to be held by such a slender chain as that, she must be a poor-spirited damsel indeed. One consolation is, 'tis a mere toss-up which of them snaps the chain first."

"I've bored you long enough with my uninteresting private affairs." Travers' voice put an end to his friend's cynical reflections. "Thanks for your patience in giving ear to them. I must be off now—I've heaps of things to do. Good-by—if I don't see you again."

"But why should there be any 'if' in the matter? I'm not leaving town at all this week. And you?"

"Oh, I—I shall have to go down again into the country almost immediately. To-night or to-morrow, very likely."

"To see your people—and take leave, eh?"

"Well, yes. They expect me, naturally."

"Most naturally. Go, and my blessing go with you, dutiful son. I trust the performance of your filial duties will bring a fitting reward."

"Meaning——?" with an embarrassed laugh.

"That I wish you luck in *all* your undertakings."

"Thanks," Travers returned briefly. Then, half-way to the door: "Lyon, if—if anything comes of this, I shall never forget—I don't know how to put it——"

"Don't put it at all," Lyons interposed quickly. "Did you send your horse home? Do you want a hansom? Better have one called. Wilson, a hansom for Mr. Travers. Where shall I send those letters, by the way? To your club?"

Travers safely off the premises, "What in Heaven's name had I done," demanded Lyon of himself, ruefully contemplating his right hand, which his lately vanished guest had nearly wrung off in fervent acknowledgment at parting, "that the poor fellow should feel impelled to crush my unfortunate fingers to a jelly? Given him a piece of very doubtful advice indeed; induced him to believe that, by dint of making a greater fool of himself than he has done already, he may yet persuade a flirtatious young woman—clearly too prudent to engage herself honestly to a pauper—to make him some kind of shadowy promise she certainly won't keep. Well, the innocent delusion that she is pledged to him may keep him quiet for a few months, till he has got over his soreness about leaving the army, and begins to take some interest in railway con-

struction ; by that time it will have served its turn. It was all
very boyish—that talk about going to the devil if she wouldn't
have him. Impossible to deal with such a juvenile being as if he
were a grown man. Before she is ready to throw him over most
likely he will long have ceased to crave for her, either in a moral
walking-stick capacity or any other. Possibly he may not even
leave the throwing-over process entirely to her. His affections
are not of the constant kind, poor boy ! though he certainly
seems harder hit than usual this time."

Mr. Lyon turned to look for his pipe ; found and relighted it;
then, subsiding into the big arm-chair lately occupied by Travers,
resumed his somewhat disjointed consideration of the case under
review.

"Suppose Travers does take the initiative ? " he reflected, leaning back comfortably with his eyes half closed. "Rather morti-
fying for the unknown fair in that case. I'm afraid I hardly considered her dignity, or her interests, sufficiently, in counselling
Travers to this new appeal. However "—easily—" I don't suppose I need reproach myself very severely on that score. Probably the maiden is quite capable of taking care of herself."

Part 1

CHAPTER I

OVER HILL, OVER DALE

"The whole earth
The beauty wore of promise ; that which sets
The budding rose above the rose full-blown."

A JUNE evening—such an evening as Keats might have sung of
delightedly ; sun-warmed, zephyr-fanned, balmy and spicily sweet
with the scent of new-mown hay. Overhead, in the country lanes,
the trees were still dressed in fresh green garments—for the bud-
ding-time had been a late one, and the vivid coloring of spring
was not yet grown pale and languorous in the heats and dust of
summer ; by the waysides the hedges were prolix of bloom, showing, almost unbroken for miles, one continuous tangle of dog-roses,
elder-flower, and wild-cherry blossom. The very ditches were
brilliant ; and the small brown-faced urchins who, evading the
stern prohibitory eye of the "collector," had stolen on to the
narrow platform of the bare little station at Donnington to enjoy
the ever novel excitement of " seeing the train come in," had their
battered straw hats and chubby hands full of freshly gathered
ragged-robin and wild phlox. Anthony Lyon, stepping from one
of the short string of railway carriages which, four times a day,
travels soberly to and fro over the single line of rail connecting
the great junction of Heydon and the small hill-village of Donnington, and finding his eyes and nostrils at once assailed by agreeable
rustic sights and scents, congratulated himself warmly on the prospect of a full idle fortnight, to be spent in the heart of a district
seemingly so pleasant.

In a moment or two he discovered that this desirable neighborhood—like most neighborhoods in an imperfectly constituted
world—had its disadvantages. It had, indeed, one disadvantage
going far to nullify all its charm : means of locomotion from one

part of it to the other were not to be procured for love or money. Seeing that Lyon's host had his dwelling-place fully five or six miles from Donnington, this lack of conveyances placed that newly alighted traveller in a decidedly awkward predicament. Not that a walk of half a dozen miles had any terrors, in itself, for the muscular ex-emigrant; unencumbered, he would have tramped twice the distance cheerfully. "But I can't carry all my personal property on my back," he reflected, ruefully considering his two portmanteaus, hat-box, rod-case, and other impedimenta, which, piled into a formidable heap in the middle of the platform, confronted him inexorably.

He took counsel with the station-master, who had little solid comfort to offer him. Yes, Heyford was quite five miles off; not a very good road either—two bad hills. Any trap to be hired on the way between this and that? The official thought not. One or two of the small farmers about had traps; but then they had no license to let them, and would be afraid to hire them out, lest they should be pulled up by the police. That some charitably disposed individual might be induced to stretch charity so far as to lend a trap without payment, was evidently a possibility too remote to be taken into account. The gentry mostly sent their carriages to meet their friends at the train, the man in uniform wound up. Clearly he thought Lyon was being cavalierly treated.

"Is it the rectory you're for, or Mr. Creighton's?" he enquired.

"Mr. Creighton's."

"Strange he shouldn't have sent, isn't it?"

"Very strange, since things are as you say. This seems a strange place altogether," muttered Lyon, who, in spite of the engaging fact that a nightingale was just beginning to warble faintly in the dark clump of copse at the end of the station-master's garden, was on the verge of losing his never very placid temper. "Heaven knows what's to be done with all that luggage!" He spoke in an aggrieved tone, as though the luggage had belonged to somebody else. "But, anyway, it's clear I can't stay here all night. I must get out of this somehow. How does one go to Heyford?"

"Well, through the village, first of all. Then turn to your right, and down the hill. If you'll step outside, I'll show you." The station-master led the way through the empty booking-office and out on to the sandy plateau at the edge of which his station was built. "That's Heyford, down yonder in the vale," he said, pointing a tanned forefinger in the direction of the declining sun. "See the church tower?"

Lyon, shading his eyes with his hand, turned them toward the spot indicated. But his gaze missed the building which was its primary object, and ranged onward to the horizon.

"What an outlook you've got up here!" he ejaculated admiringly.

"Yes, you can see a long way on a fine evening like this one. I forget how many miles exactly, but 'tis a smart few, I know."

"I should think it *was* a smart few," Lyon responded.

He was standing, so he found, on the edge of the Loamshire Downs. Below him the great cultivated plain lying between the university city of Milford and the cathedral city of Oldbury lay unfolded like a map, reaching on his right and left to the very confines of the horizon, while immediately opposite him it was closely bounded by the stony range of the Blithewold Hills. It was a summer land of plenty he looked down upon : a land of pastures dotted over with thousands of sheep and cattle; of meadows rich either with mown grass or clover and sainfoin only waiting the scythe ; of cornfields cheerful with green promise of later gold; of frequent villages and homesteads innumerable. The sight was so pleasant to the eye, as well as to every natural, unspoiled human instinct, that the spectator, in contemplating it, forgot for a moment his personal preoccupation of a minute earlier. The station-master's voice, with its strong Loamshire accent, speedily recalled him, however, to previous considerations.

"Made it out, sir?"

"What, Heyford? No—yes—ah! I suppose that's it, the square tower on the left?" Lyon measured the distance of that tower from the spot where he stood with a critical eye. "More like seven miles off than five, I should say," he remarked.

"Well, they *call* it five, mostly," dubiously returned the station-master, who was looking down the road toward the village. "Why, I believe"—with a sudden access of animation—"yes, that's certainly Mr. Creighton's pony-cart coming along! And Miss Temple in it, if I'm not mistaken. They've sent to meet you, after all, sir, you see," turning to his companion. "I might have made sure they would, I suppose—only Mr. Creighton is rather a curious gentleman in some of his ways. Yes, it is Miss Temple driving. And without a man, too."

Lyon had not time to enquire who Miss Temple might be before the light two-wheeled vehicle she drove, in build a cross between a gig and a dog-cart, actually dashed up to the door of the booking-office and stopped there.

"Oh, Mr. Lyon!" cried the occupant of the driving-seat in a clear, girlish voice, "I am so sorry! It *is* Mr. Lyon, isn't it?" interrupting herself suddenly.

Lyon lifted his hat with an assenting smile.

"I thought it must be," responded Miss Temple, preparing to dismount from her perch. "Oh, thank you, Jakes!"—to the stalwart black-bearded porter, who came forward to the pony's head with a quite unrustic show of alacrity. "I am so sorry to have kept you waiting," she resumed to Lyon, springing deftly to the ground before he could advance to her assistance, and knotting up the reins in swift, dexterous fashion. "I knew I was late, and I made Charlie fly along the level. But I dared not urge him very fast up Donnington Hill. You will see on the way back that it's a hill which *must* be taken quietly."

"The station-master was just telling me there were some formidable hills between this and Heyford," returned Lyon. "I am sorry you should have hurried either yourself or your animal on my account."

"Oh, we were bound to hurry!" the girl answered. She was quite a girl; certainly not more than one or two and twenty. "I was afraid you would think my uncle had forgotten all about your arrival—you know, I dare say, that he has a very bad memory. As it happens, he took it for granted that I had ordered the cart to meet you, when he had never even so much as told me he expected anyone by this train! Consequently, of course, no orders were given, and Wilson, the man, went out haymaking, and wasn't to be found anywhere, when I discovered by the merest accident that he ought to be on his road to Donnington. Is your luggage here, Mr. Lyon? We ought to be making the best of our way home at once, else we shall be late for dinner."

"My luggage is on the platform," Lyon said. "But there's quite a heap of it, I'm afraid; far too much for your pony to carry behind him. Indeed, I couldn't think of troubling you to transport all those things. If you'll let me take my bag in the cart—— "

"Oh, I dare say we can manage everything," interposed Miss Temple cheerily. "The cart lets down behind; and Charlie is very strong. I'll just go and look at it for a moment."

She flitted into the station and out again in the twinkling of an eye. For so tall a young woman—she was " more than common tall," her head being very little below the level of Lyon's own— Miss Temple was peculiarly brisk and active in all her movements.

" It will all travel with us quite easily—with just a little management," she pronounced confidently on reappearing. " Now, Mr. Manns,"—to the station-master—" if you'll be kind enough to hold Charlie for a moment, Jakes can fetch the luggage out, and I'll show him how to stow it."

This young lady seemed eminently practical. In a very few moments she had taught the clumsy-handed porter how to dispose of all Lyon's belongings in safety in the decidedly limited space available for their reception, had taken a friendly farewell of him and his superior officer, and, with Lyons and his bag beside her, was spinning briskly down the sharply sloping road on her return journey.

" This is the village of Donnington," she said, with a little flourish of her whip, as the cart, reaching the bottom of the slope, rounded a corner, and turned into a steep " street," lined on either side with cottages, each standing in its own little patch of garden, for the most part, rising one above another up the sheer face of the hill. " When we get up *there* "—pointing to the topmost roof —" you will have a better view of the country than the one you were looking at just now."

It did not take them long to get up to the point of vantage she indicated. The pony was a gallant animal, and his young mistress handled him firmly as well as kindly—not making impossible demands upon his strength, but at the same time exacting from him a full amount of work. The hilltop attained, she drew rein for a moment.

" Isn't it beautiful ? How I wish I lived up here ! "

She looked out over the wide rolling champaign as she spoke ; and Lyon looked, for the first time since their informal introduction with anything like attention, at her. His scrutiny was hardly rewarded ; for in appearance his new acquaintance was nowise remarkable. Yet, while devoid of all pretensions to real beauty, Miss Temple, like so many other English girls of her rank and age, was by no means disagreeable to the eye ; she was fair and fresh-complexioned, had a bright, honest smile, good teeth, plenty of rather light brown hair with a strong tendency to curl, and a set of features that were prettyish, if quite unclassical. A pair of clear, well-opened hazel eyes contrasted effectively with the lighter coloring of her hair and skin.   As to her figure, it was impossible to decide positively on its merits or demerits, since she wore with her dark blue serge skirt one of those very unbecoming upper garments yclept blouses—garments which, by effectually deadening and flattening every natural outline of the female form divine, have the undesirable result of reducing the most graceful and the most angular of women alike to a common level of shapelessness. Taken altogether, Dorothy Temple might be accounted a pleasant-looking girl enough.   But there was nothing striking about her ; no special piquancy, no fascinating peculiarity in form or feature, voice or expression, such as would be likely to stir the languid interest of a man caring nothing, as a rule, for mere ordinary specimens of girlhood.   Mr. Lyon's eyes returned quickly to their previous study of the landscape at his feet.

"Yes, there's always something rather impressive in a great sweep of open country like this," he said, answering his companion's exclamation.   "And the air on these heights must be very fine.   Heyford, I see, lies quite in the plain."

"Quite.   We are in the valley of the Cray.   It's only the infant Cray with us, of course.   Still, we are very proud of it."

"Is it navigable at Heyford ?"   Visions, highly attractive visions, of long boating expeditions undertaken alone, or in company with a book only, when the society of Mr. Creighton and his amiable niece should begin to pall unendurably, suggested themselves at once to Lyon's imagination.

Miss Temple's reply put an end to these radiant dreams.

"Not really navigable.   I get out in a punt sometimes, but it's very slow work.   I'm afraid you'd consider it ' slow ' in the other sense, too," she added, laughing.   "One gets stuck in the weeds so *very* often ! every ten or twelve yards, on an average.   Still, if you would like to try some day——"

"Thank you," Lyon responded, without any effusion.   "She has ideas of taking me out herself, I fancy," was his mental reflection.   "Very kind of her, I'm sure—still, one may be permitted to hope she won't be too prodigal of small attentions ; that sort of thing is so fatiguing to the recipient.   Rather a nuisance, now I come to think of it, her being at Creighton's at all.   A girl in the country never has anything to do, and she will probably be *en evidence* from morning till night about the garden and on the stairs."

Aloud he remarked, somewhat abruptly, having arrived at his remark by the silent and not too civil process of thought above recorded :

"I wasn't aware—Mr. Creighton never told me he had a niece living with him."

Miss Temple smiled, as she touched up Charlie, who was by this time gingerly descending Donnington Hill, a declivity fully justifying, by its abnormal steepness, her care for his lungs in ascending it.

"I have lived at The Haulms for nearly five years now—ever since I left school, in fact," she replied. "But I'm afraid my uncle hardly thinks me of sufficient importance to talk about me to his friends." She spoke with perfect sweetness, and in a tone that was almost gay, yet Lyon fancied that he detected a note of sadness in her voice. "He has a very poor opinion of women altogether," she added lightly. "I'm afraid he assigns us an extremely low place in the scheme of creation."

Now, it is to be feared that Mr. Lyon's opinion of the weaker sex in general was scarcely more favorable than Mr. Creighton's. Nevertheless, he was conscious of a sudden inexplicable movement of dislike toward that elderly misogynist, as he answered rather stiffly :

"I can hardly claim to be reckoned among Mr. Creighton's friends. Our intimacy, such as it is, grew out of a travelling acquaintanceship made a year or two ago in Germany. I was surprised when his letter of invitation reached me last week ; I fancied he had forgotten my existence long ago."

"Oh, you mustn't suppose he forgets people he likes !" was the eager rejoinder. "And I know he took a great fancy to you. It was only the day and hour of your coming that escaped his memory. Now that he has fairly begun writing his big book, he often loses all count of time. Even the dinner-hour passes over him unnoticed !"

"That habit of his must be rather inconvenient to you, as his housekeeper."

"But I'm not his housekeeper, unfortunately. I wish I were ! I should feel myself of some use to him, in that case. Unluckily, he won't be persuaded that a girl *can* be of any use, under any circumstances ! All the years that I've been with him he has never so much as allowed me to do the flowers. I have to leave them to Lewin, the parlor-maid, who arranges them as she might

watercresses for the market. I hope, by the way, Uncle Mervyn
has told her to get your room ready, Mr. Lyon. One comfort is,
at least, she will be in the way when we get there ; she won't have
taken herself off for the afternoon, like Wilson."

"I'm afraid Wilson's absence necessitated your taking this long
drive to fetch me."

"That was a treat to me, not a hardship in any way, I assure
you. I'm very fond of driving. And, as a rule, I haven't much
time for it, except on Saturdays. The only difficulty I had was
with the buckles. I never knew till to-day how many buckles
there were in a set of pony-harness ! "

"You don't mean to say you had to harness the pony yourself ?
Really——"

"It didn't matter in the least," she interrupted, cutting short
his polite regrets. "It was good fun. And my efforts were successful, as you see, which is satisfactory. I shall be proud for
Wilson to see that harness. This is the last hill," she added,
changing the subject quickly, and indicating with her whip the
slope up which, having safely descended "Donnington," the
cart was now slowly climbing. "Once down the other side, and
we are in ' the Vale ' proper."

"The Vale," viewed at close quarters, proved to be quite as
prosperous a country as it had appeared when seen from a distance. The level ground reached, Charlie trotted swiftly for five
or six miles between double lines of rich lush meadows, in which
bands of haymakers were busy or herds of handsome sleek short-
horn cattle feeding, interspersed here and there with a well-clothed
field of corn-land. The scent of the new-mown hay was everywhere. Even on the waste grounds bordering the roadsides the
grass lay in long, thick, fragrant swathes, drying in the last fervent rays of the June sun, and filling the evening air with pungent
sweetness. "It was the finest crop they had had in this part of
the country for ten years past," Miss Temple informed her companion. He noticed that she seemed well-informed in agricultural
matters, and appeared to take a considerable interest in the operations of the hour. This he gathered, not merely from her occasional remarks to himself, but from the brief conversations she
held with one or two wayfaring farmers whom they encountered
on their road. Apparently she knew everybody in the district,
for she never passed man, woman, or child without a word of
greeting, and rarely without pulling up for a moment's chat.

About two miles from Heyford, at the juncture of a steep lane, running down from a wild-looking bit of common, with the high-road, she was eagerly hailed by a group of small children, with an older girl, evidently eager to put some question, at their head. She stopped to listen to them, rather to the annoyance of Lyon, who was getting weary of such frequent halts, and there ensued a dialogue of some length, having for its main point the date of the commencement of the summer holidays at the school where the youthful persons assembled by the roadside received their educa-tion. The young lady who acted as spokeswoman, and who betrayed a keen anxiety that this fixture should coincide with the beginning of "pea-hacking,"—an operation which she declared likely to be in progress by the end of July,—appeared, as far as Lyon could make out her plea, to be supplicating Miss Temple for a change of day, which the latter showed distinct unwillingness to grant.

"Well," she said at length, gathering up her reins to move on, "you can tell your mother I will see about it, Polly, and make enquiries. If I find there's any reasonable prospect of the farmers beginning as early as you say, of course I'll try to make some change. Otherwise, we must keep to the old date. Unless you are really wanted in the fields, there would be no reason for chang-ing—don't you see? Good-night, all of you."

"You seem to be autocratic in matters parochial," observed Lyon, with an amused smile, as Charlie clattered onward.

"This wasn't exactly a—parochial matter," returned Miss Temple, looking amused in her turn. Indeed, the little smile on her fresh lips was slightly enigmatic.

"I beg your pardon; I gathered that the appeal presented to you related to the school."

"Not to Heyford school."

"Indeed? Well," said Lyon, a little nettled by his com-panion's reticence, "your young friend's Loamshire accent made her speech very liable to false interpretation. I had hard work to understand her at all."

"Poor Polly! I'm afraid I shall never—I'm afraid all the schooling in the world will never cure that accent of hers! But it isn't a Loamshire accent, Mr. Lyon, excuse me. We crossed the shire-ditch into Hillshire about ten minutes ago. When you've been in this country a little while, you'll discover a vast difference in the way they talk north and south of the ditch."

"Are we in Hillshire now?" Lyon spoke with unusual animation. "I had no idea Heyford was over the border. East Hillshire, isn't it? Yes, of course. I used to hear a good deal of this division of the county some years ago from a friend of mine who once lived here. He is in Australia now—went out there a couple of years since. But I fancy his people still have their abode somewhere in this neighborhood. I wonder if you know anything of them, by chance?"

"I don't know very many people," Miss Temple admitted frankly. "My uncle does not care much for society. Still, I may have met your friend, or heard of him. What is his name?"

"Travers—Brian Travers. His father is a parson, and I know has a living somewhere in East Hillshire. You seem amused, Miss Temple. Then you do know these good folk?"

"Very well indeed." Miss Temple's frank eyes were full of laughter. "Mr. Travers is rector of Heyford, and our next-door neighbor. And Brian is my cousin—let me see, twice removed, I think it is. I know his mother and mine were something a little less than first cousins."

"This waxes interesting. Rather curious, too, isn't it, that I should ask you casually about these people, as strangers you might just possibly have met, and discover them to be your relations?"

"It's certainly fortunate you didn't accompany your casual enquiries with any uncivil remarks."

"No danger of that, in any case. I haven't the pleasure of Mr. and Mrs. Travers' acquaintance as yet; and Brian, as I said, is a friend of mine. I might almost call his brother Jem a friend too, though I've seen very little of him since I left Oxford. By the way, this should surely be the long vacation. Is he at Heyford, by any lucky chance?"

"He is always at Heyford now. He lives here."

"*Jem?*" Lyon's voice for once lost its level tone, and sounded a clear note of genuine astonishment.

"Yes. He has been acting as his father's curate for the last eighteen months."

"Really? You must excuse my gaping surprise, Miss Temple, but indeed my imagination refuses to picture old Jem a country curate. *Jem!*" repeated Lyon musingly. "Certainly I shouldn't have thought him cut out for a village life. Besides, I heard he had some imposingly magnificent appointment in Oxford."

"So he had. It was a splendid thing, from the money point of view; and the work suited him exactly. But his father was getting old; and the parish needed a second clergyman, if it was to be properly looked after; so Jem resigned his appointment and came here," said Miss Temple in a quiet, matter-of-course tone. "Look!" as the cart swung round a last corner; "that is the rectory gate."

CHAPTER II

AT THE HAULMS

"This man's metallic; at a sudden blow
His soul rings hard."

LYON caught sight of a wide-open gateway, the iron gates that should have closed it flung fully back, and looking as though they had not stirred for years on their rusty hinges; of a broad, sloping, mossy drive completely overshadowed by magnificent trees; and of a group of quaintly fashioned red-brick chimneys mellow with time. Heyford Rectory stood so literally embowered among the beeches and chestnuts blocking it in on every side from the gaze of the curious that only its chimney-tops and loftiest gables were visible from the road. But a little to the left, where the church of which it was the humble neighbor loomed lofty above the great yews and cypresses of a crowded ancient churchyard —making the venerable trees look mere stunted shrubs beside its walls—there was no leafy screen to intercept the view of the passer-by. Not the lofty central tower alone, but the crockets and gargoyles of the chancel roof, and the entire long line of the high and narrow Norman nave, stood out sharply defined against the brilliance of the western sky.

"You have a grand church here, it seems," Lyon said, leaning back for a second look, as the cart turned afresh to the right.

"And such an interesting one! There are innumerable historical associations attaching to it, dating from the Wars of the Roses—and even earlier—downward. Jem has its whole history at his finger-ends, and loves to tell it," Miss Temple rejoined. "No doubt he will tell it to you at the earliest opportunity. Here we are at The Haulms"—checking Charlie suddenly at a gate some fifty yards from the rectory entrance and on the same side of the road. "Up yonder," pointing with her whip-hand, "over that bridge, is the village."

"And under the bridge flow the beginnings of the Cray, I suppose?"

"No, that bridge crosses the canal only. The river flows lower down, at the bottom of the garden, and on through the church meadow. Perhaps I ought rather to say it meanders along there; its pace, at this part of its career, is very sober indeed. Thanks, Mary; much obliged," as a decent-looking woman issued from the gardener's cottage, which served as a lodge, and proceeded to unlatch the gate. Unlike his clerical next-door neighbor, Mr. Creighton was not apparently in the habit of leaving his doors hospitably open to all comers.

He came briskly out to the porticoed entrance of his house as his guest alighted at it: a man whose age, between the limits of fifty-five and seventy, it was difficult to guess precisely; remarkable for exceedingly broad, stooping shoulders, but otherwise small and spare of person, especially as regarded his nether limbs. His face seemed to be formed on the same principle as his body; that is to say, all its power and vigor resided exclusively in the forehead, which was quite peculiarly massive and imposing, while the remaining features were thin, pinched, and insignificant. This singular insistence, so to speak, on the same physical idea in face and figure—the one presenting a kind of counterpart of the other—gave a touch of oddity, almost of grotesqueness, to his personality. The tendency to a top-heavy formation appeared even in the man's eyes, which, themselves unusually small, were overhung by immensely large and bushy eyebrows; and these, like his fairly thick hair and long early Victorian whiskers, were white rather than gray, so that he wore, at a slight distance, a distinctly venerable appearance. But, close at hand, you soon discovered the small eyes under the bristling brows to be still extremely bright and piercing; while a mere moment's observation would suffice to convince you that Mr. Creighton's movements were not those of a very old man.

"Glad to see you, very glad," he ejaculated in a deep, rather harsh voice, shaking Lyon's hand hastily. "Sorry there should have been some mistake about sending to meet you—hope you hadn't to wait long? No? That's all right. Come in, come in."

"But Miss Temple?" Lyon made demur. Some little effort of politeness in behalf of his charioteer, left sitting, groomless,

in the pony-cart by herself, seemed to be absolutely demanded of
him. "Your man, perhaps, may be still out of the way. In
which case——"

"Oh, he won't be long; it's close upon his supper-time!"
interrupted Mr. Creighton, leading the way into the house. "My
niece can take care of the pony till he comes. You had better
drive round to the stables at once, Dorothy, and wait for Wilson
there," he commanded over his shoulder. Then, turning again
to Lyon, "That little brute kicks the gravel all over the place if
he is kept standing any time in front of this door," he said in
an explanatory tone, with a significant glance at the smoothly
rolled drive.

Lyon paused, his conscience only half satisfied. "Surely I
might be of some assistance?"

"Oh, no!" ejaculated the niece, and "Oh, no!" asseverated
the uncle, in a breath. And Creighton added almost irritably,
"Dorothy can manage perfectly well alone, I assure you. Pray
come in at once."

Lyon yielded without further ado, feeling he had done enough
for honor, and assailed, not only by pleasing visions of approaching dinner, but also by a keen anxiety to escape, as soon as
possible, out of the dusty clothes in which he had been travelling
all day, into fresher and more comfortable habiliments.

Evidently the servants *had* been warned, despite Miss Temple's
doubts, of his approach, for he found a tolerably spacious room
set apart for him, and everything needful for comfort laid out
therein ready to his hand. This prevention of his wants came
upon him as a kind of surprise; as, indeed, did the exquisite
orderliness which, like an atmosphere, seemed to pervade the
whole house. One or two remarks of Miss Temple had rather led
him to expect a happy-go-lucky bachelor establishment, in which
he should have to struggle for the necessaries of life; where the
supply of clean towels would possibly be limited, and it might be
needful to go on exploring expeditions in search of your boots.
But the actual domestic economy of The Haulms appeared to be
conducted rather on the severely correct lines approved of well-
to-do old maiden ladies. Lyon, as he tied his cravat, felt
inclined to compliment Mr. Creighton on his choice of a housekeeper. No wonder he had declined to dispossess that lady (who-
ever she might be) in favor of so very inexperienced, and,
presumably, inefficient, an aspirant to the post as Miss Dorothy!

The house whose internal arrangements struck Lyon as so admirable was not a large one, as he discovered when, his toilet completed, he had leisure to descend and examine it cursorily. In construction it was a compromise between two styles. More pretentious than the ordinary parsonage, less spacious than the ordinary country house, it presented points in common with both; its numerous gables and mullioned windows giving it, without, the conventional semi-ecclesiastical air considered proper to the "modest mansion" of the modern "village preacher"; while, within doors, bigger and loftier rooms than it is usually the lot of the country clergyman to inhabit, a decidedly handsome oak staircase, very massive as to balusters, very wide and shallow as to steps, and a square, oak-panelled hall, adorned with the customary foxes' heads and sets of antlers, hinted rather at worldly and sporting proclivities on the part of the owner. Misleading hints, these last, as Lyon happened to know. "I wonder how much old Creighton gave for the collection?" he mused, thoughtfully contemplating the trophies of the chase aforesaid, in the intervals of listening, somewhat impatiently, for the sound of descending feet upon the stairs. It was now fully five minutes past eight. At what hour did these people intend to dine? A quarter of an hour elapsed before Mr. Creighton came bustling down. "I believe I'm a little late; hope you're not tired of waiting? The cook is, I dare say; I fear I'm rather frequently in her black books. Well, we won't keep her waiting any longer," touching a bell as he spoke. "This way. All the sitting-rooms in my house look out into the garden at the back—a great advantage, to my thinking. Secures one absolute quiet—in so far as such a thing can be secured at all in this world—and protects one from the curse of spying visitors altogether. One can be 'not at home' here whenever one pleases."

The dining-room, into which Mr. Creighton, thus speaking, conducted his visitor, was a pleasant room with a pleasant outlook. A turfed terrace, broken here and there by brilliant flower-beds, ran close under the large bay window occupying one entire end of it, and below this stretched an expanse of well-kept sloping lawn, bounded, at the bottom of the slope, by an imposing line of witch-elms, their dark array varied, here and there, by the presence of a great horse-chestnut shaking its big light-green fans in the soft evening light. Beyond the belt of trees the ground, clothed with a sort of thicket, appeared to fall again more sharply than before, descending, doubtless, to the edge of the unseen river.

Lyon cast a comprehensive, sweeping glance out of window before obeying his host's signal to seat himself. Then he took a place in silence. Only, as he unfolded his table-napkin, his eyes rested for a moment interrogatively on the vacant chair opposite his own.

Mr. Creighton's observant, if diminutive, orbs noted the unspoken question.

"My niece has been detained, I suppose ; she will be down before long, I dare say. I will not ask you to wait any longer for her."

Lyon, as in duty bound, protested his willingness to do what was not asked of him. But Creighton cut him short unceremoniously.

"Nonsense ! you must be famishing. Take the cover off the soup-tureen, Lewin."

The poultry stage of dinner had been reached, and the affairs of the nation pretty fully discussed, or rather descanted upon by Mr. Creighton, Lyon contenting himself, for the most part, with the listener's *rôle*, before Miss Temple appeared, her flushed cheeks and imperfectly arranged hair giving unmistakable evidence of the fact that her evening toilet had been made in very hurried fashion. That the lateness of her arrival on the scene was due to the pressure of unfortunate circumstances, and not to any carelessness, much less to deliberate choice, on her own part, was sufficiently proved by the manner of her entry. This was nervous, breathless, deprecating, and so manifestly the result of determined effort, that Lyon felt certain she had stood for at least a minute or two at the closed dining-room door before summoning courage to make it at all.

Guessing this much, he felt an impulse of pity for her—recollections of his own shy boyhood had kept him pitiful toward timid youth—and, in a blundering, masculine fashion, attempted to rush to her assistance. Frustrating her endeavor to slip into her place as nearly as possible unobserved, he leaned across the table, and, prompted by wholly excellent motives, unwisely addressed her with:

"Your uncle, out of kindness to my supposed starving condition, insisted on our sitting down without you, Miss Temple. Though I assured him I was capable of supporting the pangs of hunger a few minutes longer—— "

"Oh, I am glad you did not—I am glad Uncle Mervyn didn't wait for me!" Miss Temple spoke fast and low, with her eyes on the tablecloth.

"Dorothy knows I never wait for her," Mr. Creighton put in dryly.

Still Lyon blundered on. "I'm afraid you were detained mounting guard over that pony. It's too bad you should have had so much trouble on my account."

"On the contrary, it's well she should have had an opportunity of making herself useful—for once," said Creighton.

"Wilson came in very soon," Dorothy added quickly, addressing Lyon, and trying her best not to look annoyed. "It was really of no consequence—my being detained—except that it made me a little behindhand with my dressing."

Here her eyes entreated so plainly, "Please say nothing more about the matter, for pity's sake!" that Lyon was at last made aware of his error. Discomfited, he applied himself afresh to his dinner; and his *vis-à-vis* found instant refuge in hers—such as it was. She took up the meal only at the point where she found it, letting slip the rest. When the parlor-maid suggested soup in a benevolent undertone, she received a hasty and nervous negative in reply.

Mr. Creighton, having launched the two remarks above recorded at his niece's head, took no further heed of her presence. Still the girl did not recover either her composure or her spirits; she remained unmistakably ill at ease. Her uncle's proximity seemed to affect her like an evil charm, withering her natural vivacity, and shattering her natural fearlessness. When Lyon, after a discreet interval, addressed her again on some ordinary subject, she answered only by flurried monosyllables. He could hardly believe her to be one and the same with the frank, self-possessed creature who had greeted him outside the station, or the benevolent young despot who knew how to refuse wayside petitions with such lofty firmness. One thing, at least, was clear: his good-natured efforts to include her in the conversation going on between himself and his host were quite misplaced; she evidently preferred being ignored when Mr. Creighton was by. Lyon ignored her, therefore, with an easy conscience, for the remainder of dinner.

The silent figure at his board did not, apparently, exercise any depressing effect whatever on Mr. Creighton's spirits; he talked on with growing fluency and animation. When the dessert had been put on the table, he glided easily from politics to letters; and, in discussing the books of the day, touched lightly on his own achievements in the latter field. Lyon was, fortunately, fairly well posted on the subject of his host's writings—whether he had a very extensive acquaintance with them at first hand is perhaps matter of question, but at least he knew a good deal *about* them— and was therefore able to respond in such kind as satisfied the author. Finally, he made civil enquiry concerning the work just now on the stocks.

Mr. Creighton snapped at the question like a hungry dog at a bone. He was only too delighted to explain the scope and purpose of his new book. Certainly, his plans for it seemed to be of the widest and most complicated description, involving nothing less, to begin with, than a general survey of human history from the earliest to the latest times, as a kind of preliminary introduction to the treatment of the main theme—which he defined as " an attempt to ascertain the laws by which environment, acting as a formative influence on human character, tends to produce different degrees of moral and mental receptivity in different divisions of the human race; so that while one people displays capabilities for civilization that are practically boundless, another is found to possess these capabilities only to a very limited extent, while a third shows utter impotence to attain to any true civilization at all." Lyon sat, figuratively speaking, clutching his forehead. Yet Creighton's statement was made in fairly simple language, and, for all its baldness, could not be called uninteresting; Lyon noticed that Dorothy Temple, on the other side of the table, was drinking it in with all her ears.

" You have set yourself a large problem to solve," he said, after hearing the philosopher to the end of his thesis. " Have you fixed on a title yet ? "

" No. Does one occur to you ? "

" Well, it struck me the book might not unfitly be called ' The Natural History of Civilization.' "

" Not a bad idea. In that case, what would you say to this for a motto : '*Die Geschichte des Menschen ist sein Charakter*' ? "

" Striking enough ; but, surely, only summarizing half your conclusion ? Goethe, there, seems to leave the doctrine of heredity quite out of account."

" Only if his words are taken in their mere surface meaning. Dive deeper into them, and you have the whole truth. Depend

8

upon it, when Goethe spoke of 'a man's history,' he was not thinking exclusively of the history that began in the man's own cradle ; he had too much of the scientific spirit to fall into such an unscientific error. By the way, if you feel an interest in the heredity question, I dare say you may like to look at a pamphlet of ——'s "—naming a distinguished German philosophical writer of the day—" which he was good enough to send me last week. I should be glad to hear your opinion of it."

" It won't be worth hearing, I assure you. My very scanty knowledge of the question has been picked up from magazines in club reading-rooms ; not a very scientific method of study ! "

" But you are convinced of the truth of our doctrine ? "

" It would be too much to say that I feel any conviction concerning it. I remember I thought the doctrine a very comfortable one when I first encountered it, and likely to be useful, from an argumentative point of view, to the good people who are so anxious to abolish capital punishment, and reform desperate characters by sending them to live in country cottages rent free."

" Don't you think—excuse me—that's a somewhat shallow view to take of a well-established scientific truth ? "

" Oh, if it is actually well-established ! " interjected Lyon in a semi-murmur.

"A well-established scientific truth, which has already succeeded in dealing a death-blow to legendary religion, which is fast revolutionizing our canons of morality, and must before long revolutionize our entire system of law and government ? "

" All my views of the subject are necessarily shallow, seeing I know next to nothing about it," was Lyon's cool response. " By the way, since such questions are interesting to you, it's lucky you should have a near neighbor who has gone in for them pretty deeply."

Mr. Creighton drew his bushy eyebrows sharply together.

" A near neighbor ? I don't follow you."

" When I knew Jem Travers at Oxford, heredity was his pet subject. He positively revelled in little enquiries sketched on the lines of your great one."

" You know Travers ? I wasn't aware of that," Mr. Creighton interrupted.

" I used to know him rather well, at one time. It's over ten years now since we met last."

"H'm! You'll find him considerably changed, then."

"He used to be an uncommonly brilliant fellow."

"Used to be! used to be! He's nothing in the world now but a petticoated parson, whose soul doesn't seem capable of rising above the candlesticks and gewgaws with which he insists on adorning his unlucky father's church." Here Lyon perceived Dorothy Temple start forward in her seat, resolutely check herself, and lean back again. "Once James Travers had an intellect, I grant you——"

"We used to think so at Oxford."

"And rightly, in those days. But his powers are hopelessly gone now; smothered to death, long since, under feather-beds of credulity and ceremonialism. He has put his mind into petticoats as well as his body, until it's come to this, that I'd as soon take a female *dévote's* opinion on any critical point likely to clash with her preconceived convictions as Master Jim's. No, no! he might have been very useful to me once; but he is worse than useless now. The very sight of him is irritating to a sensible man."

"I was surprised to hear of him established here—in a country village."

"No wonder. At Oxford—those last four or five years—he had the ball literally at his feet. He might have done anything —anything! He was fast becoming an intellectual power; a few years more, and he would have been a commanding influence with thousands of able minds. It's true, even then the old musty prejudices had too much weight with him. At no time did he ever shake himself quite free of the conventional shackles; his taking orders so early in life was a great misfortune, a terrible hindrance to his after-action and development. But the time of complete emancipation would have come for him, no doubt, as it has come to so many others, orders or no orders, had he remained where he was, subject daily to a hundred enlightening influences. Unluckily, he chose to throw up his appointment and bury himself down here, in order to provide a handful of laborers, who laugh at him to his face, with services at unearthly hours—which they very reasonably and sensibly decline to attend—and from that day his doom was sealed. He has been retrograding steadily ever since. And no wonder! What chance has a man's mind to make intellectual progress, when the man spends his mornings pattering prayers in an empty church, and his afternoons gossiping with village wives over the wash-tub?"

"Certainly, it seems a curious step for a man in his position to have taken deliberately," Lyon said musingly.

"Not if he considered it his duty to take it, surely?" Dorothy Temple suddenly struck in.

It was so long since she had spoken that Lyon was almost startled by the sound of her voice. Before he could recover his surprise sufficiently to reply to her challenging question, Mr. Creighton resumed, ignoring his niece's remark as completely as though it had never been uttered:

"A perfectly inexplicable step. The most deplorable part of the whole business, to me, at least, is that he seems to regret nothing of what he has done. He has settled down calmly into the life of petty things, of virtual uselessness, which he leads here, and seems to desire nothing better."

Here Miss Temple pushed her chair back suddenly from the table, and Lyon, rising to open the door for her, lost a sentence or two of her uncle's diatribe. When he returned to his seat, it was to find Mr. Creighton, leaving James Travers' personal misdemeanor for a moment on one side, engaged in fulminating an indictment against the entire family to which he belonged. No wonder James had disappointed his friends, and belied his early promise—seeing the miserable stock he came of. There was Travers himself, a good sort of fellow, indeed, but narrow in the extreme ; narrow with the double narrowness of Toryism in things secular, and Puritanism in things sacred ; an old-fashioned Evangelical who had never outgrown his early creed. Then the mother —a bundle of nerves and emotions, a creature with no backbone and undetachable tentacles, a sort of moral octopus in her combined weakness and obstinacy : what was to be expected in the son of such a pair? The inherited tendency, in cases like these, was too strong to be crushed out by any system of education ; the inborn bias toward superstition was certain, sooner or later, to reassert itself in some form or other. James Travers was, in reality, his own father over again, the only difference being that in the one case credulity showed itself in readiness to give credit to revivalist miracles, and in the other, to swallow sacerdotal legends whole, without any admixture of salt.

Lyon remarked—chiefly by way of stemming the tide of his host's indignant eloquence—that, whatever hereditary lineaments might have shown themselves in James Travers, there did not, as yet, seem to be any striking recrudescence of the Puritan father in his brother Brian.

"No, he takes after the mother. Same mixture of weakness and obstinacy, exactly. Unstable as water; and, at the same time, perfectly intractable while he remains set on any course. I have no patience with that young fellow. Failure as he is, and always will be, his self-confidence beats that of any man I know."

"There's pluck in him as well as brag, though. It takes a good deal of pluck to go on picking one's self up after repeated falls, and showing an unabashed front to the bystanders."

"Brian Travers certainly has plenty of that kind of pluck, if pluck it is to be called. I hope he's not a particular friend of yours?"

"We were never specially intimate. He's a good many years my junior. But I own to a very strong liking for poor Brian."

"A pleasant fellow, no doubt—very pleasant. But sadly wanting in ballast; and quite without any ambitions worthy the name. A young man without ambitions is always more or less in dangerous case. No; the only member of that family really worth anything is Isabel—these boys' sister. A good deal might be made out of Isabel Travers by a man who had her completely in hand. Unfortunately, she's headstrong, and takes her own way far too much; besides, like all these girls who go in for masculine studies, she's intoxicated with her own achievements."

"A distinguished girl-graduate?"

"Yes; she made herself remarkable at Girton, or Somerville, or some place of that kind, I believe. Very foolish of her father to let her go to college at all; she would have been much better employed making herself useful at home. I believe he did offer some kind of feeble opposition; but my lady was rebellious, and carried the day. And now, instead of putting the learning she has, very unnecessarily, acquired to some sound use—for instance, she would have been very useful to me as proof-reader and secretary, I could have given her plenty to do all the year round—instead of this, what must she needs do but rush off to London and plunge head-foremost into wild schemes of social regeneration, so-called. One knows what those schemes are at bottom: mere expedients for making the men and women—more especially the women—who run them conspicuous in the eyes of the world."

"An unfortunate choice," said Lyon, struggling with the corners of his mouth.

"Very unfortunate. It will be the ruin of the girl. All her parents' fault, though, in the first instance, at least. She was made too much of at home; her vanity fed to repletion by adulation of her pitiful little talents. Still, for a woman, she is a capable creature. She might have been of great assistance to me, in a certain way." Mr. Creighton stifled a sigh. "Are you certain you won't take any more claret? Then we'll go into the drawing-room."

The lamps in the drawing-room were already lighted, but the room itself was empty. It was a large room, handsomely and heavily furnished, and as precisely orderly as the rest of the house. Not a chair was out of place, not a book lay open, not a vestige of needlework appeared on any of the tables. Lyon began to find the unvarying primness of his surroundings somewhat oppressive. His eyes wandered wistfully through the French windows, and lingered on the twilit lawn.

Mr. Creighton interpreted his guest's half-longing gaze aright. "I did't ask you if you cared to smoke? I don't smoke myself, and I've no room in the house convenient for smoking; but if you feel inclined for a turn in the garden——"

"Thanks, I'll have one cigar, if you'll allow me."

"Then, if *you'll* allow *me*, I'll leave you to enjoy it alone." Mr. Creighton was evidently not a punctilious host. "I have a mass of notes—which I was getting in order against your coming —to finish looking over to-night. To-morrow I shall ask you to run your eye over them, if you will."

Lyon expressed becoming pleasure at the prospect of being introduced to these interesting MSS.

"They'll be particularly interesting to you, I hope, seeing they deal with people and scenes you must be thoroughly familiar with. I am pausing just now in my general survey at Australia and New Zealand, and should be very glad of some information from you on one or two points."

"I'm sure," Lyon said—he had already one foot across the window-sill, and was busily engaged in extracting his cigar-case from his pocket—"I'm sure, if I had any useful information to impart about Australia or New Zealand, it would be quite at your service. But, as it happens, I'm really the last person in the world to apply to. When I was out in Queensland, I virtually lived with my eyes shut—to everything, that is to say, except the cutting capabilities of the strata through which I was trying to force a permanent way for my railway company."

"So!" he said to himself a moment later, as, having first dropped down the terrace-bank to the lawn, and there set his cigar carefully alight, he started on a stroll across the thick, smooth turf; "behold the motive that prompted my very unexpected invitation to The Haulms! The right moment for picking the ex-emigrant's brain had arrived. Shall I succumb gracefully; shall I be telegraphed for to-morrow; or shall I remain on, and rebel, like Miss Isabel Travers—for whom I feel, at this moment, profound respect and unqualified admiration? I rather think, inspired by her excellent example, that I will elect to stay and rebel. Decidedly, unless I get too much bored in these rural solitudes, that will be the most amusing course. And retreat is always open to me as a last resource. Meanwhile, it would be a meritorious deed to teach this old tyrant a lesson. His behavior to his niece, a most inoffensive girl as far as I can see, is really quite ruffianly."

CHAPTER III

UP AND DOWN THE LADY'S WALK

"A mind consciously, energetically moving with the larger march of human destinies, but not the less full of conscience and tender heart for the footsteps that tread near and need a leaning-place . . . capable of the unapplauded heroism which turns off the road of achievement at the call of the nearer duty whose effect lies within the beatings of the hearts that are close to us."

THE grounds at The Haulms were not extensive. They consisted, Lyon speedily discovered, simply of the sloping lawn, or rather lawns—for there were two, one falling straight to the river, the other, more rambling and irregular in shape, lying at right angles to it—which he had first seen from the dining-room window, and the winding, shrubbery walk below it, together with a fairly spacious walled kitchen-garden running parallel to the smaller lawn on the left. Beyond the farther wall of this garden the gnarled boughs of a group of ancient apple-trees proclaimed the beginnings of the rectory orchard, and the limits of Mr. Creighton's demesne.

Leaving the exploration of the kitchen-garden for a daylight hour, Lyon sauntered, cigar in mouth, toward the river. The night—it must now have been hard on ten o'clock—was delicious to every sense : clear, calm, balmy, here and there delicately fragrant with the scent of tea-roses. A clear young moon was ascending out of the east ; at the zenith the sky had taken on a deep violet hue, and the stars showed themselves distinctly as points of white light on the dusky background ; but in the western horizon the last pale opal and aqua-marine tints of a glorious sunset lingered yet. In a bit of larch thicket hard by the moss-grown river-path a nightingale was singing. Lyon felt that it would probably take him a long time to finish his one cigar.

Having taken a few steps along the path, and reached a point where the brushwood grew less closely, and he could get a view of the stream below, he stopped for a minute or two. The famous river was here to be seen in most modest guise : as a mere narrow line of slow-moving water, half-choked with reeds, rushes, and floating weed. Certainly Miss Temple had in no wise exaggerated the difficulties of attempting to navigate such a stream.

As Lyon stood looking out over the flat expanse of water-meadows forming the opposite shore, watching idly the countless thin threads of silver mist rising from a hundred unseen pools and spreading themselves over the dim face of the land, he became aware of a sudden crackling of twigs and rustling of branches on the bank just below him ; sounds quickly followed by the equally sudden appearance of a white-robed figure, which, springing up the slope, all but precipitated itself against him.

"I beg your pardon, Mr. Lyon !" exclaimed Dorothy Temple, regaining her balance with difficulty, for it was on the very edge of the bank that she had recoiled, only just in time to avoid ignominious collision with the massive person of her uncle's guest. "You were so completely in the shadow that I didn't see you."

"I think I ought to beg *your* pardon," returned Lyon. "I'm afraid I startled you. Have you been braving the waters in your famous punt ?"

The girl looked at him searchingly a moment before replying. Good-humored banter was evidently no part of her daily experience ; under raillery she half suspected some covert unkindness. Reading none in Lyon's face, she answered frankly :

"No ; I've only been sitting by the river for half an hour. I often sit there after dinner."

"By yourself ?"

"By myself, certainly. Surely you wouldn't imagine my uncle likely to do anything so frivolous?"

"Well, hardly. He has gone to work now, I believe. At any rate, he is preparing work for to-morrow—devotion to labor, indeed, on such a night! That's the worst of authors; their time is so taken up in laboring for immortality that they have next to no leisure to bestow on their perishing fellow-creatures. I dare say Mr. Creighton doesn't give you much of his society at any time?"

"No. But in any case, even if he were a less busy man, I could hardly expect him to do that, of course."

"Why 'of course'?"

"I am not a very fit companion for him, as you may easily guess. I don't understand the subjects that are his main interests in life; I never had any chance of studying them. You have, no doubt——"

"Indeed I have *not!*" interposed Lyon with fervent emphasis. "Whatever you do, Miss Temple, for goodness' sake don't encourage your uncle to think that I can be of any manner of use to him in his enquiries! If you should perceive him inclined to cherish such a delusion, try, I beg of you, to disabuse his mind of it. Tell him I know no more of the scientific doctrine of heredity than I do—say, of the philosophy of the Rig Vedas!"

Miss Temple laughed outright at this vehement appeal—frankly, easily, with all her first cheerful fearlessness of manner. Then Lyon laughed also; and matters were immediately replaced on their former pleasant footing between the two.

"But, if you don't care for the doctrine of heredity," Dorothy said when she had had her laugh out, "I'm afraid you will have a dull time of it in Heyford; for my uncle cares for very little else; and there is next to nothing to do—this is a particularly quiet neighborhood. It's impossible you should find a visit•here amusing."

"Mere lack of amusement won't make me pine. I'm not particularly given to gayety at any time, and just now I feel in the frame of mind to enjoy lying on the grass all day, and communing with nature—chiefly with my eyes shut. I'm a fearfully lazy mortal, and there's this good point to set against many ill ones in a lazy man : he is very little trouble to entertain."

Dorothy shook her head incredulously.

"I doubt your being quite so fond of an absolutely stirless existence as you'd have me think."

"Well, when I tire of dreams, I shall throw myself on your charity. Will you undertake to amuse me occasionally ? "

" I have so little time," was the grave reply. " You see, I am scarcely ever at home, except in the evenings. But the cart and pony will be at your service, I am sure. You could drive yourself anywhere you pleased—if you care for driving ? "

" Thanks." Lyon felt he had been quietly put down. Had the girl taken offence at his light tone ? Certainly, there was no offence visible in her manner, which, for all its gravity, remained perfectly sweet and serene. Nevertheless, clearly she had no intention of lending him her companionship whenever he chose to ask for it.

A momentary pause. Miss Temple, shivering slightly, drew the light fleecy shawl she wore over her shoulders a little closer at the throat. Her head was bare, and the thick fair waves of her hair caught the growing moonlight prettily.

" You seem cold," Lyon remarked. " Hadn't we better be moving ? I have my doubts about the sanitary virtues of that seat of yours—when the mists are rising," he added, as she turned by his side, and they strolled along the path together.

She did not make any immediate rejoinder. But after a moment or two she exclaimed, with apparent irrelevance :

" It isn't often that people do exactly what one wants of them."

" Very rarely indeed." Lyon wondered to what discourse this exclamation was serving as introduction.

" And though I hadn't the slightest expectation of your coming out here this evening, I was wishing just now with all my heart that you would come."

Lyon's wonder became perplexity. He began to think Miss Temple a decidedly curious girl. Inwardly he breathed a hope that her unconventionality might not assume any very seriously embarrassing form.

" I wanted so much to get a chance of saying a word to you in private," the girl went on—" about my cousin. I am afraid Uncle Mervyn may have prejudiced you against him. And, indeed, he does not understand Jem in the very least. He is the last person likely to judge him correctly."

She paused, not in any apparent confusion, but rather because her eagerness had made her a little breathless. Lyon, who had till now been holding his half-smoked cigar between his fingers, flung

it suddenly away into the bushes, and called himself secretly by
an opprobrious name before he answered :

"Pray have no further misgivings on that point. It is true I
haven't seen Travers for a good many years, but no one who knew
him at two-and-twenty would be easily brought to believe that
any lapse of time could have transformed him into the man of Mr.
Creighton's sketch. It's easy to see that your uncle and James
Travers are too differently constituted to be likely to understand
one another's motives. I've no doubt Mr. Creighton spoke in all
sincerity; he drew Travers exactly as he appears from his own
particular point of view. But one may be allowed to question
whether that point of view is the right one from which to regard
a man like James."

"Will you come and see for yourself ? " Dorothy appealed.
"It's not two minutes' walk to the rectory ; and we shall most
likely find him in the garden. Do come ! " as Lyon seemed to
hesitate. "He is so cut off from all his old friends here. I know
he will be delighted to see you again."

Lyon yielded, but not without secret misgivings. "That Jem
could lose his honesty of purpose, or his mental energy either,
seems very unlikely," he reflected. "All the same, it's scarcely
probable we shall find ourselves still in touch at this time of day.
For it's clear that he has quite abandoned his old Oxford
positions ; and, good Lord ! what have I in common with a
ritualistic parson ? "

The riverside path melted insensibly into a winding walk of the
rectory garden, neither gate nor boundary-mark of any kind
interposing itself where the one ended and the other began.
Dorothy led her companion through a corner of plantation first,
then over a lawn, more steeply sloping and much less scrupulously
kept than the lawns at The Haulms, and so out on to the mossy
sweep of gravel in front of the parsonage. Part of this, low-
roofed and lancet-windowed, was manifestly of very ancient date,
and such additions as had been made to it in more modern times
did little to disturb its general air of hoary antiquity. Not only
were the newer parts of the house in perfect architectural harmony
with the older portions, but both were now so thickly covered with
creepers that it was difficult, even for a practised eye, to discover
where the old ended and the new began. Twenty yards distant
from the entrance-porch lay the churchyard, separated from the
garden merely by an open iron railing, so that, standing on the

threshold of the house door, the inmates of the rectory could look straight up a narrow path between lines of venerable headstones to the noble south doorway of the neighboring church, with the escutcheon of the house of Lancaster still prominent in fair bold carving above its lintel.

The rectory shutters were all closed ; no sign of life appeared about the place.

" Mrs. Travers is half an invalid, and shuts up the house early," explained Dorothy Temple, seeing Lyon glance at the darkened windows. " And the rector never goes out after nightfall. I wonder we haven't met my cousin. Perhaps he is in the Lady's Walk. We will go and see."

She led the way again across the lawn downward toward the river ; then, stopping short of the path along the bank, branched off suddenly to the left. A moment later Lyon found himself in a straight turf-covered walk, closely overhung on the left hand with trees, but bordered on the right by the remains of a fine old brick wall which had clearly, at some time or other, formed part of the ramparts of a feudal mansion. In one or two places the embrasures for bowmen, and projections on which the culverins of ancient warfare were mounted in time of siege, remained in perfect preservation, while in others their former existence could be more or less distinctly traced. From below, the river, whispering softly through great clumps of reeds and bulrushes, sent up a pleasant murmur.

" This is the Lady's Walk," said Dorothy.

" A ghostly lady, I presume ? "

" Yes. It is a sad story, poor Lady Helen's. Her husband killed her." Dorothy paused in her walk, plucking a little nervously at the ivy covering a projecting mass of brick close by her. " It was during the Wars of the Roses. Her brother, flying from the victorious party, came to her for shelter ; and she hid him in the well that is at the farther end of the walk, there where you see the two cypresses, without telling her lord, who, being on the other side—the victorious side—himself, might have refused to harbor a fugitive. Somehow or other, a suspicion that someone was concealed in the well got about, and reached Lady Helen's husband. He watched, saw her pass to and fro at night with food for the unknown man, heard her talk with him ; and the second evening, as she was stealing back to the castle, fell upon her and killed her, without giving her time to explain the truth. Now the legend goes that she wanders up and down this walk at night, searching for her husband, unable to rest till she *has* explained."

" Granting to disembodied spirits a power of wandering, and a capability of concerning themselves with their past histories, that is just the sort of thing a female ghost would be likely to do, I dare say. A woman's impulse would naturally be to come back and insist on explanations."

" Or a man's either, I should think, in such a case."

" I'm not so sure."

" Why ? Are men so willing to be misjudged, then—to *die* misjudged by the persons they care for most in the world ? "

" No, I fancy not in the majority of instances. But I think our sex accepts the inevitable with a better grace than yours, as a rule. And personally, I've always fancied that death would probably have a wonderfully *cooling* effect on one's mind ; that one would probably wake up on the other side, supposing there *be* another, very much in the mood in which one wakes up in the morning here after a good night's sleep, having gone to bed in a shocking bad temper ; wondering, that is, how one could ever have made such a fool of one's self about a pack of trifles. But then "—with the slightest of smiles—" I speak only for the coarsely constituted masculine nature. A woman would probably feel differently."

" I cannot imagine being content to be misunderstood, certainly, living or dead."

" It's a thing one grows used to, I assure you. After a while— do you know ?—one ceases to set any extraordinary store by the opinions of one's fellow-creatures. It must be the delightful diffidence of youth that makes young people—so long as they remain young—so extremely anxious to be thought well of by their neighbors, I fancy ; for it's a craving which soon wears off. As one learns to esteem one's own judgment more lightly, one finds it quite easy to disregard the judgment of other people. Of course I'm supposing that one is lucky enough to have a pretty good conceit of one's self to begin with. When all's said, self-satisfaction is the only abiding source of solid comfort."

" Do you suppose anyone is really and thoroughly self-satisfied ? " questioned Dorothy abruptly. Moving on again, without waiting for an answer, she added, " Ah, here is Jem ! I thought we should find him."

A short and rather thick-set black figure moved out of the shade of the cypresses and a cheery voice called :

" Is that you, Dorothy ? "

" Yes, Jem. I've brought an old friend of yours to see you—Mr. Lyon."

" Lyon ? Not *Anthony* Lyon, surely ? Why, old fellow ! "—the dusky apparition was upon the pair already, and seized Lyon's hand as it spoke—" where have you sprung from so suddenly ? And what good fortune brings you to Heyford ? "

Lyon explained; taking stock, meanwhile, of his old friend and new acquaintance from head to foot, an operation rendered easy by the moonlight.   Barring the precision of his clerical costume, and the presence of the significant little cross hanging at his watch-chain, there was certainly nothing in the appearance of the Rev. James Travers to mark him out as the typical " ritualistic parson " of Lyon's uneasy fancy.   His air was neither stern nor unctuous, and conveyed no hint of lofty sacerdotal pretensions on his part, no suggestion of saintliness flaunting itself aggressively in the face of a wicked world.   His voice had a hearty, boyish ring ; his pleasant, open countenance bore no special traces of asceticism, while his figure inclined to decided squareness of outline.   For the rest, he had a fair complexion, light hair, with a strong dash of red in it, eyelashes and eyebrows strictly to match, and blue eyes in no way remarkable for size or vividness of coloring.   His head was for the present in great measure concealed by his soft felt hat, but the little that could be seen of the brow and temples would have led an observer to suspect that it contained brains.   The feature most noteworthy in his face was doubtless the chin, square as Lyon's own, and eloquent of strong will and unflinching resolution.   His mouth, on the other hand, though too wide for beauty, with its regrettably long upper lip, had a sensitive sweetness of expression, curiously at variance with the uncompromising firmness of that heavily moulded jaw.   It did not require much power of divination to guess that a man possessing at once such a mouth and such a chin must occasionally have a hard time of it with his conscience.

Lyon, making his explanation, perceived that Miss Temple had not erred in asserting James Travers' certain delight at the sight of himself, for James stood, meanwhile, openly beaming upon his old friend, his whole countenance radiant with genuine satisfaction.

"This *is* a rare piece of luck!" he ejaculated when Lyon came to a stop. "You'll stay and have a chat, won't you? Mr. Creighton is gone to his writing as usual, I suppose, Dorothy?"

"Oh, yes."

"I know nothing is ever allowed to interfere with two four-hour periods of labor; nine to one in the morning, and nine to one at night. You'll stay, then?" to Lyon.

"And pray don't feel obliged to hurry back at any particular hour," Dorothy put in. "I will tell Lewin to leave the drawing-room window open for you. Good-night, if I don't see you again. Good-night, Jem."

She flitted briskly down the moonlit walk into the shadow of the trees. Lyon glanced after her for a moment.

"Your cousin is a young lady of prompt action," he remarked.

"And quick instincts. She imagined, I've no doubt, that she might be in the way, and spoil our talk. Lyon, I warn you that I'm brimming over with feminine curiosity. I shall ask you questions. Don't answer them if you'd rather not."

"My dear fellow, there's so little to tell one way or another. I suspect you know already all there is to know."

"Well, I have to congratulate you to begin with, haven't I?"·

"To—Heaven forbid! Oh, I perceive! You allude to that lucky windfall in the shape of Yorkshire mines? Thanks, that *is* matter of congratulation. I was pretty low in the world when the wind shook that beneficent apple down, as you are probably aware."

"I heard of your sudden dash to Queensland, of course. That was not so long after——" Mr. Travers checked himself rather suddenly.

"After I had to leave Oxford, you mean? You needn't be afraid to mention that sore subject now. I know I behaved like a fool at the time; I must have bored you and Mallam—you recollect Charlie Mallam?"—("Don't I?" with boyish emphasis from Travers)—"bored you both to death with my tragic groanings under that first stroke of ill fortune. But I've outgrown that misery, thank Heaven, as I've outgrown others. It's astonishing, but very comforting too, to find how utterly reconciled one gets to things as they are."

"You've turned philosopher, apparently," observed the other, directing a searching look that was half incredulous, half compassionate, at Lyon's dark, impassive face.

Lyon did not see the look. His eyes were fixed on the moonlit sward at his feet.

"Every man's bound to turn philosopher when he finds himself gliding down the thirties. More shame to him if he doesn't!"

"Always supposing he can—that the root of philosophy is in him, as old Creyke used to say. You've not forgotten old Creyke? He's at St. Boniface still; same set of rooms behind the gateway, into which the sun never looks. I saw him when I went up to vote last week, and Mallam, too."

"How is Mallam prospering?"

"First rate. Tutor at the old place now, with heaps of private pupils besides. By the way, another old chum of yours has come back into college lately."

Oxford news, Oxford reminiscences sufficed to keep the conversation in full flow for the best part of half an hour. It was rather a one-sided conversation, certainly, Travers doing at least two-thirds of the talking. Lyon, however, seemed well pleased to play the listener's part. His expression, as the two men paced up and down the Lady's Walk together, became quite animated.

"You haven't mentioned Cartwright," he remarked, at the end of the aforesaid half-hour. "I used to like that fellow, and he certainly was very brilliant. He ought to be doing well."

"He *is* doing well—very well. Quite one of the leading men among the younger sort. They prophesy great things of him."

"Is he in Oxford still?"

"Very much so, indeed. Why, didn't you know he had stepped into my old berth?"

"No, I hadn't heard. Well, if you must needs vacate the place, I suppose it would have been hard to find a better man to come after you. To tell truth, though, Travers, I can't think why on earth you gave Cartwright that chance."

"My dear fellow, I had simply no choice in the matter. My father was responsible for this parish, and needed help here which only I could give him. It was impossible for me to stay on at Oxford."

"My dear Travers, excuse me, surely there were other available parsons in this realm of England two years ago? I haven't an extensive clerical acquaintance, but I believe I could name half a dozen men quite fit to be curate of Heyford. On the other hand, I don't know one, parson or layman, whom I should have cared to nominate to your old post."

"My father's means wouldn't have borne the strain of a curate's stipend," returned Travers brusquely. "Of course I dare say you'll think that difficulty might have been met in a different way. But you don't know my father. He is not a man to whom anyone, even his son, would dare to offer pecuniary help. Besides, he saw no need for a curate at that time. He sees none now. In his view, the work here was, and is, such as he can easily cope with single-handed. Even my presence he merely tolerates—as a kind of superfluity, a sort of unnecessary spiritual extravagance."

"Well, I can't help thinking you have made a mistake."

"I trust to God I haven't." The words were so gravely, albeit simply, spoken that Lyon, who was at the moment leaning over the parapet of the ancient wall, looking down into the river below, turned involuntarily to glance at the speaker. "That's what I fear sometimes I may have done. You see, unluckily, my father's way of thinking is not altogether mine. It doesn't seem fair to run counter to his ideas in his own parish. I feel bound to work, as far as is possible, on his lines. On the other hand, there's the higher duty. And it's often difficult to feel sure one isn't acting too much as a son, and too little as a parson. The precise point at which the question of expediency ends, and the question of right and wrong begins, is hard to determine," said Travers, with a nervous twist of his sensitive mouth.

"These things are rather beyond me," Lyon responded. "Only to the plain, non-religious man it certainly seems that, given two religious men who agree in essentials—as I presume you and your father may be said to do—there ought to be no great friction between them with regard to things that are merely accidental."

"True, as far as it goes. But how decide what constitutes an essential, and what an accidental, in such matters?"

"Oh, if you come to that, Travers, unless you wish to squander the not inconsiderable amount of brains nature endowed you with on mere hair-splitting for the remainder of your life, it strikes me you'd better go back to Oxford, or up to London, by the first train to-morrow morning. You haven't enough to do in this idyllic village."

"I don't want for work, I assure you. There's more to do in Heyford than you imagine, old chap. And the air's not a bit more conducive to moral uncertainty than the air of Oxford. Long before I left St. Boniface, years before I had any idea I

4

should ever be wanted here, I had my doubts as to whether I could honestly go on holding that professorship. I had been put into it as the nominee of the progressive party, you see—the party to which we all belonged in the old days. I gather that you belong to it still ? "

" My dear fellow, I belong to no party whatever. To belong to a party, one must believe, or, at the least, disbelieve something ; one must have made up one's mind either for or against. My mind isn't made up at all on any one point, except it be the worthlessness of human nature in general, and my own individual nature in particular ; not much of a foundation to build upon."

" I beg your pardon," returned Travers quickly, with another swift, sidelong glance. " However, as I was saying, they certainly gave me that post with the idea that I should make it a vantage-ground from which to advocate a certain definite set of *in*definite opinions. When my own views on certain subjects changed utterly, it seemed scarcely fair to stay in office and lecture the doctrines of my electors down. Then, on the other hand, one felt bound to use the opportunity. Well, Heyford's need of a curate cut the knot of that Gordian difficulty," he broke off, with a sudden return to brightness of manner.. " And as to going back, my dear chap, they wouldn't have me at any price ! I'm a sort of reactionary, you see ; a kind of traitor. The Heyford villagers are a bit suspicious of me, I believe, as a possible secret emissary of the Papacy. But in Oxford I should have to encounter much worse suspicions."

" I think I should prefer the most distrustful cold-shouldering in Oxford to the intellectual stagnation of a country village," quoth Lyon, heavily persistent.

" Oh, if a man stagnates anywhere, with a tolerable collection of books on his walls, and a post-bag twice a day, it must be the man's own fault," retorted Travers cheerfully.

He accompanied his friend to the foot of the neighboring garden, descanting on the past history of Heyford, and giving, incidentally, a humorous account of the last visit paid to the place by the local archæological society. Brian had made a sketch of the party of provincial worthies ascending the church tower, which Lyon must really see.

Here Lyon, suddenly awakened to a sense of his omissions, enquired for the vivacious ex-lancer. Travers reported his brother to be doing very fairly well in Australia, sticking to work, and keeping steady as Old Time ; apparently engineering was the profession for him, after all. At this point he had to suppress so unmistakable a yawn that Lyon, pulling up short in his walk, insisted on saying good-night at once.

"Why, you're half asleep, man ! What have you been about to-day ? Poring over the Fathers in MS. ? "

"Haven't so much as opened a book. It was our Benefit Club fête-day, and I had to preach to the members, and then preside at their annual feed, which lasted all the afternoon and a good part of the evening as well. I suppose the carving, with singing and bad tobacco *ad lib.* afterward, has made me a bit sleepy."

"A Benefit Club dinner ! What an ordeal ! " Lyon murmured.

"Ordeal ? Not a bit of it ! I enjoyed it very much ; they're awfully nice fellows, many of them. Good-night, Lyon. I'll look you up to-morrow as early as I can."

"And that's the end of the most brilliant scholar in Oxford," mused Lyon, as he proceeded on his upward way. "Truly, the man burdened with a conscience has precious little chance of getting on in this world. When will people learn that there's nothing on earth worth worrying one's self about sufficiently to spoil one's night's sleep ? "

He found the French window of the drawing-room open—Miss Temple had been faithful to her promise—and a light still burning in the hall. Possessing himself of his candlestick, he was marching upstairs with it, on his way to his room, when, at a sudden turn of the staircase, he came full upon Mr. Creighton's niece in the act of descending, with the shawl she had worn in the garden still wrapped about her shoulders.

"I—I thought you had come in before," she said in some confusion.

"I apologize most humbly. I know I'm outrageously late. But Travers and I got talking Oxford ; and, you know—or, rather, you don't know—what that means to old college chums ! It seems, though, that you, too, keep late hours. May I take that as a sign that you are not extra early in the morning ? "

"*I* am rather early," returned the girl. " I have to be. But my uncle does not breakfast till nine ; you will not have to rise with the lark. Good-night once more." With a friendly nod, she skimmed past him downstairs, disappearing into the dark, deserted drawing-room. Men are slow of intuition. It was not till Lyon heard the cautious grinding of bolts below—his room was over the drawing-room—that the reason of Miss Temple's unexplained nocturnal vigil occurred to him.

CHAPTER IV

AT THE RECTORY

"Les hommes ne sont justes qu'envers ceux qu'ils aiment,"

LYON's vague fear that he might possibly see too much of his host's niece during his sojourn at The Haulms did not seem at all likely to be justified. Not only was Miss Temple absent the following morning—as she had intimated would be the case—from her uncle's breakfast-table, but she did not even put in an appearance at luncheon. Mr. Creighton made no apology for her absence—did not, indeed, by word or sign, let fall any hint that he recollected so much as the fact of her existence ; and Lyon, as the day wore on, found himself indulging more than once in passing speculations as to her whereabouts. Two or three times during the long hours of the morning, which he spent with Mr. Creighton in his library, now languidly resisting, now lazily yielding to, the process of determined pumping to which that thoroughgoing disciple of the doctrine of heredity persistently and unblushingly subjected him, he glanced out of the half-open window, expecting to see a tall slim figure in dark skirt and light blouse pass by, laden, perhaps, with a trowel and basket—for, to his eye, Miss Temple had looked just the sort of young woman likely to spend a good deal of her time in gardening. No such figure, however, appeared to divert the somewhat oppressive monotony of his *tête-à-tête* with his philosophic entertainer ; and, if Miss Temple accomplished any garden work at all that day, her labors must have been performed in some extremely out-of-the-way corner of her uncle's modest property. Otherwise, her uncle's guest could hardly have failed to light upon her as he strolled about that very limited demesne in the afternoon.

The day was brilliantly fine, and the heat of the sun-charged atmosphere decidedly unfavorable to physical exertion. Lyon felt no inclination whatever to avail himself of the proffered services of Mr. Creighton's horse or Miss Dorothy's pony, and shrank with positive distaste from the notion of extensive exploration in the village. For some time, pleasantly accompanied by a book and a pipe, he made himself perfectly happy on the river-bank in the shade of a huge thorn. When the company aforesaid began to lose something of their absorbing charm, he sauntered over to the rectory in search of Travers.

Half-way to his destination he met the person he was going to visit. Travers came hurrying up, hot and apologetic.

"So sorry I haven't been able to look you up earlier; haven't had a moment! In the early morning, of course, there's church, and school, and what-not. And ever since eleven o'clock I've been engaged in trying to quell a parochial disturbance—a mere tea-cup tempest; but it bothers my father. Come up and be introduced to him. Seeing you will divert his mind a bit from old Crowther and his grievances, may be."

"What does the grievance relate to? Tithes and offerings?" enquired Lyon, as the two men climbed the steep ascent of the rectory lawn.

"Wish it did! Pecuniary grievances are at least tangible things to deal with. No; this is a case of Protestant panic, whereof I can't at present discover the originating cause. Unfortunately, Crowther, who has constituted himself spokesman in the matter,—he is our leading farmer, and a thoroughly worthy old chap in his way,—has been my father's churchwarden for thirty years, and understands exactly how to drive him to the verge of desperation. He has nearly driven him *over* the verge this morning. And the absurd part of it all is, that after two mortal hours' talk my father seems to be still quite in the dark as to the exact head and front of my present offending."

"Possibly the excellent Mr. Crowther is a little in the dark on that point himself."

"Possibly. However, he left word that he would call again this afternoon; and then *I* mean to tackle him, and get to the bottom of the matter, once for all. Ah, here comes my father!"

If Mr. Travers' elder son had indeed inherited, as Mr. Creighton so confidently asserted, his father's mental idiosyncrasies, this similarity of disposition was not heralded forth by any physical resemblance between the two men. In James Travers, short, plain-faced, irregular in outline and undecided in coloring, it was impossible to trace even the faintest likeness to the tall, distinguished-looking old man, dark-eyed and snowy-haired, with features cast in the purest aquiline mould, who wore his shabby clerical coat with the grace of a fallen French aristocrat, and stepped off the threadbare mat at his parsonage door to greet his son's friend with the courtly affability of a Spanish hidalgo. On the other hand, it was easy to recognize Brian's father in this stately old clergyman. Upon the scapegrace younger son of the house of Travers the mantle of his progenitor's good looks had fallen in no scant measure ; and Lyon found himself imagining Brian, some forty-five years hence, presenting the very counterpart of the figure in the rectory doorway.

"I am glad to make your acquaintance, Mr. Lyon. We have often heard your name from James," the old man said with dignified cordiality. "Though I believe you have not met for some time past ?"

Lyon explained that he had been in Australia for the best part of the last ten years.

"Indeed ? We have taken a special interest in Australia and the Australians of late years," Mr. Travers responded, with a smile. "My younger son went out to Queensland the summer before last. You know him also, I believe ? His brother has told you, no doubt, that he seems to be taking kindly to colonial life. Where are you going, James ?"

Mr. Travers' tone, in putting this abrupt question to his son, was marked by a sudden and complete change of tone, a change so sudden and so complete that Lyon could hardly fail to be struck by it. From the extreme of suavity the old man seemed to have passed in a moment to the extreme of irritability. His voice, till now so smoothly modulated, sounded harsh and rasping ; his manner, losing for a moment all its polished calm, betrayed keen annoyance, smouldering suspicion, even a suggestion of positive rooted antagonism.

"I see Crowther turning in at the farther gate," returned his son promptly. "I intended to intercept him and carry him off to the study before he could bear down upon you."

"Well, well," said Mr. Travers, still somewhat suspiciously, though with a note of relenting in his voice, "it might not be amiss for you to do so. I have no objection to your speaking to him yourself, if you choose." He uttered these words with the air of a schoolmaster granting a doubtful permission to a somewhat presuming schoolboy. "But be careful what you say to him. It does not do to put these people's backs up, especially when, as in the present case, the right is unfortunately on their side. Perhaps, on second thoughts, I had better be present myself at the interview."

James Travers flushed to the roots of his light hair.

"As you please, sir, of course. I merely fancied you would be glad to keep out of the fray."

"There need be no fray, as you call it, if you are commonly judicious," retorted his father oracularly. "Well, be it as you wish ; see Crowther alone, by all means, if you prefer to do so. Mr. Lyon,"—this with an easy resumption of his momentarily abandoned grand manner—"will you sit with me on the lawn for a few minutes, until James is at liberty to return to us ? "

Lyon sat down, wondering within himself how much longer James Travers would continue to hold the curacy of Heyford. "If the St. Boniface Common Room could have witnessed this little scene ! " he said to himself. " ' Verily, I think thou'rt fallen far,' my poor James."

"My son," Mr. Travers pronounced with dignity, "is very well-meaning, extremely well-intentioned. But, like most young men, he is highly injudicious. He never showed his want of judgment more than in flinging up his Oxford appointment, and planting himself at Heyford, on the plea that the parish required more supervision, and more services, than I could give it. A most mistaken notion from my point of view. I have never considered the multiplication of services an aid to spiritual religion. James, however, has become unhappily imbued with the ideas of that pernicious school which sets an exaggerated value on externals, and he thinks otherwise. Consequently, he insisted on becoming my curate, almost, I may say, against my will. And what is the result ? My parishioners, so far from welcoming his new fangled ceremonies, resent them."

Lyon, in some embarrassment at the turn given by Mr. Travers to the conversation, delivered himself of the highly original remark that country folk were usually averse to change of every kind.

"Yes ; *stare super antiquas vias* is their motto in most things. And a right good motto, too. I wish James would consent to follow its teaching ! His doings are a constant source of strife in this quiet place. This very morning my senior churchwarden, a most estimable man, who has served his responsible office faithfully during the whole period of my incumbency of thirty-two years— this worthy man comes to me in great distress, because of some symbolic words in an unknown tongue—he did not know whether Latin or Greek words; he is naturally not a scholar, good man !— which James has introduced into the ornamentation of the church. A very foolish prank on James' part—certain to give rise to scandal, as he might easily have known beforehand.''

"What are the words in question ?" Lyon asked languidly, not feeling much interest in the matter, but obliged to feign a slight curiosity, for politeness' sake.

"I really cannot inform you. I had not noticed them myself until Crowther came to lodge his complaint against them. Indeed, I have not seen them now, for I have not been able to go into the church since he left me, to make examination. I suffer a good deal from asthma, and the damp atmosphere of our venerable church is trying to my weak chest—especially on week-days, when the building is empty. Ah ! my son is taking Crowther into the church, I see !" Lyon, turning in his seat, caught a glimpse of Farmer Crowther's burly form disappearing under the archway of the south porch, in the wake of James Travers' diminutive black figure. "Why does he do that, I wonder ? What good can he possibly expect to effect by showing a man afresh the very object that has roused his dislike ? James should have better sense. But all this unwisdom springs from his fatal tendency to overestimate the importance of mere ornament.''

At the end of about ten minutes—a rather trying ten minutes for Lyon—James Travers reissued from the churchyard with Farmer Crowther, and, having shaken hands warmly with that sturdy Protestant, who tramped off with an air of stolid satisfaction in the direction of the village, came running across the grass like a schoolboy, waving his clerical hat in sign of victory.

"James," his father began in a tone of the utmost severity, "what does this mean ? I trust——"

The whilom professor fell into a fit of convulsive laughter. "My dear father, excuse me—don't think me absolutely crazy, Lyon—but really it's too good a joke altogether ! I've been keeping a straight face before Crowther, for the honor of my order, and now I must let myself go, or perish." He threw back his uncovered head, and laughed again boyishly.

"Let us into the joke, when you can," Lyon said.

Travers struggled for composure. "Oh, delicious ! The dear old man, pouncing upon a pair of new altar candles with a word in an unknown tongue stamped into the wax of each, thought he had lighted on a Popish symbol, of course. And the word turned out to be 'Ozokerit,' the brand of Messrs. Field & Field." Travers fell into fresh ecstasies of mirth.

But his father austerely refused to smile. "An unfortunate blunder," he remarked. "It shows how careful one is bound to be in these matters."

"The occurrence of such a blunder as this could hardly be guarded against by any amount of care, I should fancy," Lyon observed dryly. "Errors of sheer ignorance are hard to foresee. This would make a good story for *Punch*, Travers," turning to the younger man.

"First rate, if one only had Keene here to put in the figures," responded James. "Typical farmer and typical curate—Crowther and I make fairly tidy models for those characters, eh, Lyon ? Well, I'm happy to say he has departed content, his wrath thoroughly mollified."

"I hope you explained the matter to him properly," Mr. Travers interrupted. "These people do not understand levity in treating of such things."

"I should never think of trying it on with Crowther after that fashion, I assure you," James replied. Lyon saw Mr. Travers shudder at the slang phrase. "In his presence I didn't indulge in so much as the ghost of a smile ; I pointed out the mistake into which he had fallen with the utmost gravity, I may say solemnity, of countenance."

"You seem to be a primitive folk hereabouts," Lyon remarked.

"We are ; not a doubt of it. Has my cousin Dorothy told you the story of the hedger who objected to the keeping of Ascension Day ? No ? I thought she might have related it ; it's rather a pet story of hers. Well, this good man was dead against the multiplying of festivals—a new-fangled custom, it appeared to him, of my presumptuous making. 'Till you come into Heyford,' he said to me, as a final clincher on the subject, ' us had but three veasts a year : Christmas, Easter, and ship-shearing. And they be enough for I.' "

Once more Mr. Travers utterly declined his son's invitation to him to make merry. "William Hewer had, after all, some touch of right on his side," he said coldly, getting up. "To persons of

simple faith this insistence on a formal observance of times and
seasons is often more of a stumbling-block than anything else.
Will you come into the house, Mr. Lyon, and let me present you
to Mrs. Travers? She is, unfortunately, something of an invalid,
and receives few visitors. But any friend of my son Brian will
be welcome to her, I know."

And it was wholly as Brian's friend, ignoring quite his older
and closer connection with Brian's brother, that Lyon found
himself greeted by the lady of the rectory : a pretty, faded,
untidy-looking woman, lying on the sofa in a room, pretty, faded,
and untidy-looking as herself. For twenty minutes Mrs. Travers
talked eagerly and incessantly of her younger son, in whom, it
was easy to see, her maternal soul was completely bound up.
When Lyon, James being temporarily absent from the room,
made some passing reference to the elder, the response he elicited
was neither ready nor cordial. Of James his mother spoke, when
she spoke at all, with indifference, almost with impatience ;
clearly his ideas and methods met with no greater sympathy from
her than they received at his father's hands. Lyon perceived that
his old friend was, to both his parents, a source of irritation rather
than pride. He was at once too simple and too transcendental, too
unworldly, after a very antique pattern, and too unconventional,
on the modern plan, to present aught but the appearance of an
inconsistent and annoying problem to their understandings,
cramped by early training in the straitest sect of the Philistines,
if not of the Pharisees. His nature did not fall within the
compass of any measuring-rod these two elderly persons had ever
learned to mete withal. Broad and easy-going in his views and
practices where, according to the traditions of Mr. and Mrs.
Travers' youth, he should have been decorously narrow and rigidly
immovable; sharply dogmatic and obstinately unyielding when,
from his parents' point of view, a modest vagueness and teacha-
bleness of spirit would have better become him, he was doubtless
a perpetual prickle in the sides of a father and mother whose
mental range, originally limited, was every day growing shorter
by reason of the failing vision of age. What wonder if he
received, as Lyon suspected he did receive, scant justice at their
judgment-bar ?

For Brian, on the other hand, the mother, at least, had nothing
but indulgence. It was plain that she chose to regard his faults
as the simple outcome of his circumstances, that she excused his

worst failures as chiefly due to the unkind action of an adverse fate. For his newly developed qualities of industry and perseverance no praise seemed to her too great.

Mrs. Travers talked, and Lyon, after his wont, proved a patient listener, by this means so far winning his new acquaintance's heart that, when he rose to go, she took a most gracious leave of him, making him at the same time a pressing general offer of the rectory hospitality at all times and seasons.

He thanked her, deciding, as he did so, that, in Mr. Creighton's unflattering picture of the Travers family, this figure at least had not been out of drawing. Mrs. Travers' thin, tightly compressed lips, oddly at variance with the soft delicacy of her other features ; the little spurts of ill-concealed temper in speaking of her elder son, which contrasted so strangely with her flowing eulogy of his brother ; even the sudden dictatorial enunciation, now and again, of an opinion—usually highly illogical—on some indifferent subject, breaking forth in the midst of a stream of rambling and rather inconsequent talk; all these things accorded accurately with the portrait of her as a woman weak and obstinate at once, "a kind of human octopus," limned by the unmerciful hand of her next-door neighbor. Lyon's pity for James Travers waxed strong.

However, James did not seem, at the moment, at all inclined to pity himself. Strolling back to The Haulms with Lyon he was in the highest spirits, joking and laughing like a boy of fifteen. Only once did his voice take a melancholy tone, and that was when he lamented the enforced loneliness and monotony of his mother's life. An invalid, all her friends living at a distance, she had to pass most of her days in something like solitude.

Lyon suggested that Mrs. Travers must find Miss Temple's near neighborhood an advantage.

James reddened slightly. "Well—at one time——" he said in evident embarrassment. Then, pulling himself together: "Dorothy has always been most kind and attentive to my mother ; and at one time they used to see a great deal of one another, I know. Latterly there has been some little—I won't call it coolness, exactly—but some little uncomfortableness between them. However, I quite hope and believe the—the feeling will wear off ultimately. And my cousin was not really to blame in the affair, as my mother fancied; naturally enough, I admit. You haven't seen much of Dorothy yet ? "

"Since last night, nothing whatever. Your cousin appears to be a much-occupied young lady—unless it is an uncommon love of solitude that keeps her apart from her kind."

" Oh, Dorothy has no fancy for solitude; she's a socially minded creature ! A visitor at The Haulms must be quite a pleasurable excitement for her, poor girl. Creighton is not a very genial guardian, I'm afraid, and Dorothy does so enjoy chattering when she can get anyone to chatter to."

"She doesn't seem inclined to exercise her conversational powers on me, at any rate. I hope I didn't show myself extra forbidding last night."

"Well, at least you needn't take it so hastily for granted that she is keeping out of your way intentionally ! She's always off to her school by eight in the morning, and doesn't get back much before five, as a rule. I've started a small school for an outlying hamlet of ours, more than two miles off, on the Donnington road," Travers added explanatorily, " and Dorothy acts as mistress."

" Rather stiff work for a girl of that age, eh ? "

" Just what hundreds of professional school-mistresses, younger and weaker than Dorothy—who is as strong as a young lioness, by the way—have to do year out, year in, for a living. In stuffy town schools, too. No, I don't think the work is too hard for her. And it gives her an object in life, which, until recently, was a thing she sadly needed. She felt the need herself."

" Doubtless you've infected her with your own notions in such matters. Now, to my mind, the principal thing in life is to be without any ' object.' It's the only prophylactic against disappointment."

"And the condition in which one is most certain to sink quickly and easily from the level of a human being to that of a jelly-fish."

"Ah, your jelly-fish threat has no terrors for me," Lyon smiled. " I only wish we could approximate a little more closely than, even under the most favorable circumstances, men seem capable of doing, to the state of those colder-blooded creatures. We humans are far too much and too consciously alive nowadays. With fewer red corpuscles in our veins we might worry through life with less of fret and fever perhaps."

" One may buy quiet too dear," Travers said rather brusquely. " As a matter of fact one *must* buy it too dear. Absolute quiet means absolute indifference, general insensibility, to pleasure as well as to pain."

"Considering the proportions in which pleasure and pain are distributed in this best of all possible worlds, I should say the balance of advantage was on the side of the wholly insensible man."

"There I can't agree with you," returned the other. "Besides, no man ever made himself really insensible at all joints. There's always a vulnerable joint somewhere in the harness. Five o'clock!"—as the church clock began to chime the hour—"I must be off." He turned back quickly, calling over his shoulder as he went, "By the way, you'll find my cousin come back from Owlswick by this time, I should think. She always has tea in the drawing-room at five, if you care for tea."

CHAPTER V

ACROSS THE TEA-CUPS

"A very pitiful lady, very young—
Exceeding rich in human sympathies."

MR. LYON, on mature deliberation, decided that, at the close of so hot an afternoon, he did care for tea; and took his way to the drawing-room in order to obtain the desired refreshment. Stepping through the open window, he descried in the middle of that primly ordered apartment a small tea-table duly set out, and a diminutive brass kettle hissing cheerfully on a stand beside it; while in an arm-chair close by, her head thrown back, and showing almost golden in its fairness against a dark blue velvet cushion, half sat, half lay, Dorothy Temple. He was just opening his mouth to wish her an ironical "good-morning," when his eyes, travelling upward from the skirt of her lavender cambric gown to her face, gave him warning to check himself. The girl was sound asleep.

Overcome either by the heat or the labors of the day, she appeared to be slumbering most luxuriously in the great chair, her hands folded peacefully in her lap, while a pair of slender feet, clad in extremely dusty shoes, displayed themselves unabashed beyond the skirt of her light dress. On the floor beside her, where she had evidently tossed them down on entering—lay sunburned straw hat, and a brown canvas satchel full of school-books.

Lyon stood studying the quiet figure attentively. Asleep, Dorothy looked younger than in her waking hours—and also prettier. Her placid face, with its closed eyelids and slightly parted lips, wore a serene innocence of expression that was almost childlike, coupled with a seriousness that was not without its pathetic suggestions—at least to Lyon. Why the sight of a young woman, very naturally asleep after a long walk on a hot summer afternoon, should touch an emotional chord in him, who was certainly not given to sentiment, he could hardly explain to his own satisfaction. The fact remained, however, that the chord *was* touched for an instant—touched, as it might have been, say, by the sudden recurrence to his memory of a line from Tennyson, the hearing of a yearning melodic phrase in the midst of a symphonic storm, or an unexpected glimpse of snow-mountains with the sunset glow upon them. Unemotional as he was, these things, even of late years, would occasionally stir in him just such a wave, or rather ripple, of feeling as now ruffled the calm waters of his nature for a moment.

His tread, like that of many massively built men, was quiet if heavy, and his entry did not rouse the sleeper in the big chair. Neither did his scrutiny of her unconscious face appear to disturb her slumbers in the least. He might have continued his study until dinner-time, had he cared to do so, but for the accident of the kettle suddenly boiling over with much fuss and ceremony. Before he could advance to the rescue Dorothy was awake and on her feet, exclaiming:

"How stupid of me to go to sleep and forget! Clean water, mercifully"—hastily extinguishing the spirit-lamp; "it can't have done the carpet any great harm. Oh, Mr. Lyon, how do you do? You must think me a shocking bad hostess. I am so sorry! Have you"—with a slight accession of color—"been here long?"

"Barely two minutes, I assure you. I beg to add that, during those two minutes, I was as quiet as any mouse. *I* am not responsible for waking you."

"I know; it was the kettle. I am much obliged to it."

"Really? You looked so extremely comfortable, it seemed a thousand pities you should be disturbed."

"I should have been grateful to anyone who would have disturbed me sooner. There is nothing I feel so ashamed of as this absurd falling asleep in the daytime. I am not surprised when my uncle is severe on the subject. Cream? and sugar?"

"Both, please. Do you do this often, then?" enquired Lyon, taking his cup.

"Falling asleep, you mean?" coloring again. "No, not very often. Only when it is extra hot, as it has been to-day, and I get a little bit fagged in consequence. The road to Owlswick, where I go every day," she added, "is quite unshaded; and that makes it rather a tiring walk."

"Travers, your cousin, has been telling me about this Owlswick undertaking of yours," Lyon said in a would-be non-committal tone, through which, however, some undertone of disapproval must have made itself audible, for Dorothy retorted, with a laugh:

"You speak of the ' undertaking ' as if you considered it rather reprehensible."

"It strikes me as formidable—for a young lady."

"Not if the young lady is as strong as I am."

"And, excuse me, something like a waste of the young lady's powers besides."

"Aren't you a trifle hard upon me, Mr. Lyon? It mayn't be a very lofty occupation to teach a score of village children to read and write and say their catechism; and it certainly isn't one requiring much talent in the teacher—luckily for me! But I've always considered it a harmless employment, perhaps a useful one."

"My dear Miss Temple, I haven't a word to say against its usefulness. I only intended to suggest that you might possibly be more pleasantly and profitably employed than in a drudgery which any board school pupil-teacher would plod through with just as good results."

"And much better ones," Dorothy chimed in readily. "Only, unfortunately at present we can't afford to pay that board school pupil-teacher! If we could we certainly would, for, of course, an untrained mistress like myself is a great disadvantage to any school. I do my best; but it's a very bad best. And then we suffer financially, too, in consequence."

"Why, don't you get good government grants?" rather sarcastically.

"How should we get *any* government grants? I'm not certificated, you see," and there was a merry twinkle in the clear hazel eyes. "Mr. Lyon, your political education appears to have been neglected. I really must lend you the Education Act of '70 to read! Another cup?"

"Thanks; I won't refuse so good an offer. Well, you'll think me obstinate, I dare say,—perhaps impertinent,—but I must repeat that this thing seems to me rather a reckless expenditure of strength, physical and mental, on your part."

"Ah, that's because you don't know!" Dorothy rejoined, not very lucidly. "There are so few useful things that I am at all capable of doing, unluckily. Just this one thing I *can* do, and therefore I feel bound to do it."

"You seem to have a sort of passion for being useful."

"I don't care to feel myself a complete cumberer of the earth. No one likes to do that."

"Pardon me, you are generalizing at too great a rate. Some people have no feeling at all on the subject; it's a pure matter of temperament. Take me—I suppose I ought to blush to say it—for an instance. The Scriptural phrase you made use of just now most aptly describes me. And yet I'm afraid I don't repine at my lot; while, as to craving opportunities of usefulness——" He shook his head expressively.

Dorothy knit her smooth young brows in silence for a moment or two before she answered:

"You are differently situated. I suppose your work is already cut out for you. A man with a profession——"

"But I haven't any profession, now! I'm a mere holiday-maker. To contemplate the doings of such people as yourself and Travers fills me with wonder and awe—and shame besides. I feel as if, when dinner-time came, I should hardly be within my right in presenting myself."

Dorothy smiled. "Even Jem takes a holiday now and then; once a year or so."

"Does he? I'm heartily glad to hear it. But my holiday—do you understand?—is continuous. You perceive that I'm not leading a very active or useful life down here? Very well. That's the sort of do-nothing existence I lead everywhere, from one year's end to another, since I gave up work."

"Then you acknowledge that you did work once?"

"Certainly, I admit the soft impeachment. I worked once; during some years I even worked extremely hard—for the simple reason that I had to. At that time, if I had stopped working, I must have starved. So I went on. There's nothing like Hunger at a man's elbow for keeping him going. But as soon as the vulgar necessity for industry ceased to exist I gave up being industrious."

Dorothy's face wore a half-puzzled, half-incredulous expression.

"Aren't you laying on the colors a little too thickly, Mr. Lyon? You must do something—you can't live absolutely without occupation!"

"No. Even of myself I wouldn't assert that to be possible. Complete inertia is beyond even me, so I still hunt a little and shoot a little. In the summer I generally attempt some mild climbing, and in the winter I go occasionally to the play. I dine out when people are good enough to ask me. Also, in the course of the year I manage to get through a fair number of books and an outrageous number of pipes. I'm afraid the sketch of my existence strikes you as decidedly unimpressive."

"I fancy you must be caricaturing it."

"Not a whit, I assure you." Lyon shot a quick, searching glance, that had an underlying suspicion in it, at his companion; a glance which perplexed and took her aback, though she did not understand its meaning in the least; then he set down his cup rather hastily, and got up from his chair. "Do you like this school-work of yours?" he asked, returning abruptly to the former topic of conversation. "Do you enjoy it?"

"No," she replied, with some reluctance, "it would be too much to say that I *enjoy* it, now. I did for a while, at first, when it was all new and interesting, and the children behaved like a troop of little angels, and I quite believed I was going to turn every one of them into a prodigy of learning and goodness. But those days soon came to an end. And then——"

"There came a reaction?"

"Such a reaction that I believe I should have thrown up the whole scheme in disgust if it hadn't been for Jem."

"He holds you to your bargain, then? Tyrant! There are no tyrants like these parsons. I suppose he put the idea into your head, to begin with?"

"No, the idea was my own. Of course I knew he was distressed that the Owlswick children should have no school, but he never suggested that *I* should try to teach them. Indeed, I thought he would refuse me when I offered; and he told me frankly that he was doubtful whether I should do. Only, when

5

once I had begun, and, to a certain extent, succeeded, he would not let me give the work up. It was a very good thing he stood firm in the matter.''

" Else you would have yielded to temptation ? ''

" It's more than likely, I'm afraid. Jem says it's my constitutional failing to rush into sacr—into undertakings without properly counting the cost, and then repent myself and want to back out of them.''

" Your failing is shared by the majority of mankind—and womankind, too, I fancy, Miss Temple. However, you seem to have conquered it honorably in the present instance—a most trying one, I should say. Those imps you once fondly imagined budding cherubs must make large calls upon your stock of patience. Don't you find them difficult to manage ? ''

" Oh, at times they are simply maddening ! '' the girl confessed frankly. " To-day, for instance—how I should have liked to box their ears all round, half a dozen times during the afternoon ! and I really believe it would have been good for them.''

"And how about yourself ? Miss Temple, in the end you will find that I have right on my side, when the fiendish gambols of the imps have succeeded in utterly ruining, as ultimately they infallibly will ruin, your naturally excellent temper.''

" But my temper isn't naturally excellent, I am sorry to say. It's rather hot. No, I must learn to keep it in better order, that's all. My cousin Isabel Travers always declares it's an admirable discipline to have your temper thoroughly tried every day,'' said Dorothy, laughing a little, " and I am trying to believe her. I know she speaks from hard experience, as one great in organizing committees. From what she tells me, school-children must be a joke to committee-women as temper-tests. I'm glad to think you will meet Isabel, Mr. Lyon. She is coming down to the rectory from Saturday to Monday.''

Lyon expressed becoming pleasure at this intelligence. " Miss Travers is a very learned lady, is she not ? '' he asked politely.

" She took a very good place in the classical tripos. But she isn't merely learned ; she's very clever in a practical way, besides. She does no end of useful work in London. I really should like you to know her very much.''

" I believe you fancy she might convert me from the error of my idle ways ! I fear I'm past praying for there, Miss Temple ; indolence has eaten too long into the marrow of my bones. But

I've no doubt "—with a somewhat enigmatic smile—" that your cousin is a most interesting and admirable person. I shall look forward with pleasure to Saturday."

CHAPTER VI

BY THE RIVER

"A tale
Not new, nor joyful, but a common tale."

SATURDAY, however, did not, after all, bring Miss Isabel Travers to Heyford. That young lady, finding herself even more than ordinarily hampered by her business engagements, so she wrote to her cousin, postponed her flying visit for a week ; and during ten days nothing whatever occurred to vary the uneventful course of Lyon's life at The Haulms. A morning spent in Mr. Creighton's library ; an afternoon passed in the congenial companionship of book and pipe under Mr. Creighton's trees ; tea, followed perhaps by a stroll in the garden, or along the river-bank, with Miss Dorothy ; after dinner a more extensive ramble, usually shared by James Travers : such was the monotonous sum of his daily history. He did not chafe against this monotony—found it, in fact, rather pleasant than otherwise. The weather remained steadily fine ; his host's excellent library was his to ransack as he pleased ; while frequent intercourse with Travers preserved him from any danger of sinking into that condition of intellectual stagnation which speedily conduces to boredom—in the case, that is to say, of any man to whom mere animal comfort is not the be-all and end-all of life. Then Mr. Creighton's society, if not exactly delightful to Lyon, was not disagreeable to him. He took some idle pleasure in studying the cranks and angles of his host's decidedly cranky and angular individuality, and felt almost disposed to deem the insight hereby afforded him into an order of human nature of which he had, up to this time, encountered few types, sufficient payment for the trouble of answering an innumerable number of questions bearing on his Australian experience. In this matter he had fallen completely into Creighton's toils, and suffered himself to be exploited, morning after morning, with a secret grim amusement at his own folly in submitting to the infliction.

Nor did he confine himself exclusively to Creighton's character, as a subject of study, during these ten days. In a fitful way he took observations on that of Creighton's niece ; with the result, so far, that he was half inclined to believe he had lighted on that which, in his estimation, might be ranked among the rarest of rare phenomena : a perfectly honest and unaffected young woman, with no taint of feminine insincerity corrupting the wholesomeness of her straightforward, unsophisticated nature at any point. Only half inclined, however ! He still suspended judgment on Dorothy Temple ; still thought it extremely likely that, under sufficient provocation, she would betray herself as being, at heart, no better than the rest of the sisterhood, and watched, with something like interest, for an occasion of such self-betrayal to arise. But in the meantime he found himself compelled in common fairness to give her, woman though she were, the benefit of the doubt.

If Dorothy's idiosyncrasies interested Lyon a little, those of her cousin James Travers interested him much. This brilliant scholar and man of letters subdued to a humble country curate, this daring speculator of earlier days become an obedient mouthpiece of the authority of the Church, this *ci-devant* leader of men and thought submitting himself patiently to the petty tyrannies of a narrow-minded old man incapable of understanding so much as the alphabet of a nature immeasurably deeper and loftier than his own, presented to Lyon a problem over which he pondered constantly. Every day added something to the difficulty of arriving at any solution of the enigma, since every day showed Travers in some novel and, to Lyon, incomprehensible light. Once he let drop a hint of his perplexities on the subject of her cousin to Dorothy.

She answered quickly, " There is nothing particularly mysterious about Jem, that I can see, Mr. Lyon."

" Perhaps you hold some clue to his motives that I haven't found as yet," Lyon remarked.

Dorothy let the remark pass. " The whole explanation of Jem lies just in the one fact that, unlike most people, he lives for another world."

" But I've met men before who did that, or professed to do it, and in nearly every one of those cases the transcendental ambition to live above the earthly plane seemed to have killed out all genuine human nature. The men in question were not men at all, from my point of view ; they were imitation, artificial monks—only they generally seemed to bar the ascetic part of the business of monkery. It's not so with Travers; he's real and human enough."

"I think it's given to few people to be so absolutely real as Jem," Dorothy responded thoughtfully. "I fancy even the best men can hardly help posing a little at times. Jem wouldn't know how to pose." She laughed softly at the idea.

"He must be a unique specimen of his kind, then."

"He is!" indignantly.

In his heart Lyon leaned to agreement with this assertion. And he found Travers as a specimen, if not unique, at least of a singularly uncommon kind, so well worthy his continued investigation, that, when Mr. Creighton begged him to lengthen the term of his visit, originally fixed at a fortnight, by the addition of another week, he permitted himself to be over-persuaded.

This promise to extend his stay was given by him on the morning of the day fixed for Miss Travers' deferred arrival at the rectory. True on this occasion to her engagement, the renowned damsel did actually arrive at last, though not before she had twice telegraphed a change of train; and after dinner, in the garden of the The Haulms, Lyon was presented to her in all due form by her cousin.

The results of this introduction were not quite satisfactory to Dorothy. It is true, Mr. Lyon listened most politely and respectfully to the fluent disquisitions on many subjects of the gifted Isabel, a small, eager, dark-skinned creature, with restless eyes, and tiny brown hands perpetually in motion as she talked; but Dorothy had her doubts, nevertheless, whether he were taking her cousin seriously. She more than suspected that, smirking under his decorously lowered eyelids, playing a game of fiendish hide-and-seek behind his grave air of almost exaggerated attention, there gambolled a mocking spirit, to whom poor Isabel and her schemes for the regeneration of society—her guilds and libraries and halls of science, her woman's suffrage meetings and associations for the spread of the higher education—were mere matter of scoffing amusement.

Her suspicions were well-founded. Miss Travers, with her mixture of ignorance and assurance, her real inexperience and her lofty assumption of a profound knowledge of the world, did amuse Lyon immensely. So entertained, indeed, was he by her talk that for a while he altogether forgot to be angry with the strain of unreal sentiment that ran through it. To his mind, there was something exquisitely ludicrous in this girl of three-and-twenty, who had passed, perhaps, some twelve months of her life in London, setting to work in all gravity to lay down the law on matters of city government and morals with all the authority that might have befitted an acknowledged master of social ethics, or an experienced metropolitan magistrate.

For quite an hour the cynical spirit in him remained absolutely quiescent, tickled into unwonted good humor. Then, roused by one or two unlucky gushes of manifestly false sentiment on the fair Isabel's part, the demon began to bestir himself. Moved by him, Lyon deliberately provoked Miss Travers into fresh absurdities; and Dorothy, sitting ·by, perceived what was afoot, and was deeply angered. She was powerless, however, to interfere in the matter, for whenever she presumed to enter the conversation it was only to be quietly snubbed out of it again by Isabel, who liked having the field entirely to herself. Dorothy, therefore, could only continue to look on and listen, in rising indignation.

And now Lyon had the malicious satisfaction of seeing Miss Travers recoil from an exemplification of her own pet principles. She had spoken great things earlier in the evening concerning the dignity of labor, and of her strenuous endeavors to impress upon the young men to whom she lectured thrice a week the elevating truth that any and every kind of work is ennobling, no matter where or by whom performed—with other platform platitudes of the same kind. It chanced that she saw fit, later on, to discuss the feasibility—much under discussion in the public prints just then—of making a certain projected railway through a certain district of Africa. The chief difficulty in the way of this enterprise was supposed to consist in the nature of the geological formations through which the line would have to pass, certain engineers having asserted that one at least of these was too hard for cutting.

Lyon met this assertion with a blunt negative. He knew, he said, that the stone in question could be cut.

Miss Travers enquired, "How?"

"Because I've cut a good many cubic yards of it myself in my time. An up-country section of a railway I once helped to make in Queensland ran through a precisely similar formation."

"You cut?" Miss Travers echoed blankly. "You don't mean with your own hands?"

"With my own hands, aided by a pick—certainly."

Lyon was enjoying himself immensely.

Miss Travers murmured something altogether incoherent. Then —"Oh, I see!" she exclaimed in relieved accents; "you were engineer of the line, and you used to work with the men for their encouragement." She would perhaps have added some word of commendation of his conduct in so doing, had not he interrupted her with:

"No, my inducement was a daily wage. I wasn't engineer of the line at that time; I was a simple navvy."

"Really? How—how very interesting!" stammered the prophetess of the dignity of labor, with a nervous laugh.

"I am glad it should appear so to you. Personally, I must confess that I found stone-cutting horribly uninteresting. However, it doesn't do to be particular when one is out of work. I'm sure you'll agree with me there?" Lyon said, with an appealing smile.

"Oh, yes; certainly—entirely!" Isabel made haste to respond. Anxious to turn the conversation into a fresh channel, she added—she flattered herself, with considerable adroitness: "That experience of yours, the having mixed for a time with workingmen and shared their life at all points, must be very useful to you now in dealing with your people in the North."

"My—people?" Lyon lifted his dark eyebrows interrogatively.

"My brother told me you had mines in Yorkshire," Miss Travers explained rather falteringly.

"I beg your pardon—I did not quite catch your meaning for the moment. Yes, I have some coal-pits in Yorkshire. They came into my possession about three years ago. But I must make a humiliating acknowledgment on the subject of those pits. I've never yet seen them."

"But you have been down to the district? you know something of the people who work in them, surely?" Isabel said.

Dorothy leaned forward a little in her seat, her eyes seeking Lyon's face anxiously.

"No; I blush to say. Shocking confession—isn't it?—for an employer of labor, in these philanthropic days. However, I have an agent who seems to be of the right sort. He certainly looks after my interests admirably; and I dare say looks after the pitmen's equally well."

Lyon glanced involuntarily under his eyelashes at Dorothy, a little curious, maybe, to see how she took this last speech of his. She had her lips set very hard one upon another, and he fancied also that she looked paler than usual. But she gave her feeling, whatever it might be, no expression in words.

Miss Travers was not so reticent. Very fearlessly she took Lyon to task for his manifest dereliction of duty in failing to visit his property and ascertain the condition of the human creatures who spent their lives in exhausting labor under the earth that he might be able to dwell at his ease in upper air. And this time she was perfectly sincere in her outspoken indignation. The note of sincerity rang in every word she uttered, as Lyon acknowledged to himself, even while he laughingly parried her attack in a fashion which, though she indubitably had right on her side, speedily reduced her to a condition of stammering discomfiture, and left him, most unrighteously, master of the field.

Seeing the futility of her efforts to awaken her new acquaintance from his state of moral insensibility, and sorely wounded by the shafts of his ridicule, she before long took occasion to bid both her companions a somewhat sudden good-night, and beat her retreat to the rectory.

Her cousin gone, Dorothy, too, got up from her garden chair, with the evident intention of retiring within doors. To her surprise, Lyon intercepted her movement in the direction of the house with a quickness foreign to his ordinary manner.

"Why should you go in yet? This is just the best hour of the day," he said.

Dorothy murmured something touching the lateness of the hour.

"Only ten minutes to nine as yet—honor bright!" He held out his watch as a guarantee of good faith. "Don't you feel inclined for a stroll by the river, before immuring yourself for the night?"

"Well, we might go just a little way, perhaps," Dorothy responded in a somewhat doubtful tone.

Taking her at her reluctant word, Lyon struck at once into the riverside path, turning to the right, and thus setting his face away from the rectory, and the girl obeyed his lead.

For two hundred yards or so the path, thickly shaded by trees, ran fairly straight ahead. Then it crossed a narrow swing bridge to the other side of the stream, and performed a more devious course along the top of the opposite bank, where a thick-set coppice of thorns and alders divided it from the expanse of great flat meadows stretching westward to the downs. A rough unmortared wall, low enough to serve as a seat, formed the boundary between path and coppice.

"Suppose we sit down here for a few minutes," Lyon suggested.

Dorothy assented ; but again somewhat unwillingly. She was aware of feeling nervous and self-conscious, a most unusual state of things with her, save when in her uncle's formidable presence. Until to-night she had always been quite at her ease in Lyon's society. To-night she felt almost afraid of him. Something, she could hardly define what it was, in his manner disturbed her vaguely. She had a sense of actual physical oppression, such as is the result of an impending thunderstorm in the air.

The two sat down, the full moon throwing a long white track across the river at their feet, and so complete a stillness wrapping them round that the feeble lap of the sluggish water against the sedges just below sounded almost loud in the midst of the brooding silence. Once a dog barked at a farm-house far up the bank they had left ; his bark rang out on the quiet air with a distinctness actually startling.

Dorothy let fall a remark or two on the beauty and calmness of the evening, to which her companion vouchsafed scarcely any rejoinder. Presently, however, he said abruptly:

"I'm afraid I succeeded in thoroughly shocking you just now. Come, tell me honestly—I *did* shock you ? "

Dorothy, with those disconcerting eyes of Lyon's fixed full upon her face, faltered and looked down. "I—was sorry," she said, with some hesitation—" sorry——"

"That I should give myself away so completely before your cousin ? " Lyon helped her out. "That was very kind of you, and I guessed as much. Believe me, I am duly grateful to you." Sarcasm seemed to be momentarily contending for the mastery in Lyon's usually passionless voice with a rare note of emotion. "I fear," he continued, finding that his companion remained silent, "I very much fear this isn't the first time, by any means, that I have been unlucky enough to shock you."

Still Dorothy said nothing.

"Isn't it so ? " Lyon persisted.

"I—I believe—I think I would rather not discuss the matter, Mr. Lyon."

"But I want to discuss it, particularly ! Don't you think I

have some little right to insist on such a discussion if I please, just for once ? You'll do me the justice to acknowledge that it is not my habit to talk very much about myself."

"You never talk of yourself at all !" Dorothy interjected quickly. If the truth must be told, she had more than once, during the past fortnight, found herself wishing that Mr. Lyon would be a little less reticent on this special subject.

Lyon inclined his head slightly.

"Thanks. That's satisfactory testimony. But to-night it so happens that I do want to talk of myself, for the space of five minutes. No more than that. I won't keep you lingering long over such an uninteresting theme. The truth is "— he continued in a slightly different tone, speaking less deliberately than usual, and kicking a small pebble that lay close to his foot dexterously into the river—" the truth is, that though Miss Travers is welcome to hold what opinion of me she pleases, I should be sorry that *you* fancied me—well, something even worse than the good-for-nothing I undoubtedly am." His eyes were cast down, as usual ; he did not see the sudden flush that leaped up the cheeks of the girl beside him as he spoke. "I prefer, if possible, not to be classed by you with the monsters in human shape among whom your cousin, I know, is ready to class me. Though you may hardly be able to grasp the fact, I assure you on my faith and honor, if you kindly give me credit for possessing either, that there really are bigger villains in the world than—your humble servant."

He laughed a little as he ended, a singularly unmirthful laugh.

"Mr. Lyon ! I—I never thought——"

"I fancy I have divined your thoughts pretty accurately, Miss Temple. I don't for a moment wish to imply that they do me any wrong. Of course I know very well that my life's a contemptible one—not worth calling a life at all, in fact. Unhappily, I'm not capable of making it any less contemptible. To *live*, in the proper sense of the word, one must do and one must feel. I can't do, to any effective purpose, now ; it's too late to think of that. As to feeling, I confess frankly that I fight shy of it, as a burned child who dreads the fire. Who is it that says somewhere, ' To have in general but little feeling, is the only safeguard against feeling too much on particular occasions,' or words to that effect ? That's a maxim I can heartily endorse. It *is* the only safeguard."

"And is it worth while, do you think, for the sake of going

armed against one kind of pain, to—to turn one's self into something not quite human, to *petrify* one's self, in fact ? " Dorothy asked.

" There spoke Jem Travers' pupil ! " said Lyon, with a smile. " Yes, I think it's worth while—in certain cases. I don't say I would recommend petrifaction to *you*, at present. But take me : seeing all my ambitions had perforce to die a violent death when I left Oxford twelve years ago, surely it's a good thing that I should have ceased to regret their decease ? "

" Perhaps ; I don't know, " Dorothy responded, with a note of sadness in her fresh voice. Possibly it was the hearing of this note that drew Lyon on to add:

" I made outcry enough at the time, I assure you. I wasn't ' petrified ' then "—with a second unmirthful laugh. " And the blow fell very suddenly. We had always supposed ourselves rich people, my mother and I. All at once we found ourselves worse than poor—worse than poor ! " He bore with painful emphasis upon the phrase.

Dorothy's fingers locked themselves tightly together in her lap. She had heard the story of the Lyon family disaster some days since from James—a disaster, according to her cousin, due wholly to the wanton extravagance, if not to the fraudulent dishonesty, of Lyon the elder, who had put himself beyond the reach of enquiry in the matter by dying opportunely immediately after its occurrence—and her heart thrilled in sympathy for her companion. All the stronger was the compassionate throb for her recognition of the manly self-restraint that would have made Lyon's utterance hieroglyphic to a less well-instructed listener, the pride that forbade him to let fall a word on his father's share in effecting the ruin he hinted at.

" However, I should have recovered that ugly knock in time, no doubt. At two-and-twenty one is extraordinarily elastic, one gets over the loss of a fortune with astonishing rapidity—even the loss of a career, because at that age one so easily persuades one's self that one will be able to carve out a new one in no time. Yes, and even the worse loss of one's respect for a number of people in whom one had had an ingenuous youthful faith ! For, I need hardly say, our experience of the steadfastness of friends in time of adversity didn't differ from that of our neighbors ; the rats, according to their nature, made haste to run from the falling house, to me, at the moment, their desertion mattered little, as I could continue to believe in my mother—and one other woman.''

He paused there for an instant, taking off his hat, and pushing back the heavy hair from his forehead with his right hand.

'' We had only been engaged a few weeks when the crash came. As long as she stood by me, nothing else seemed of supreme concern. My one idea was to get work which would enable us to marry soon. Fortunately, as I thought then, she herself was poor—had always been poor ; I did not suppose she would shrink from a life without luxuries. With that idea moving me, I decided to try my luck in Australia. I could have got a small appointment at home that would have maintained me, and, personally speaking, I would have preferred living on a dry crust in England to feasting on the fat of the land at the Antipodes, but I wanted to do something more than maintain myself. And there seemed a better chance of making a decent income within a few years' time in a new country than in the old one. So I went to Queensland. For a time I didn't get on there at all; nothing prospered with me—— I'm sure I hardly know why I am boring you with this very commonplace story,'' he broke off suddenly.

'' I should like to hear the end of it—if you care to tell me,'' Dorothy said in a remarkably subdued voice.

'' I'm afraid the end is even more commonplace than the beginning, if possible ! It's a story that's been told so many hundreds of times before. Of course she got tired of waiting. I might have known beforehand that she would be sure to get tired. She hinted as much, in a delicate, ladylike fashion,—she had a particularly refined way of expressing herself, and wrote charming letters, when she wrote at all,—such a delicate fashion that I quite failed to understand her drift. At last, finding, I suppose, that my dulness was impenetrable to hints, and finding also that things were looking blacker and blacker as regarded my prospects,—those were the navvy days of which I spoke just now to your cousin,—she resorted to plain words, and kindly but firmly insisted on relieving me from the fetters of a useless and hopeless, etc., etc. She did not feel herself fitted to encounter a life of hardship, she said, nor to bear the strain and suspense of a prolonged waiting upon Providence. I dare say she estimated her powers very correctly. I need not tell you the sequel—or, rather, the real explanation of this sudden awakening to her own deficiencies.''

Dorothy gazed at him, white and bewildered.

"Nevertheless, I don't understand," she half whispered.

"Really? Oh, there was tangible cause enough! Another man, with ten thousand a year—no, fifteen, I believe, to do her justice. The temptation was a great one, you'll acknowledge."

"It should have been no temptation at all." Dorothy's cheeks glowed suddenly in the moonlight. "Not if—if——"

"She had cared for me, you mean? But how could she be expected to care for a lover four thousand miles off, getting his living ignominiously with a pick, and presenting a revolting image of fustian-clothed, clay-covered poverty to her mind's eye, when she had a spick-and-span admirer close at hand, with five figures to his annual income? Certainly *I* should not expect it of her, or of any other young lady similarly circumstanced—now. *Then*, I was ten years younger."

"She could never have been worth your—anyone's—caring about," said Dorothy hotly.

"I am quite of your opinion—at the present time," Lyon returned with great calm. "Unfortunately, in those old days I thought differently, having endowed her, in my foolish young imagination, with qualities approaching the angelic. So the discovery that she was—well, merely an ordinary young woman of the nineteenth century, came upon me as a considerable shock."

"I think—I am sure—that there are very, very few women of this or any other century who would have acted in such a fashion!" cried Dorothy, roused to indignant defence of her sex.

"I wish I could share your belief," said Lyon politely. "To resume, as they say in novels: Soon after this naturally-to-be-expected catastrophe, the tide of fortune turned a little with me. It would hardly have seemed worth while to take advantage of this tide-turning just then, but for my mother's sake. But she was living very poorly and hardly in England, and if I didn't greatly care what became of myself at that moment, I still felt anxious that she should have a decently comfortable home, if possible; so I pulled myself together as best I could. However, by the time the home was ready for her, she didn't need it."

"She—died?" Dorothy asked very softly.

"No. She married again. Married a rich man, whom, in the old days, *I* should hardly have accounted fit to wait upon her at table. So the last of my old illusions, or delusions, whichever you prefer to call them, went by the board. And since then, build no castles in Spain, that's all. I've found them too ruinous a speculation."

Dorothy was speechless, reproaching herself vehemently in secret for certain past uncharitable judgments.

"To come to the moral of this tale : Seeing that I've been rather unfortunate in the specimens of human nature it's been my lot to study at first hand, perhaps you'll not be so surprised in future at my absence of enthusiasm for the race in general? To love humankind, to be very eager about its welfare, one ought to be able to believe in it. I must confess that my own faith in the deity of the Positivists is not profound."

"Mr. Lyon, you once told me that I generalized at too great a rate. I feel inclined to retort upon you. Surely you don't mean to assert that you have no faith in *anybody?* You must know that there are some men and women who are honest and true."

"As long as their circumstances permit the exercise of such virtues, I quite believe it. Indeed, I fancy everyone prefers being ' honest and true,' if the being so involves no serious cost to themselves."

"And, in many cases, when it does involve very serious cost," emphatically. "Take such a person as my cousin James, for instance."

"Oh, if you quote individual instances !" interposed Lyon. "Besides, in making sweeping assertions of this kind, of course one is always understood to exclude present company, with its whole body of relations and friends. In society one only talks of humanity in the abstract, naturally."

Dorothy got up from the wall, with a little unconscious move-ment of displeasure.

"It is getting cold here," she said brusquely. "We had better be moving homeward."

Lyon walked by her side in silence till they reached the swing bridge. Then, as he held out his hand for her guidance across the narrow plank, he said abruptly :

"I wish I had not troubled you with my foolish little tale. I have only succeeded in making you angry."

"No," Dorothy interposed, almost under her breath, "not angry—sorry. More sorry than I can well say."

And, lifting his eyes to look at her, he saw that hers were full of tears.

CHAPTER VII

ON THE LAWN AND IN THE FIELDS

" Und sprich, woher ist Liebe ?
Sie kommt und sie ist da ! "

THAT evening talk by the riverside was not without its consequences, although these were hardly of the kind Dorothy might
reasonably have expected to ensue from it. Whether Lyon resented
her fashion of receiving his sudden and unlooked-for confidence, or
whether he was simply annoyed with himself for having been led
by some singular and scarcely explicable impulse into making such
a confidence at all, the girl found it impossible to decide ; but
that for some reason or other he regretted his action in the matter
was abundantly clear to her. That hour in which for a brief space
he had drawn strangely near to her, so far from deepening the
semi-intimacy that had previously been growing up almost imper-
ceptibly between her and her uncle's guest, seemed to have pushed
them suddenly apart. Conscious, so it would appear, that he had
drawn for a moment *too* near,—nearer than either his pride or his
natural reserve could endure to recollect,—Lyon now, in a revulsion
of feeling, removed himself·to a distance which neither kindness
nor curiosity should be able to bridge. He took up an attitude
absolutely unapproachable in its buckram stiffness ; and, fearful of some unwelcome expression of the sympathy he had himself
done his best to provoke, held his hapless confidante, figuratively
speaking, ever at arm's-length. The better to check the rush of
any possible wave of sentiment in his direction, he gave his cynical demon full rein ; took frequent occasion to stab Dorothy
deliberately in what he supposed likely to be the tenderest places
of her beliefs and aspirations ; turned her enthusiasms into polite
ridicule ; or silently expressed a shrugging incredulity touching
the idols he perceived her to worship most devoutly. The girl
came to fear him, in a few days' time, almost as she feared her
uncle himself. Indeed, it is doubtful whether oftentimes the mute
curl of Lyon's lip—cruel, unspoken comment on some girl
expression of delight or admiration—was not even more pai

her than Creighton's harshly snapped phrase of contemptuous retort.

Withal, she could not bring herself to resent Lyon's changed behavior with all the spirit which the circumstances seemed to require of her. And for this reason : She could not disabuse her mind of the fear that there might, indeed, that there surely *must*, have been some error on her own part, some want of kindliness or sympathy, some rash and over-hot expression of opinion on the facts of his story, to account for this curious alteration in his demeanor. Formerly, after a languid fashion, he had appeared to feel a friendly interest in her, a good-natured liking for her. Now she perceived, or thought she perceived, that he regarded her with actual dislike. Dorothy's simple mind could not conceive of such a complete transformation of Mr. Lyon's sentiments taking place wholly without cause. It was plain that she had been unfortunate enough to offend him.

He took care, if this were the case, that she should have no chance of setting herself right in his estimation. For the most part he sedulously avoided her society, and on the rare occasions when he sought it, as would still happen now and again, did so with a manifest reluctance, an air of being compelled to the act almost against his will, and altogether against his better judgment, which the girl found intolerably irritating. She, on her side, drew back from him, as he from her ; and for several days they saw but little of each other.

Lyon took refuge in the company of Travers, and solaced his hurt pride—hurt, in his own esteem, almost to death by what he angrily styled his inexplicable and contemptible self-exposure in a moment of sentimental weakness—by plunging the stiletto of satire into the vitals of Jem's most cherished ideals. Travers argued with him, then laughed at him ; finally, suffered him to rail unchecked. "One can't expect a man with a smarting wound to be either calm or considerate," he said to himself good-humoredly.

The metaphor started a whole train of new ideas in his mind. Wounds, it is well known, are commonly most irritable when on the point of healing. Was Lyon's beginning to heal ? It would be quite like Lyon to resent the process—supposing him to be conscious that it was going on—and try to arrest it. James had his thoughts as to the nature of the curative unguent in this case. But he wisely kept them to himself, till a woman's quick suspicions, scenting danger, forced him into reluctant confession.

It was his regular habit every Wednesday to hold a kind of mission-service in one of the cottages of Owlswick, the isolated hamlet in which Dorothy taught her school. The Wednesday following the Sunday of his sister's visit chanced to be a cool and pleasant day, and Mrs. Travers, tempted abroad by the beauty of the afternoon, offered to drive him to his destination in her pony-carriage. As a matter of convenience he would have preferred walking, having made up his mind previously to think out his Sunday evening sermon by the way ; but he was pleased and touched by the offer—few such offers from his mother falling to his share—and he accepted it.

The pony-carriage left the rectory about four o'clock. Half-way to Owlswick its occupants descried two figures, the figures of a man in straw hat and light-colored tweeds, and a girl in a blue cotton gown, coming toward them along the level, lonely road.

"Dorothy," observed James, who was driving, pointing forward with his whip—the pair were still nearly a quarter of a mile off—"and Lyon with her, I think. Yes, it is Lyon. I wish——" He checked himself quickly.

But not quickly enough. Mrs. Travers caught him up with startling briskness.

"James ! You don't think there is anything between that man and Dorothy ? "

"No, mother ; not as yet."

"But you hope there may be, will be ? You said just now you wished——" Mrs. Travers' pale cheeks were deeply flushed ; her indignation seemed to choke her.

"To be honest, I should be very glad if Lyon were to take a fancy to her—and she to him. It might be the saving of him."

"And what of your brother ? *His* salvation is of no account, it seems ! "

"Brian is out of the question, in any case. You know that Dorothy has said over and over again that she does not care for him—cannot marry him."

"I know that she has behaved very cruelly and heartlessly to the poor boy——"

"No, mother,—pardon me,—there you are unjust to Dorothy. It was not her fault that he fell in love with her, and wouldn't

6

take ' No ' for an answer. She was perfectly plain with him from the beginning. She has never hesitated or wavered in her refusal."

"That is all you know about the matter! Brian could tell a different tale, I fancy. Indeed "—with significant emphasis and a faint touch of triumph—" I *know* he could. I know more than you imagine. And now, if she is to begin playing fast and loose in this fashion——"

"Where there is no tie, there can be no playing fast and loose with it," was James' retort. And he might have retorted further had not the two persons under discussion been now fairly within earshot.

He pulled up the pony, and halted a while talking to them, to the displeasure of Mrs. Travers, who was in no mood for amicable converse. James, however, scarcely observed his mother's manifest ill humor. He was both surprised and rejoiced at Lyon's appearance as Dorothy's escort, for he had not failed to notice the odd estrangement that seemed to have taken place between the two, and his speculations as to the cause of this apparent renewal of friendly intercourse occupied his attention entirely for the moment.

Dorothy, on her part, was fairly bewildered by the thing that had come about. When, her children dismissed for the day, she had stepped out of the school-house porch at Owlswick, satchel on arm, and discovered Lyon waiting for her a few paces off, she had been scarcely able to credit the evidence of her senses. As he vouchsafed no explanation of the very unusual step he had taken, but merely remarked that the afternoon was pleasant for walking, she had no choice but to swallow her amazement as best she could. The state of perplexity into which his appearance had thrown her was not lessened by the utter absence from his talk, during their walk to Heyford, of the cruel and gibing note that had been so constantly present in it of late.

If this fresh change bewildered, it also delighted the girl. She so hated to be on bad terms with any person who had once been kind to her! This much she acknowledged to herself, even while endeavoring to dissemble, as out of sheer self-respect she felt bound to dissemble, all the relief she really felt. Since Mr. Lyon could bring himself to overlook her unknown offence so soon and so easily, it stood to reason that it could never have been a very serious one; and in this case she felt herself to have been unfairly treated by him in the past. Her sense of having suffered wrong at his hands made her less talkative than usual, less readily responsive; throughout the walk her manner remained a little cold, a little proud. Nevertheless, under assumed coldness and genuine pride, Lyon failed not to discern hidden satisfaction.

And now it was his turn to discover that, in a different quarter, he, too, had given unwitting offence. Mrs. Travers, hitherto always unvaryingly suave and gracious in her bearing toward him, gave him to understand with sufficient plainness that he had forfeited her favor. Her greetings became icy, her few reluctant words—for she only spoke to him when she could not decently avoid doing so—stiff and formal in the extreme. Lyon, quite unconscious of having given the poor lady any pretext for looking blackly upon him, was at first merely amused by this sudden assumption of frigid loftiness on her part. After a while, however, he became aware of a similar change in the demeanor of the old rector himself, and grew puzzled. It was in vain that he considered the puzzle; no explanation thereof that was even plausible presented itself.

The mystery was cleared up at last, in a fashion that left him in no further doubt concerning the true origin and meaning of this seemingly causeless unfriendliness.

Sauntering over to the rectory late one afternoon in search of the son of the house, he came suddenly upon Mrs. Travers seated in her invalid chair in a shady corner of the lawn. Beside her stood Dorothy Temple, drawn up to her full height, her eyes and cheeks unusually brilliant, while her mouth wore an expression oddly compounded of annoyance and determination.

"You cannot deny it!" Mrs. Travers was exclaiming in querulous tones. "There is his letter, the letter I received from him only last Monday, to prove what I say."

"I don't deny it." Miss Temple spoke with a heightened color, but she had her voice well under control. "All I say is, that he had no right to tell you—no right whatever. Merely by telling you he has produced a false impression."

"Here is Mr. Lyon!" Mrs. Travers interposed hastily, catching sight of the approaching visitor. Poor Lyon came forward, doing his best to look quite unconscious of having intruded on a serious difference of opinion between the two ladies.

He announced his errand. Mrs. Travers said that James would appear in a few minutes, and in a manner slightly more cordial

than usual invited him to sit down.   He sat down, feeling
thoroughly uncomfortable.   Dorothy, who, if her looks did not
belie her, was equally ill at ease, soon took occasion to slip away,
leaving him alone with Mrs. Travers.

That lady talked civilly for a few minutes of indifferent
matters ; then, after a moment's lapse into thoughtful silence,
said, looking suddenly up into her visitor's face :

" I wonder, Mr. Lyon, whether I might venture to make a
confidence to you, and an appeal as well ? "

" To me, Mrs. Travers ? "

" Yes.   You are my son Brian's friend, are you not ?   Really
and truly his friend ? "

" I've a great liking for Brian, as he knows.   If I can be of any
use to him, pray command me."

" You could be of the greatest, the most priceless use, if you
would.   My young cousin, who has just left us, has, I know, an
immense respect for your opinion."   Mrs. Travers paused.

" You must allow me to question that."   Lyon filled up the
pause, with a slight, incredulous smile.   Inwardly he asked himself what on earth the woman could be driving at.

" Oh, I assure you !   You see, if you'll excuse my saying so,
you are the first clever, cultivated man of the world she has ever
had to do with."   Lyon's upper lip curled afresh.   " Naturally,
she esteems your judgment, of men and things both, very highly.
Now, if you would use your influence with her——"

" I am not aware of possessing any influence with Miss
Temple," Lyon interposed, stiffening suddenly to a cast-iron
demeanor.

" Brian's friend must have *some* influence with her, I feel sure,"
responded the maternal serpent.   " If you would but use it, Mr.
Lyon, in his behalf !   You know, of course, that he is devoted to
her ? "

" No, I did not know.   Brian has been devoted to so many
charming young ladies in his time," said " Brian's friend " with
somewhat brutal frankness.

" He was always susceptible, poor boy ! " with an indulgent
smile and sigh.   " But this is different.   Here it is question of
a real, lasting attachment, I firmly believe.   I did not wish to
believe this at first, I will own.   Dorothy is a good girl, but she
is ordinary—decidedly ordinary ; both Mr. Travers and I felt
that our boy might have looked higher for a wife.   Now, how-

ever, that he seems to have made his choice irrevocably, now that they are virtually engaged, it's my earnest hope and prayer that nothing may occur to prevent the marriage. If anything did, Brian would be driven to despair. And then in many ways it is suitable enough : a really excellent girl, in his own position in life, with a little money of her own, too. Oh, I should be broken-hearted if Dorothy were to show any sign of wishing to change her mind *now !*'"

Lyon's dark face remained impenetrable as a mask to the keen eyes watching it. "I should imagine you might make your mind easy on that score, Mrs. Travers. Miss Temple does not appear to be a changeable person. Brian is to be congratulated on his good luck," he added, after a scarcely perceptible pause.

"Only he is so far away ! And—and I have always feared Dorothy was a little inclined to rate his devotion too cheaply, to take it rather as a matter of course than a gift to be thankful for. The very fact of their being cousins, who have known each other intimately from childhood, takes away from the romance of the affair, no doubt, in her girl's eyes. A girl's ideas of romance are so limited and conventional ! Otherwise, there is far more of real romance in the story of a love like my boy's than in half the stories one reads in novels. Don't you agree with me, Mr. Lyon ?"

"I'm afraid I am not a good judge on points of romance."

"At least you will not refuse me your assistance ?"

"To speak frankly, Mrs. Travers, I hardly see where my assistance should come in. Remember, I have known Miss Temple barely three weeks as yet. If you recollect this, you must, I think, recognize the impossibility of my setting to work to instruct her in her duties toward your son. To attempt anything of the kind would be an intolerable impertinence on my part. More especially as Miss Temple has never but once, that I can recall, mentioned Brian's name in my hearing, and never even once hinted at the existence of the engagement you speak of. The matter is much too delicate for my interference—or that of any outsider. Ah !" in accents of unmistakable relief ; "here comes Jem !" Lyon added to himself as he rose from his chair, "And in good time he comes. I should certainly have flung manners to the winds in another minute or two."

"Ready for a ramble, Lyon ?"

Travers' voice rang out cheerily as he crossed the lawn.

The alacrity of the " Quite ready, old fellow ! " that answered
his enquiry, surprised him. Lyon's fashion of assenting to the
propositions made to him was not often so prompt or so eager.

Nevertheless, poor Travers' *tête-à-tête* stroll with his friend did
not, despite this promising beginning, prove a very lively one.
Once clear of the rectory gates, Lyon fell into a fit of abstraction. Either he was bored by his companion's choice of subjects
of conversation, or his mind was distracted by some private care,
for during the first half-hour he scarcely opened his lips except in
monosyllables, and Travers' most extravagant nonsense—Travers
could be very extravagantly nonsensical at times, when in a
whimsical vein—barely provoked him to a mechanical smile.

The truth is, he was busy cudgelling his brain for an accurate
remembrance of his last conversation with Brian Travers—that
conversation held two years ago, just before the young man sailed
for Queensland. Brian had come to his rooms, he recollected, and
there talked wildly of his absorbing passion for some steely-
hearted divinity whose relenting, if only she could be brought to
relent, would surely be his salvation in this world and the next.
Now, it appeared that Miss Temple was the divinity in question;
no longer steely-hearted, however, if the mother's assertions were
to be depended upon. Why any " if " in the matter ? Probably
Mrs. Travers had spoken no more than the truth. Unless Dorothy
were really engaged to Brian, Brian's mother would hardly have
gone the length of giving another man such clear and unmistakable hints to keep his hands off her son's property. Poor woman!
her proceedings were not in very good form, perhaps, but she
doubtless meant well. Lyon's keen enjoyment of the humor of the
situation had not suffered him to give her the veiled assurance
which would have set her mind completely at rest on the subject
of his half-suspected rivalry with Brian—so he told himself.
Otherwise, he would certainly have done so, since it was a pity
she should continue to suffer from a perfectly groundless anxiety.

" Travers," he said suddenly, interrupting a disquisition of his
companion on the iniquity of diverting trust-funds from their
original uses, which was just approaching an effective peroration,
with no ceremony at all, " is it true that your brother is engaged
to be married to Miss Temple ? "

Travers, considerably surprised alike by the matter and the
manner of the question put to him, turned and stared for a moment
at his questioner, who was leaning on the top of a five-barred

gate, his arms planted on the uppermost rail, and his stick dangling negligently between his half-open fingers. But his enquiring gaze told him nothing. Lyon was looking straight across the flat meadow in front of him with his usual impassive and slightly fatigued air. James pulled himself together to reply.

"Dorothy engaged to Brian? How did you hear? Were you told there was any such engagement?"

"The idea would hardly have occurred to me of itself, my good fellow. Nor, if it had, should I have been likely to ask you point-blank questions on the basis of a mere idea. I may possibly have misunderstood Mrs. Travers, but she certainly gave me to understand that the matter was one which might be spoken of."

"My poor mother! In this case, the wish is father to the thought with her. She has never quite forgiven Dorothy for refusing to marry Brian."

"Then—they are *not* engaged?"

"Certainly not. Decidedly, you must have misunderstood my mother very seriously, if you understood her to say that there was any question of engagement between them." Lyon here made some rather impolite reflections on female incapacity for speaking the truth, which the circumstances, unfortunately, obliged him to leave unspoken. "Of course," the unconscious Travers continued, "we were all aware of the boy's wishes in the matter, some years since. But there never was any hope for him in that quarter. And I know—from himself—that when he made a last effort, just before leaving England, he was refused definitely and finally. No, there is nothing whatever between them. Just as well, perhaps. She might be the wife for him; that's possible. But I'm by no means sure that he would ever be the husband for her."

Lyon re-entered his room at The Haulms an hour later, in a frame of mind quite incomprehensible to himself. To begin with, all his sensations, physical and mental, were those of a man who has lately experienced a severe shock; yet nothing had occurred during the afternoon which could legitimately have had such an effect upon him. Secondly, he was conscious of an inexplicable feeling of relief—a feeling which had surged up in him suddenly at Travers' stout assertion that there was "nothing whatever between" his brother and his cousin, and taken form in the instinctive, silent exclamation, "Thank God!" Why should he, of all men, thank God that Dorothy Temple was not going to

marry Brian Travers ?   What possible business, concern, or interest could it be of his whom she married, now or at any future
time ?

"At this rate, Mrs. Travers might almost appear justified in her
anxiety," he said angrily to himself as he set about the business
of dressing for dinner.   "Folly !   Absurdity !   A mere girl—
whom I had never seen three weeks ago, and whom, after Monday,
I shall in all probability never see again—who is nothing, and less
than nothing to me——"

There he suddenly caught sight of his own face in the glass, and
half started, struck by its curious pallor.   A man who for long
years past had made it his rule to be, as far as poor human nature
would permit him, absolutely honest with himself, he could not go
on lying to himself now.   He gave a sort of groan commingled of
incredulity, indignation, and profound self-disgust.   "No, no !"
he ejaculated half-articulately in his impatience.

But when a still small voice in his breast retorted upon him with
a merciless "Yes," he did not venture to contradict it in his turn.

CHAPTER VIII

OUTSIDE THE SCHOOL-HOUSE

"Les violences qu'on se fait pour s'empêcher d'aimer sont souvent plus cruelles que les
rigueurs de ce qu'on aime."

LET no one suppose, however, that because Anthony Lyon felt
and acknowledged a hit, he had therefore any intention of throwing
down his arms and yielding the field peaceably to the foe against
whose attacks he had so long believed himself entirely proof.   So
far from allowing what he contemptuously styled his ridiculous
infatuation to take its course, he rebelled furiously against it.   He
told himself that, let the effort cost him what it might,—and he did
not pretend, even to himself, that it would be likely to cost him
nothing,—he would put a speedy end to his folly.

An impulse of self-defence moved him to deal thus summarily in
the matter.   When he told Dorothy Temple that he dreaded anything like strong feeling " as a burned child dreads the fire," he
had described his own state of mind with perfect truth and accu-
racy.   One such scorching experience as he was not likely ever to

forget had followed on his early yielding to sentiment ; he had no
desire to repeat, in mature manhood, the painful history of his
youth.   By dint of ruthless self-repression, he had brought a
nature, orginally hotter and less easily governed than most men's,
to a condition of chilly quiescence ; but he knew very well that
the capacity for passion was only scotched in him, not killed.
Once let him lift the heel of his will from the serpent's head, once
permit the venomous thing to rear its snaky crest on high, and
there would be all the old hideous battle to fight over again, every
one of the old stinging miseries to endure afresh.   For it was
characteristic of Lyon's mental attitude toward the whole question of love between man and woman, that he never for a moment
pictured this new-born passion of his becoming to him, under any
circumstances, a source of joy or a means of healing.   He saw
in it merely the ominous beginning of a new tale of doubt, disillusionment, humiliation—above all, of suffering.   And he had
suffered quite enough already ; he was determined not to suffer
after that particular fashion again, if he could possibly help it.

It should not be difficult, he thought, for a man gifted with an
ordinary amount of common sense to get the mastery of a mere
groundless fancy.   From a logical point of view, he would not,
should the fancy prove too strong for him, have an excuse to
offer for himself.   The girl was not beautiful, scarcely even passably pretty.   Beside the heroine of his youth's love-story she
would have looked a farthing candle competing with the sun.
Her lack of striking external charms was not atoned for by any
exceptional mental gifts ; impossible, by the extremest stretch of
courtesy, to call her either clever or accomplished, brilliantly witty,
or remarkably wise.   She was, no doubt, a sensible girl and a
good girl.   But sensible girls are as plentiful as blackberries, and,
according to the general verdict, good ones also ; so that these
qualities of sense and (supposed) goodness in no way distinguished
this particular girl from a whole crowd of her sisters whom Lyon
had met and known, more or less intimately, at one time or
another, without finding his dearly bought indifference to the sex
in any way disturbed.   No ; so far, Mrs. Travers was right.   In
the generally accepted sense of the term, Dorothy was " decidedly
ordinary."

And yet—he had fallen in love with her.   There was no blink-
ing or disguising that unwelcome, uncomfortable fact.   He might
summon all the strength of his will to combat it, shed forth all the

vials of his ridicule on so preposterous an idea ; it refused obstinately to be either strangled or mocked out of existence. Already
Dorothy's power over him was greater than he could bear to
acknowledge. A man singularly indifferent to the esteem of his fellows—careless of the opinion of men, contemptuous of the opinion
of women—he had felt himself wince and smart once and again,
under the sentence of unspoken condemnation written in Dorothy's
eyes. He had even fallen so low as to offer a craven *Apologia pro
vitâ suâ* to this untaught, inexperienced country girl—fool that he
was ! Well, not all fool, mayhap. His self-abasement had not
gone altogether unrewarded. He remembered her wet eyes, the
look that she had turned upon him, the broken phrases that fell
from her lips at the crossing of the bridge ; and the remembrance
of these things was sweet to him—sweet as the first ray of warmth
striking through the cold atmosphere of utter loneliness within
which, for the last dozen years of his life, he had resolutely shut
himself up.

Of one thing he felt convinced : Illogical, irrational, as was the
whole affair, its very illogicality and irrationality, as well as his
knowledge of himself, assured him that, were he to permit himself
to love this " ordinary " girl, he would love her, not wisely, not
prudently, not with the temperate warmth of an affection given on
any reasonable ground, but passionately, absorbingly, to his own
certain torture and probable undoing. Therefore, he very wisely
resolved to deny himself the permission in question.

Fortunately, as he was glad to remember, his visit to Heyford
was drawing fast to a close. He was no coward, but he perceived
clearly that it would naturally be an immense advantage to him, in
his task of conquering the weakness he despised, to fight out the
battle elsewhere than in Dorothy's actual presence.

Acting on this view, he managed to see very little of her during
the day following on his unpleasant discovery. As this day
happened to be Sunday, some ingenuity on his part was needed to
avoid a *tête-à-tête ;* and it was forthcoming. Church services and
Sunday schools aided him to attain his end during the earlier hours
of the day, and a long evening walk with Travers, followed by a
talk (at the rectory) which lasted till past midnight, not only filled
up the remainder, but at the same time averted the danger of a
farewell. Before Lyon returned to The Haulms Dorothy had, of
course, gone to her room ; he reckoned that she would have started
for Owlswick a full hour before he came down the following morn-

ing. Thus any leave-taking was rendered impossible, in a perfectly easy and natural manner.

Whether the fashion in which he had arranged matters would be agreeable to Dorothy as well as to himself, Lyon did not stop to enquire. He was fighting for his life; it simply never occurred to him that the blows he dealt in self-defence might have painful consequences for her.

Monday morning arrived. He went down to the breakfast-room at nine o'clock with an unreasonable semi-expectation, in which hope and dread played about equal parts, that he should, on this particular morning, find her there, and that thus the good-by he had striven to avoid would yet be thrust upon him—or granted to him. His groundless prevision turned out to be a false one. Dorothy, as on all previous mornings, was absent, and Mr. Creighton, according to his custom, made no reference to her.

Then Lyon's conscience smote him, or else the fierce yearning of a desire, that spoke louder than the voice of prudence and struggled painfully in the grip of resolution, got the upper hand for a moment, and he began to cast about for some means of repairing his last night's lack of courtesy. Throughout his stay of three weeks at The Haulms Dorothy had borne herself kindly and friendlily toward him ; it were worse than boorish—absolutely brutal—on his part to go away, making no acknowledgment of her kindness and friendliness, treating her, after her uncle's manner, as a thing of no account, unworthy even the common politeness of a common leave-taking. Should he write a note before he went—a few lines of apology and regret—or, better still, supposing he took occasion, on his way to the station ? Owlswick, he knew, was little more than half a mile off the Donnington road, and the morning was cool and overcast, pleasant for walking. He surprised his host by observing suddenly that he should be ready to start at half-past ten.

" You needn't go quite so early as that," Creighton answered. " The pony does the distance easily in three-quarters of an hour."

" I thought of walking—part of the way, at least."

" That makes a difference. You'll probably be caught in the rain before you get to Donnington if you walk, though ; we shall pretty certainly have a downpour by eleven. But perhaps you don't mind wet."

" No, I am happily impervious to weather."

" All right, then ; half-past ten be it," said Creighton, getting

up with some alacrity to ring the bell. He had quite done with
Lyon now, and was perfectly willing that the young man should
take his departure. Lyon recognized this, and knew that he
need not stand in fear of further invitations to The Haulms in
time to come.

Mr. Creighton's predictions with regard to the weather were
fully verified. When, at the bottom of the steep lane leading up
to Owlswick Green,—a triangular scrap of rough wild common
forming the head of an equally wild valley,—Lyon leaped down
from the pony-cart, and, requesting Wilson to drive on with his
luggage to Donnington station, announced his intention of doing
the rest of the way on foot, the thick soft mist that had shrouded
the countryside since early morning was already turning into fine
penetrating rain. By the time he reached the tiny porch of the
school-house—a diminutive square brick building standing solitary.
in the middle of the scrap of common aforesaid, some hundreds of
yards distant from the little group of ancient tumble-down cottages
which were clustered together on its outer edge—his hat and
travelling-coat were getting tolerably wet.

He entered the porch, hung on either side with rows of shabby
caps and hats, a worn little cloak or two among them, and stood
an instant, listening to the hum within. A reading-lesson was
proceeding ; evidently an elementary one, for the words that some
dozen small hoarse voices uttered together in a monotonous drone
were exclusively monosyllabic. Now and then he caught the
sound of Dorothy's clear voice, checking and correcting. It
annoyed him to find that this occasional note set his heart beating
disagreeably fast ; he determined to listen no longer. With a
final admonition to himself to be on his good behavior, he raised
his stick and rapped softly at the door.

"Please, teacher, there's someone outside," he heard a shrill
voice pipe immediately.

"Very well, Mary Ann ; go and see who it is. Quietly, now.
Children, not so much fidgeting, please." Dorothy spoke
patiently, but to Lyon's ear it sounded as if she were putting
strong constraint upon herself. "Sit straight, the first class—and
go on with your writing. Mr. Lyon ! *You!*"

She was standing very near the door that Mary Ann, a fuzzy-
haired, be-pinafored monitor of twelve, had just opened with an air
of great importance ; and the unexpected apparition in the doorway
caused her to start visibly.

"I myself," returned Lyon, not altogether displeased at his reception. "May I come in?"

"No, I—I think you had better not. I will come out and speak to you, in one moment." She turned hastily to the group of "infants" who stood round a chalk circle drawn on the floor, primer in hand, gazing open-mouthed at the stranger.

"Close your books. Sit. And be quite quiet till I come back."

She stepped out into the porch, closing the door softly behind her.

"Is anything the matter?" she asked rather breathlessly. "Anyone ill? My uncle?"

"Your uncle is perfectly well, and so is everyone in Heyford, as far as I know," Lyon returned almost testily. He felt curiously annoyed at her failure to divine his errand. "I merely called to bid you good-by. Perhaps," with rising displeasure, "you had forgotten I was to go away this morning?"

"Oh, no! I had not forgotten."

To his ear, she spoke coldly, with an indifference that was scarcely even civil. His mortification got the better, for the moment, both of his prudence and his manners.

"It would have been natural enough if you had forgotten, since it cannot possibly be of the slightest moment to you whether I go or stay."

The cut told; she winced under it visibly. Her color rose; her lip trembled slightly. "Why do you say that, Mr. Lyon? On the contrary, I am truly sorry you are going. You have been very kind to me; and, as you know, I have not many friends."

A minute earlier he had been remarking with a savage kind of satisfaction that she did not look in the least pretty that morning. Her eyes were heavy; her cheeks colorless; the bright freshness of air that made ordinarily her chief attraction had wholly disappeared; her dark tweed dress, donned, no doubt, in deference to the badness of the weather, and the spotted calico bib-apron worn over it were both eminently unbecoming to her. This lack of charm in her appearance might have been a positive safeguard to Lyon—had been such, for a brief moment or two; now, by his ill-considered burst of temper, he had deprived himself of it. For his taunt, striking home, not only stirred her pulses, but transformed her face; and through the halo of the emotion which his own sharp words had created he saw it as he had never seen it before, beautiful.

The first effect of this vision was to make him feel considerably ashamed of himself.

"I beg your pardon," he murmured. "I believe I was abominably rude. I don't know if it's any excuse to say that I am in a frightful temper this morning! Possibly because I am going away; I hate travelling. However, you forgive me? You won't bear malice?"

"Certainly not. There isn't much for me to forgive," Dorothy answered quickly. "And, if there had been, I could still make allowance for you. You know I have what Irishmen call 'a touch of the temper' myself!"

She paused there, perhaps expecting him to take his leave and go. But he seemed nowise inclined toward any such decided movement. Instead of saying anything he stepped outside the little porch, and looked about him irresolutely, with an air of considering the weather.

"I'm afraid you are going to have a thoroughly miserable day for your journey," Dorothy observed, coming to the edge of the step on which she had been standing and peering out ruefully into the mist and rain. "Fortunately, the journey itself isn't very long. That is—— You are going back to London, I suppose?"

"London's my first stage. But in all probability I sha'n't stop there—for more than an hour or two. If I find the letters I expect to find at my rooms, I shall most likely"—raising his eyes suddenly to his companion's as she stood above him on the edge of the steps—"go down to Yorkshire by the afternoon express."

Dorothy's face lighted up afresh—this time with a wholly different, because wholly pleasurable, emotion.

"Not to—Creyke? To see——"

"That princely property of mine? Even so. You see, I am not, after all, so utterly impervious to reproof, rebuke, exhortation, when skilfully administered. You and Miss Travers have together succeeded in awaking me to a sense of my criminal apathy as a landlord; at least, you have made me curious to see for myself what pit-life is like. I—— What were you going to say?"

"Nothing of any consequence. Only—don't be angry with me!—that I am very glad."

"Why on earth should I be angry with you for feeling glad? I'm delighted to hear that any doings of mine meet with your approbation. You haven't had much reason, so far, to approve of them, or of me; that I freely admit."

A sound of scuffling feet with which mingled Mary Ann's shrill voice of rebuke, followed by an outburst of childish sobbing, cut short Lyon's half-uttered sentence, and made the young teacher start nervously to the door. Opening it, she discovered the "infants," no longer seated demurely on their bench, but huddled together in a disconsolate group round one of the most diminutive of their number, who was sobbing bitterly in a corner, while the juvenile monitor with the towzled locks brandished a slate threateningly over their youthful heads.

"You must excuse me a moment," she said hurriedly to Lyon, as she disappeared.

It seemed a long moment to him before she came out again looking flushed and wearing a little unconscious frown of distress on her smooth forehead. Neither was the length of her absence wholly in his impatient fancy : she had really been several minutes gone. Her reproof, indeed, took but little time to administer;. a sentence or two of grave displeasure and she had done. But the crying child had refused for a long time to be comforted.

Lyon's sentiments toward that child were by no means of a kindly nature.

And, now that she had returned, it was clearly not to stay. Closing the door behind her with one hand, she held out the other to her visitor, saying hurriedly :

"I must go back to them at once. You see how it is. I ought not really to be here at all——"

"You are a painfully conscientious school-mistress."

She made a somewhat unsuccessful attempt to smile. "No ; if I had been truly conscientious, I should have refused to leave the school-room for so much as a single minute ! "

"Seeing I had come up here especially to see you—to bid you good-by——"

"That was very kind of you," interrupting him hurriedly. "Very kind indeed. I never dreamed of your coming, this place is so far out of your way. And then the rain ! you will get so wet. Where is the cart ? "

"The cart has gone on to the station with my impedimenta. And you needn't trouble yourself about the rain ; that won't hurt me. Well, since you are clearly so anxious to get rid of me, and return to your cherubs, I will say good-by."

He took her offered hand and held it a moment, lightly, not

bestowing on it any fervent pressure, thus detaining her, whether she would or no, while he added, with a coolness which almost surprised himself, "I wonder whether we shall ever meet again?"

Her breathing quickened visibly as she answered hesitatingly, "Perhaps—perhaps you may—may be induced to pay my uncle another visit, some time or other."

"He will not ask me to pay him any more visits, I fear. I have—excuse my frank speaking—I have served his turn; and there's an end of me, as far as he is concerned. I pass out of his horizon forever. No, it doesn't seem probable that Heyford will see me again. So this is a final good-by, I'm afraid—unless you come, by and by, to London, and we encounter one another there by some happy accident. To be sure, London is a big place; it's always a chance whether one runs up against the people one knows or not."

"I don't think I am ever likely to go to London," said Dorothy quietly. All color and animation had faded once more from her face; and, with these, the transient beauty of a few minutes earlier. But Lyon took no note of this new change. Roused to fresh anger by the calmness with which she spoke, he dropped her hand without looking at her, saying briefly:

"Then, good-by, Miss Temple."

"Good-by, Mr. Lyon."

He lingered no longer after that, but tramped away over the rough turf at a vigorous pace, holding himself even more upright and squaring his shoulders even more resolutely than usual. So fast and carelessly did he walk indeed that he presently caught his foot in a great tussock of coarse grass and came very near ignominiously measuring his length on the wet hillside. Recovering from this little mishap, which had brought him to a momentary standstill, he turned and looked half-involuntarily behind him—to find, to his extreme surprise, that Dorothy had not yet returned to the society of her children. Through the veil of rolling mist and soft driving rain which now intervened between him and the school-house he could distinctly discern her slender, darkly clad figure, leaning against the entrance of the little porch. She was gazing down the valley, watching him, as he could not but think, on his departing way.

Something vaguely wistful in her attitude, in the poise of her half-bent head, in the fixity of her steady, following look, struck home, through the joints of that defensive armor of cowardly prudence and cynical distrust which he had so carefully buckled on an hour before, straight to the core of the man's heart. For a moment he forgot alike his dearly bought experience in the past, his almost panic dread of fresh suffering in the future. Moved by a compelling instinct, a passionate impulse stronger than memory, more vehement than fear, he turned to retrace his steps.

A sudden gust of light wind moving across the valley blew fresh wreaths of fog, fresh sheets of rain, between him and the school-house, obscuring wholly the slim young figure lingering in front of it. When, stumbling through them, he reached the porch, the figure was no longer there: Dorothy had re-entered her school-room, and shut to the door.

CHAPTER IX

FROM PICCADILLY TO WESTMINSTER

"With me, faith means perpetual unbelief kept quiet."

JUNE is past; July also. It is August—not the rich golden August of the country, with its fiery noons and cool, still nights, its pleasant prospects of ripe cornfields and laden orchards, but August in London; airless, cloudy, depressing; August brooding over the great city as a canopy of heavy yellow haze, and sending its attendant dust into every crevice and cranny, to make the face of all household gods, not white, but sadly grimy. The grass in the parks is burned a sickly buff color; the trees have long ceased to present even an apology for greenness; the gorgeous array of flowers stretching from the Marble Arch to Hyde Park Corner is only kept brilliant by dint of unwearied and copious watering. Closely examined, the plants look as languid as the few passers-by who halt occasionally to glance at their artificially preserved beauty.

These passers-by are mostly of the humbler sort, for everyone who can, by hook or crook, contrive to leave the dull-burning furnace to which "Town"—so lively a month ago—is now reduced, has fled away to the country, the Continent, or the seaside; and the West End consequently displays a monotonous sequence of closed shutters and lowered blinds.

7

James Travers, flying along Piccadilly with his head down, at his customary pace of something over four miles an hour, may therefore be easily excused his start of astonishment on hearing a familiar voice at his elbow enquire sarcastically :

"Are you going to cut me altogether?"

"Lyon! I didn't see you. Where on earth did you spring from? And how comes it to pass that you are perambulating Piccadilly at this season, you man of fashion?"

"In order to sustain that character I ought to answer, I suppose, that I am only 'passing through.' Unfortunately, that would be hardly a veracious answer. I came up from Yorkshire last week, and I've been rather at a loss what to do with myself since, to tell the truth. Good luck, our meeting like this! The sight of a familiar face is as a cup of cold water to a man in this hot desert. Come in and lunch with me."

"Thanks—impossible. I'm only in town for a few hours on necessary business ; on my way to Whitehall now—with no time to lose, for I must catch the 4.10 down-train, whatever happens. My mother is ill," Travers added in brief explanation, as he prepared to move on.

"I'll walk with you," Lyon said, suiting the action to the word. "Mrs. Travers' illness is not serious, I hope?"—as the two pursued their way.

"Very serious ; so we fear. Her condition has been more or less precarious for years, and now there is a fresh complication which seems as though it must prove too much for her strength. My father is in great distress, and I am anxious not to leave him alone longer than I can help. Dorothy, of course, has her hands full looking after my mother."

"Then Miss Temple is—— Then your sister is not at home?"

"Not as yet." Travers frowned unconsciously. "She hasn't appeared to grasp the gravity of the situation, so far. My fault, probably. I'm a wretched letter-writer at all times, and of course I didn't want to alarm her unduly; perhaps I softened things down too much. She knew, besides, that Dorothy was on the spot, and would do her best. Not a bad best, either. The girl has proved herself a born nurse."

"That is fortunate."

"Very fortunate. Indeed, I don't know what we should have done without her. My only fear is lest she should break down under the prolonged strain ; my mother will hardly let her out of her sight for a moment. It's curious how she clings to the girl! You remember, perhaps, I told you there had been a little coolness between them of late? That seems wholly forgotten, the very memory of it wiped out."

"I hope Miss Travers will be able to go down with you," Lyon said. The news of the *rapprochement* between Mrs. Travers and her young cousin was not welcome news to him by any means. It aroused in him, he could hardly have told why, a vague apprehension.

"Oh, she must!" responded Miss Travers' brother with decision. "I shall make it clear to her that it is her duty to go. Do you mind coming into the Stores for a moment? I telegraphed to Isabel to meet me there at two."

Isabel was in waiting at the Stores, not in the best of humors. "Your telegram quite frightened me," she said, with some indignation, to James, when her first enquiries had elicited the fact that no special change had taken place in her mother's condition. "I thought you had some awful tidings to communicate, and I gave up a meeting, a most important meeting in every way, to come here. I wonder"—looking at her watch—"if I could possibly get down to Victoria Street in a hansom before that last resolution comes on for discussion? There are one or two amendments which ought really to be pressed, and I know, if I am not there, they will be allowed to drop."

"Well, I'm afraid you must let them drop," returned James dryly. "I want you to come down with me to Heyford by the 4.10 train."

"This afternoon? Oh, Jem, out of the question! You don't know all I have to arrange before I can get away for so much as a single night from town."

"When it's a question of nursing your sick mother——"

"But I can't nurse! You know I can't!" interrupted Isabel. "I should drive mother wild if I approached her when she is in one of her spasms. My very voice irritates her nerves at those times. Dorothy is much better fitted to take care of her than I. Isn't it curious, Mr. Lyon,"—appealing to the calmly observant spectator of the foregoing scene,—"that men always imagine a woman can nurse, and cook, if only she will take pains enough? As if nursing and cooking capabilities weren't just as much a matter of natural endowment as a singing ear, or an eye for color!"

136178B

"We will leave the question of your nursing capabilities altogether out of court, if you wish," Travers put in, sparing Lyon all reply. "Let it be granted that you are of no use whatever in a sick-room, and that Dorothy can—and does—more than supply your place at home, as far as actual nursing is concerned. Still, she is not, for all that, our mother's daughter. You don't seem to take in that the case is a grave one."

"You wrote yesterday that there was 'no immediate danger,'" retorted Miss Travers, speaking a little shamefacedly, however.

"And I say the same thing to-day. I believe there *is* no immediate danger. But the danger may become immediate, without much warning, at any time. I think we have discussed this question long enough, Isabel."

"Well," grudgingly, "I'll see if I can make arrangements to go down with you. But I'm afraid it's hardly possible. I have to find substitutes to do my work while I'm away, and that takes time. Then there's the Women's Suffrage Association meeting to-night; I was to have seconded the first resolution, and I don't know of any speaker to take my place. But one thing I promise you : if I can't get off to-day, I will follow you to-morrow. You needn't be uneasy ; you know I always keep my word when I have passed it."

"Your sister seems to be involved in a network of engagements," Lyon said, to break the rather awkward silence that ensued when he and Travers found themselves again in the Haymarket, Miss Isabel having previously selected a swift hansom, and had herself driven off at break-neck speed to Victoria Street.

"Engagements that bar the claims of natural affection, it seems," returned James bitterly. With him strong feeling of any kind would always out ; he was incapable of even attempting to play a part, however powerfully circumstances might seem to demand the effort of him. And, in the present case, Isabel had, to his mind, betrayed her want of heart with such cynical frankness that the most astute special pleader would have found it impossible to advance an argument in her favor.

"My dear fellow, when natural affection and one's own supreme personal interest come into collision, natural affection, quite 'naturally,' goes to the wall," Lyon observed in his cool, level voice. "It's one of the favorite modern hypocrisies to pretend that we attach far more value to family ties than we really do. As a matter of fact, clannish sentiments have had their day, and are out of date ; but most of us are too cowardly to throw them

boldly overboard. Miss Travers is honest enough—I admire her
for it—to own openly that her work has a stronger hold upon her
than any sentiment, that's all."

"Such work!"

"You consider the Female Suffrage movement unhallowed, eh?
If Miss Travers were deferring her departure in order to take a
Bible-class, or conduct a mothers' meeting, you would be better
satisfied?"

"No, I should not."

"Then you're unlike most parsons—if their practice accords
with their theory. Half the sermons I hear wind up with solemn
exhortations on the subject of subordinating the natural affections
to the claims of duty."

"Sometimes one has to choose between two conflicting duties—
one higher and the other lower."

"And you would rank the Bible-class and the mothers' meeting
among lower duties? Look to yourself, Travers; your sentiments
are hardly orthodox. All the same,"—with an abrupt change of
manner, if not of tone,—"I wish you'd go north and preach them to
the people at Creyke. They'd make a more wholesome diet for
pitmen than the counsels of perfection weekly discoursed up there
at present—I won't say to them, but to the empty benches
intended for their occupation. If only parsons would be men
first, and 'priests' afterward!"

"You've been at Creyke lately?" Travers quietly ignored his
friend's impatient exclamation in conclusion.

"For the last six weeks, off and on."

"What sort of village is it?"

"Oh, God-forsaken enough! Ugly, of course,—a mining village
must be hideous, I suppose,—and squalidly uncomfortable. And
yet prosperous, too, in a sense; in that sense in which rump steaks
ad lib. for the men and feathered hats in fearful and wonderful
variety for the women may be said to constitute prosperity.
Appallingly dull. The popular ideas of amusement don't seem to
rise above beer and pipes, with an accompaniment of free swear-
ing, diversified by a weekly dog-fight, and a movable festival in
the shape of an occasional row."

"There is a church?"

"A charming church; mediæval Gothic as to its architecture,
and modern High Anglican as to its decorations. There is also
a refined and scholarly vicar, who held forth—on the only morning

when I had the pleasure of sitting under him—to the school-
children, a few old women, and the benches I have alluded to, on—
the duty of reviving the observance of the Black Letter Festivals,
whatever those may be."

Travers gave his friend a sharp look, but did not take up the
scarcely veiled challenge thrown down to him. Letting it lie, he
demanded brusquely, "What did you do up there yourself?"

"I? Nothing. I made a few humble suggestions on first
arrival : one touching the inadequate way, so it seemed to my
ignorance, in which the large families were housed ; and another
hinting that a reading-room, or club, or some decent shelter of that
kind, might perhaps be acceptable to the better sort, who were not
ambitious of making beasts of themselves every night ; all of
which suggestions were promptly quashed by my agent. He
assured me that the people were quite content with the present
state of things, and I had much better leave them alone. When
I expressed incredulity on this head, he invited me to go round
the village and find out for myself."

" Well ? "

" Well, I went, and found matters precisely as Harrison had
said. So I 'concluded,' as the Americans say, to take my ticket
and come back to town."

" Abandoning all your plans ? "

" Certainly. Why on earth should I bother myself trying to
elevate the condition of people who prefer remaining at their
present level ? "

" That they should prefer remaining there argues the greater
necessity for your interference."

" From your point of view, I dare say. Not from mine. I've
no commission to make my fellow-man either virtuous or refined
against his will. If he likes to remain vicious and brutal, I'm not
called upon to interfere with his preferences."

" That's a question. At least you are bound to give men,
actually dependent on you for every opportunity of rising, a
chance to rise, whether they ask it of you or not, so it seems to
me. It's a simple matter of duty."

" From your point of view, I say again, I don't doubt it. But
then you probably spell Duty with a capital letter, and regard it
as a fixed quantity—which is more than most of us nineteenth-
century pagans are able to do. That's why we all talk so much
and effect so little. An open mind and a suspended judgment

may be necessary to the true philosophic attitude ; but, as far as my experience goes, it's not the philosopher who makes the best citizen. No, it's you fanatics, you fellows who are so cocksure of everything, who do all the useful work that's done in the world, to give you your due."

"And yet," said Travers, a fleeting but singularly beautiful smile illuminating his plain face for an instant, " you despise us for that same cocksureness ! "

"No. Not invariably. Sometimes, more often than not, we envy you."

Lyon jerked out these brief sentences somewhat hoarsely.

"In that case, why not make some effort ? "

"To arrive at your state of mind ? Ah, there are obstacles in the way that you know nothing of, you to whom belief in a supernatural creed is an easy thing."

"Good Heavens ! " ejaculated Travers in a tone strangely different from any Lyon had ever heard proceed from his lips before, "do you imagine, on your side, that faith is easy to *anyone?* or that we, any more than you, are without our doubts and questionings concerning this horrible tangle we call life ? Do you suppose the explanation of the mystery we try to believe in, and do believe in, thank God ! in our better moments—do you suppose even that explanation always satisfies us ? If so, you are profoundly mistaken ! "

A block in the street traffic had obliged the two men to halt at a crossing while Travers was speaking. Now, as he finished, they turned simultaneously and looked straight, each into the other's face, with a look that in its absolute frankness, its utter want of reserve on either side, had the force of a mutual revelation. It was as though the soul of each man had been suddenly laid bare to his companion for a moment. In that moment Lyon had as clear a glimpse of Travers' passionate daily struggle to maintain his foothold on the heights of faith to which he had painfully climbed as had Travers of the unacknowledged yearning toward the creed he could not accept, which moved uneasily beneath the surface of Lyon's pessimistic scepticism. A glimpse only; all was over in a mere flash of time, the shutters of self-recollectedness shutting quickly upon the curious double vision, which had yet lasted long enough to create the consciousness of a new bond between them, new and strangely intimate.

That there was anything incongruous in the fact of this singular revelation taking place on the crowded pavement of Whitehall did not suggest itself at the time either to Lyon or to Travers. Lyon, indeed, reviewing the matter in cold blood later on, found something absurd in this circumstance; but the absurdity was not of a kind which afforded him much genuine amusement.

They walked on in silence after passing the crossing, until Travers, stopping abruptly at the foot of an imposing flight of steps, observed briefly:

" Here's my office. Well, I'm glad we chanced to meet."

" So am I. I hope you'll find Mrs. Travers better this evening. Remember me down there," Lyon responded.

He watched Travers run up the steps in his active boyish fashion, and disappear within the great glass doors at the top; then, instead of turning homeward, he prolonged his walk toward Westminster. He wanted a longer walk; rapid motion would, perhaps, help him to shake off various unpleasant feelings aroused by his late unexpected interview with his friend. So he betook himself to the Embankment at a good round pace, and strode along in the direction of Sion College, a prey to uneasy reflections.

It was not the latter, but the earlier, part of his conversation with Travers which had so disturbed, and was still disturbing, Lyon's mind. The electric shock following on Travers' heroic lifting of the veil from his own tempest-tossed mind had spent itself, so it seemed at least, in one strong thrill of mingled surprise and sympathy; he put the thought of that moment wholly by, and fell to considering, instead, the news that James had communicated on their first meeting, together with all its possible bearings on his personal destiny and interests.

One important effect on these it had had already, in precipitating him to a decision hitherto only trembling in the balance. When he ran against Travers in Piccadilly, an idea of going down to Heyford, and there making unconditional surrender to the passion he had been fighting so desperately for six weeks past, was but just beginning to take shape in his mind. He had suspected indeed for some days that his conflict with himself would probably end in some such ignominious acknowledgment of defeat; but he had been far from arriving at a fixed intention of yielding such acknowledgment without further ado. Now, however, that destiny, making use of Mrs. Travers for the purpose, had barred his approach to Dorothy Temple for the moment,—for it seemed clear that he could not insist on her quitting her sick relative's

bedside to listen to his wooing,—he quite forgot that, till he heard
of this obstacle, he had never really settled in his own mind the
vexed question whether to suffer the door she had unconsciously
shut in his face that wet summer morning at Owlswick to remain
a lasting barrier between them or no. He had now no doubt whatever of his own intentions ; he felt himself hardly used in being
debarred for a while from carrying them out.

In his vexation, his sense of baffled purpose, above all, in the
state of indefinite apprehension into which his knowledge of
the renewal of affectionate relations between Dorothy and Brian
Travers' mother had thrown him, he almost forgot to gird at himself for the folly and unreason of his love. His self-addressed
criticisms had, indeed, been losing in force, if not in asperity, for
some time past. He might word them just as incisively as ever,
they had ceased to have their old tonic effect on his mind. It was
in vain that he appealed to his past experience. Instinct, or the
illusion of a passion which seemed only to grow stronger for
the unmerciful discipline to which he subjected it, persisted in
assuring him that in Dorothy he had lighted on a new type of
womanhood, to which his past experience could apply no measuring line. Equally vain were now his efforts to analyze coolly this
girl who had stirred his nature so inexplicably, to bring her individuality under a mental dissecting-knife, and pronounce triumphantly the absence from its composition of all those charms and
gifts that could justify a man in setting his heart upon her. The
time for scientific investigation into her claims on his regard was
clearly overpast. As to the success of his suit, he was tolerably
sanguine. He did not, indeed, suspect Dorothy Temple of being
in love with him. But he knew, he had known all along, she
being of an unguarded honesty and he a singularly acute observer,
that from the outset he had aroused her interest and fascinated
her imagination ; he believed that he could easily dominate her
will. Love, with such a girl, would follow naturally ; he had few
fears on this score.

Dreading no hopeless obduracy on Dorothy's part, and being a
man with whom patient self-government had become a fixed habit,
it should not, in theory, have been difficult for him to defer for
a little the moment of taking formal possession of a kingdom over
which he believed himself to exercise virtual sovereignty already.
In practice, however, he found his enforced waiting on events
singularly trying. If he had chafed in anticipation against any

delay of his now settled purpose as he passed along the Victoria
Embankment that close morning in August, he chafed far more
restlessly against the actual delay that ensued, as September
passed into October, and still his purpose remained unfulfilled.
For over his waiting, hopeful as in one sense it undoubtedly was,
there hung the cloud of a scarce-acknowledged fear. He would
not put it into words, would hardly even allow it to take definite
shape in his thought; but as a vague, formless shadow it haunted
him continually. While he knew Dorothy to be day and night at
the bedside of Brian Travers' mother, rest was not for him, nor a
perfect confidence in the future.

CHAPTER X

UNDER THE CYPRESSES

"But when my heart
In one frail ark had ventur'd all . . .
Then came the thunderbolt."

POOR Mrs. Travers, like King Charles of mirthful memory, took,
so it seemed now and then to Lyon's impatience, "an uncon-
scionable time in dying." Not that he had any spite against the
poor lady, or cherished an unholy desire to hurry her untimely
from this mortal scene. He would have rejoiced sincerely to hear
that she had been unexpectedly restored to health; at the same
time, he was secretly of the opinion of a certain German music-
master, who observed coolly of the next-door neighbor whose
lingering progress toward the grave interfered with the daily
practisings of his pupils, that "persons who are so very ill as all
that should either get well or die."

In Mrs. Travers' case the question of recovery was, after the first,
scarcely even mooted; and when, in the last days of October, her
protracted illness found its consummation in death, her nearest and
dearest had long been fully prepared for the event, and met it with
that composure which antecedent expectation of such a calamity
scarcely ever fails to produce in the sincerest mourners. Only the
old rector tottered beneath the weight of his loss, which had aged
him, so his son wrote to Lyon, by ten years in a few days' time.
"Dorothy feels it greatly, too; all she has gone through has altered
her considerably," James added briefly.

Lyon, pondering over this bald and unsatisfactory postscript to his friend's hurried letter, decided, though it was now the middle of November, to defer his journey to Heyford yet a little longer. To go to the house of mourning with a love-tale, to pour the pleadings of passion into the ears of a sensitive girl fresh from deathbed scenes, seemed to him the height of unwisdom as well as the perfection of bad taste. On the judicious choice of time and season the very success or failure of his enterprise might depend. With the prospect of putting his fate to the touch actually close at hand, Lyon, it will be observed, had grown less confident in his own power to achieve victory.

So convinced was he of the need of proceeding cautiously that it was only on the very last day of the month that he ventured to set out for Donnington. Noon on that day found him stepping once more from an empty train into the bare little country station; but this time he did not linger there half expecting the appearance of someone from Heyford to greet his arrival. He had taken good care that no whisper of his intended coming should precede him; even refraining from writing, as for a moment he had thought of doing, to the nearest town for means of transport, lest by this means his project should get noised abroad. Unencumbered with any kind of baggage, he could, he reminded himself, easily walk the half dozen miles dividing Donnington from The Haulms.

The road leading to that present goal of his desires presented to him an aspect differing most signally from that it had worn on the occasion when he first traversed it, in company with Dorothy Temple. Thickly carpeted then with white summer dust, it was now dark and miry with November mud; at the end of a mile Lyon was already looking ruefully at his boots, and saying to himself, "A pretty sight I shall be by the time I get to Heyford!— hardly fit to go in. Probably her one desire on seeing me will be to get me out of the house again as quickly as possible, before I have hopelessly ruined the carpet in that immaculate drawing-room of Creighton's." Under the nip of a sharp white frost the previous night the hedgerow oaks had parted with their last remaining dry leaves; the beautiful overgrown hedgerows themselves, that had been so lavishly garlanded with flowers in June, were now mere tangles of naked briers, tipped with scarlet hips and haws, with here and there a clump of lighter-hued briony berries, or a melancholy trailing cluster of "old man's beard"; the fields, stripped of their very latest autumn crops, lay brown and bare on either side the way. Yet both the scene and the day had their own subtle charm. Deliciously mild, the atmosphere was full of that soothing softness peculiar to the air of a warm day in late autumn; the sun shone pleasantly, if hazily, out of a pale eggshell-blue sky; an exquisite stillness, restful, without being oppressive in its silence, hung over the landscape, and through it the commonest country sounds—the twitter of an invisible hedge-sparrow, the distant bleating of a far-off flock of sheep, even the ploughman's encouraging "chirrup" to his horses as they turned at the end of a newly drawn furrow, and the cry of a boy on the hillside scaring crows from the fresh-sown wheat—fell tenderly upon the ear.

Lyon walked on steadily, taking little or no conscious note of his surroundings, which yet were not without an influence on his mind. Only to him there seemed to be rather a suggestion of spring than of autumn in the calm, soft, quiet air. Everywhere he discerned, not evidences of "calm decay," but the germs of the new life to be —that same new life which had begun to stir and throb in his own veins so lustily. After years of cold lethargy he felt his whole nature once more thoroughly awake, all its sleeping powers roused into startling activity by—what? The mere unconscious touch of a girl's hand? Incredible!—and yet most true. Old ambitions, old aspirations, old plans and purposes were all reviving mightily in his breast. Already he had begun to ask whether he had not despaired of himself too soon, whether achievement, as well as happiness, might not yet be within his reach. Much time he had, no doubt, irrevocably lost; but something not wholly unworthy a man's efforts might perhaps even now be possible. Judged by the simple standard of her he had so strangely learned to love, his present existence, whereof he had never attempted to hide the poverty and the pettiness from himself, suddenly looked poorer and pettier than ever before; at all costs he would have to do better than *that*, since, otherwise, how could he possibly endure to meet the tender eyes that would henceforth watch his life from day to day—if all went well this morning?

He added this saving clause superstitiously, as a propitiation to Fate; for in his heart he believed once more that all would go well. On his walk the confidence he had lost for a while had, for no special reason, returned to him in full force. The vague fears that had haunted him during the past three or four months receded into the background. What could Mrs. Travers, he demanded scornfully, Mrs. Travers, dead, and silent forever with the silence of the grave, do against him, living, and able to plead his cause in burning words? While she lived he *had* feared her; he acknowledged this to himself : but now he was surely more than a match for the influence that death had reduced to a mere memory. If his heart beat uncomfortably high as he rang the bell at the closed door of The Haulms, it was certainly not with fear.

The maid who answered his ring informed him, without giving him time to put any question to her, that Mr. Creighton was not at home. He had gone to London for a few days, she added.

"It's not——" Lyon checked himself, remembering opportunely that it was needless to explain that his visit had in no case been intended for the master of the house. "Perhaps Miss Temple is in ?" he suggested diplomatically.

No, Miss Temple was out.

"Do you know at what hour she is likely to be back? Because I might be able to call again later."

"I can tell Miss Temple you are here, sir, if you wish to see her particularly. She is only somewhere in the garden ; she told me she shouldn't go farther, because she was expecting a poor woman to call during the afternoon."

"Thanks," Lyon interrupted, cutting short the worthy Lewin's intention of inviting him into the house ; "then I needn't trouble you further. I'll go into the garden, and find Miss Temple for myself."

He turned away, and strode round the corner of the porch, taking a path which led downward to the lawn ; leaving Lewin on the doorstep, somewhat scandalized at his airy waiving of all the usual formalities of a morning call.

No sign of Dorothy could Lyon discover on the lawn—nor yet by the river, nor in the shrubbery. He was beginning to fear she must have reconsidered the determination she had expressed to Lewin, when the happy thought suddenly occurred to him that it might be well to look for her in the Lady's Walk. He knew it to be a favorite lounging-place of hers.

In the Lady's Walk, sure enough, he found her, sitting at the far end of the old wall, quite close to the historic well—a slender figure, scarcely distinguishable, in her mourning garb, from the funereal cypresses overshadowing her fair head. Her back was toward Lyon as he came ; and, the thick soft turf yielding noiselessly to his footsteps, she remained unconscious of his approach until, standing at her very elbow, he said, in a voice which nervousness only rendered a trifle deeper than usual :

"Miss Temple ! "

" Mr. Lyon ! How—how you startled me ! "

It seemed that he had startled her indeed, for the face she turned toward him, as she sprang to her feet, was deadly white ; and when he took her proffered hand, it trembled palpably in his grasp.

" I—I beg your pardon a thousand times ! " he exclaimed hurriedly, changing color very faintly himself. " Your maid told me I should find you in the grounds—and I never thought—— Of course I ought not to have come upon you so suddenly; I should have remembered you have had a great deal to try you lately. You are not looking well," he added abruptly.

" There is nothing the matter with me, thank you "—sitting down again on the wall with a suddenness suggesting that she found standing difficult. " I was only very much surprised—and then, perhaps, I am a little tired and nervous. We have had such a sorrowful time since you went away."

" I know," Lyon answered gravely. Then, after a moment's pause : " I did not like to write, to trouble you with letters. But I have thought of you, constantly, these last months."

" Thank you," she responded simply and without embarrassment, taking his words, evidently, in their ordinary, commonplace signification. " I was sure you would feel sorry for us all."

The ring of this last sentence—wherein Dorothy seemed to identify herself more closely than he deemed at all necessary with the Travers family in their bereavement—displeased Lyon. Changing the subject brusquely, he enquired after James.

" He is very well. I suppose you did not tell him you were coming over ? No, of course not, or he would have telegraphed to you not to come to-day. He is at Oldbury, for a meeting of the Diocesan Conference, and I'm afraid there's not the slightest chance of his being back before the middle of the day, to-morrow. It is most unfortunate ! "

It was on the tip of Lyon's tongue to say at once that he had not come to Heyford to see James Travers ; but something, perhaps the unsuspecting calmness of Dorothy's manner, held him back from the frank confession.

" Such a piece of ill luck ! " the girl went on. " He is so rarely away ; and I know he will be so annoyed at finding he has missed you. But perhaps you will be able to come again? Are you staying quite near to us ? ”

" I am not staying anywhere,” Lyon returned, with an odd little laugh. " I simply ran down from London, on the chance——”

" Oh, but that is still worse ! A long journey for nothing ! and, to add one more unlucky circumstance to the rest, my uncle is away, too, for a few days. If he had been at home, I am sure he would have begged you to stay here, for the night, at least. Poor Mr. Travers is in no state to receive anyone——”

" I quite understand that,” Lyon interposed. "And in no case had I any intention of spending more than a few hours at Heyford.”

" Well, at least you will come in, and let me give you some luncheon ? ”

" No, thanks. I lunched at Malding on my way down. But I'll stay and talk to you here a while, if you'll allow me,” boldly seating himself at a little distance from her on the wall. " And first, tell me, how is the old rector ? Travers wrote of him as completely crushed.”

" He is better ; better, that is, than he was some weeks ago. But he will never get over the loss of her. It is as if half himself had been torn away ; he feels hopelessly maimed, I think. And yet, as you know, she could *do* little or nothing for him, only sympathize; it is her sympathy he misses so terribly. One doesn't wonder at it. Their minds always seemed to move in a sort of harmony ; it wasn't only that they thought alike—they *felt* alike, on pretty nearly every subject.” She paused for an instant. " It was very beautiful,” she added in a slightly lower tone.

Lyon made no answering comment on these words of his companion's. He was busy studying her face, noting the changes that had taken place in it, and wondering whether they portended good or evil to himself.

No doubt but these changes were both great and significant—so great as to startle Lyon, so significant as to render him uneasy. He had expected to find Dorothy looking paler and graver than in the summer, still bearing traces, it might be, of fatigue and emotion ; but he was not prepared to find her grown, in the space of less than half a year, from the mental stature of a frank, light-hearted girl to that of a sedate, self-contained woman. Yet to this astounding inner development, and to nothing less than this, did her countenance, with its new steadfastness of expression, bear witness.

Also, there was now a spiritual beauty, a depth of tender thought-fulness in her eyes which he had never discerned there before, and the discerning of which caused him, even as he recognized it, to assume a new attitude toward her, the attitude of humility. He knew now that, in any future joining of their lives, it would not be he who should condescend to her, but she who, from an altitude quite out of his reach and ken, would stoop to him.

While these thoughts chased each other through her companion's mind, Dorothy went on talking calmly of the old rector.

At first, she said, the prostration, both mental and physical, from which the old man suffered after his wife's death, had been so extreme as to make him think seriously of resigning his living, and he had even taken certain steps toward placing his resignation in the bishop's hands. His bodily condition improving, however, he had promptly rescinded his resolution, and was now as obstinately determined to stay on at Heyford as he had for a while been eagerly anxious to leave it. " I think it is a pity he should have changed his mind," Dorothy said in conclusion. " He is not really equal to any trouble or responsibility. And then, it's a little hard on poor Jem, who fancied himself at last on the point of attaining his heart's desire."

" What's that ? "

" Don't you know that for years it has been his dream to join one of the preaching Orders, and go out to India as a missionary ? A fortnight ago it seemed as if the time for realizing the dream had come ; I know Jem actually wrote a preliminary letter to Father White, and ordered his Marathi and Hindu grammars. Then Mr. Travers changed his mind—I believe on the very day the parcel of books arrived from Oxford. Was it not hard ? "

" Very, since his ambition lies that way. How does he bear his disappointment ? "

" Like himself—as being all for the best. He told me on Monday he was working hard at his Marathi, and he believed it was a capital thing he had been prevented going out at present ; the delay would give him just the time he needed for perfecting himself in the language ! "

Dorothy smiled as she spoke, but her eyes were suspiciously dewy.

" Happy optimist ! " ejaculated Lyon. " No, I never heard a whisper of the missionary plan before. But, supposing Travers had been free to carry it out, as far as this place is concerned, what would have become of the rector? He could hardly have gone to India, too."

"Oh, in that case, we should—— No, of course Mr. Travers could not have gone out with Jem. But Brian, his other son, is coming home,"—there was a slight appearance of flurry about Dorothy's manner,—"and I think the rector would probably have gone to live with him. You know he was always his father's favorite."

"Yes, I know," Lyon answered abstractedly, not much heeding what she said. He was considering how best to lead the conversation round to the desired point, which he rather shrank from attacking with absolute suddenness.

Dorothy, all unconsciously, gave him a helping hand.

"I wish Jem and his father had more ideas in common," she remarked meditatively. "It would make both their lives so much happier—Jem's especially. For the rector at least has friends near at hand, while all Jem's cronies are far away. It is all the more tiresome that he should have missed you to-day, after your travelling all the way from London on purpose to see him——"

"I beg your pardon!" Lyon interposed desperately, feeling that now or never was his moment. "I really can't let you labor under a misapprehension any longer. You give me credit where I deserve none. I didn't come here to-day to see Travers. My journey was prompted by no kind motive whatever; it had a purely selfish personal end." He found himself getting curiously out of breath, and had to pause for an instant. "I came—can you guess why?"

She shook her head. But he fancied that he could discern a shade of fear sweep over her face at the same moment, suggesting that she felt vaguely afraid of what he might say next.

What he did say was very much to the purpose. "Well, it was to see—you."

"*To see me?*"

No question but that she was thoroughly frightened now. Fear had blanched even the lips with which she repeated his words.

"Yes." He rose and stood straight before her, upright and resolute; clearly he meant to give her no chance of running away without hearing him out. "To see you, and tell you what I should have told you last June, if I hadn't been a fool and a coward. That I love you—love you passionately, as I've never loved any woman before, and certainly never shall again."

8

"No! no!" she exclaimed faintly.

"But it is yes!" he retorted, with a half smile. "Surely you might allow me to know my own mind after nearly six months' consideration? I am not a hot-headed boy, remember. I'll be honest with you; in the summer I was *not* sure. I thought, to conceal nothing, that I could live it down; and I tried to live it down. You'll not misjudge me for that; you know if I had reason to dread setting my whole heart on a woman! But I could do nothing: I was helpless as a child. I had loved you from the moment I saw you. I fancy, though, I was slow to find out the truth. By the time I did find it out the thing had become a part of me; I could no more get away from it than I could get away from myself."

Again he stopped, that curious breathlessness once more momentarily getting the better of him. When he resumed, it was in a lower and less steady voice.

"I can't make eloquent speeches. I can only tell you, in the old hackneyed phrase, that you are all the world to me. But understand that I don't speak in a figure, please. You *are* all the world to me. Everything I fancied I had lost forever—not love and happiness only, but hope and self-respect and faith in human nature—I have found again in you. Deny me yourself and you beggar me afresh—only more completely than before!"

Her face had changed while he was speaking; a veritable glow of light and color had invaded it. For a minute past she had been bending unconsciously forward, while her eyes seemed drinking in his impassioned words. But, when he ended, her color died down again, and she drew back, shivering a little, into the angle of the wall behind her.

"I am sorry—so sorry," she murmured almost inaudibly. "I didn't know—oh, I didn't know! And now, I——"

"Hush!" he interposed; "hear me to the end before you give me an answer. I know there's a great deal to be said against what I am asking you to do. To begin with, I am far too old for you—in mind and years alike. I have never in my whole life done anything that would justify you in caring for me; the chances are I never shall do anything. For my present manner of existence—you yourself cannot think it more contemptible, more unworthy of an intelligent human being, than I know and feel it to be. As to my past, two or three years of it at least, if I could bring myself to tell you of those years, you would probably consider me deserving only of the most merciless condemnation. And so I am. I offer no excuses for myself; I won't even tell you that I've been no worse than other men. In a way, I *have* been worse. So many men's sins are more or less involuntary—mine were always deliberate. Evil never presented itself to me at any time in the guise of an angel of light. I was simply reckless, because profoundly miserable, and wanted distraction. You see, I keep nothing back," he made abrupt comment. "At least you'll acquit me of trying to deceive you—of making myself out any better than I am! I can truthfully say I have never done that, with you. From the first, some demon has always been impelling me to show you the worst and lowest side of myself. And yet, if only you could and would believe it, even I am not all bad——"

"Oh, I have never thought so !" eagerly. "Pray, pray do not imagine it ! "

"It is something that you should be able to say even so much as that. Well," with a desperate attempt at lightness of speech, " I don't know that I have any further touch to add to the unpleasing portrait I have drawn. If you were not—what you are, I should feel it doubly insane *now*, after what I have told you, to ask you to stretch out a helping hand to such as I. But, you see,"—a strange smile quivered across his face,—" I know your passion for usefulness, for aiding any broken-down creature you find by the wayside, if only he or she is in sufficiently desperate case, and I think I may fairly advance that sort of claim to your mercy. If ever man wanted help, I do. Will you give it me, Dorothy ? Will you ?"

Dorothy rose quickly to her feet there. "Mr. Lyon, you must not go on. I ought not to have let you say so much."

" You must hear one word more before you silence me," he persisted. " Understand that, in my case, it lies with you, and you only, to help. For others there may be other means of redemption, other ways of struggling back to better things. For me, there is your hand to hold by—or nothing." She trembled visibly, putting her hand on the edge of the wall to steady herself. He drew a step nearer. " I don't ask you to love me—though I believe I might win your love in time, perhaps ; I simply ask you to save me. I don't promise you "—still with a kind of perverse candor putting the case rather against than for himself—" that you will be perfectly happy as my wife ; I am too little fit for you to be likely to make you perfectly happy. But this I can and do promise you : if you give yourself to me, what I give you in return will be nothing less than my whole life—to deal with as you please. Mere wreckage as it is, I believe you might yet, if you would, make something out of it. Will you try?"

Lyon's voice had almost regained its wonted firmness. But there was that in his eyes, as he put his final question, which no woman could have met unmoved. Dorothy felt herself quivering in every nerve.

"You don't know—— It is not a question of what I will or will not do," she replied hurriedly in a half-choked voice. "I cannot be—what you ask me to be to you"—she seemed afraid to say "your wife"—"because—I am engaged to be married already."

Lyon stood a moment as if stunned. Then there came to him a dreary sense of anticipation fulfilled—of having known all along that thus it would be. "To Brian Travers?" he asked very quietly.

Of course he ought not, conventionally speaking, to have put this question at all. The moment, however, was one in which conventionalities had no weight with him; he had temporarily passed into another atmosphere.

"Yes, to my cousin Brian. But—how did you know? And if you knew, why did you come here to-day?" She paused, her eyes grown suddenly severe, and her mouth almost hard.

"To play Brian this disloyal turn, you mean? Yes, perhaps I had better explain how it came about. Poor creature as I am, Miss Temple, I am not, I hope, quite such a scoundrel as to be capable of laying plans to betray my friend, nor such a dullard as to fancy I should be likely to induce you to break your word to him. No; here I can acquit myself of anything worse than an unfortunate blunder——"

And he proceeded, in few words, to tell her of Mrs. Travers' hints concerning a tie between herself and her cousin, and Jem's subsequent positive contradiction of his mother's assertions.

"After that I felt myself free to act as I would—without any disloyalty to Brian. I can only say that I am sorry my mistake should have caused you pain. The mistake was rather Jem's than mine, though—at least in the first instance. He assured me so confidently that you were *not* engaged to his brother."

"And he was right," Dorothy struck in eagerly—alarmed perhaps at the growing blackness of Lyon's brow, and anxious to exculpate the innocent Jem. "We were not engaged, at that time. There was only a—a sort of understanding—just between ourselves —that there *might* be something, perhaps, when he came home. We had not told anyone. Indeed, there was nothing to tell, no promise of any kind." Dorothy, in her inexperience, felt constrained to explain the matter fully. "It was while you were here that he first wrote to his mother; and it was only settled a day or two before she died. Till then there was nothing certain at all; nothing for Jem to know—or anyone."

Again Lyon told himself drearily that he had been right in his presentiments. Mrs. Travers, on her deathbed, had been strong enough to snatch the prize of his life from him. Yet, stay, had he not rather himself wrought the ruin of this last best hope of his manhood! A recollection of his last conversation with Brian Travers—that conversation held in Half-Moon Street two years and a half before—flashed once more across his memory, but this time it was a recollection clear and precise in all its details; he recalled not only the young man's despair in speaking of his rejection by some nameless girl in the country, but his own carelessly given counsel, and Brian's resolution, taken in accordance with that advice, to try his luck once more.

"It's all my own doing; I have less than no right to complain," he muttered.

"I don't understand." Dorothy's pale face, which had remained without a blush while she told her love-story, wore a look of bewilderment.

"No? Perhaps you can fancy, though, what the feelings of a man might be who should find out that by mistake, half in joke, too, he had signed his own death-warrant? That's my position at the present moment. It's certainly a warning not to put one's name heedlessly to any document. I see I am only puzzling you further; but really the riddle's not worth explaining. Good-by," and he held out his hand. "I'm heartily sorry to have been led into troubling you with my impossible wishes and aspirations. Do me the justice to believe, at least, that if I'd known how matters really stood, I would have spared you the infliction."

"Oh, but I do not—it was not an infliction. You can't guess how grieved I am," she responded incoherently.

"It is kind of you to be sorry for me," he answered gloomily. For a moment the old hateful suspicions mastered him; was the sop to her vanity which his subjection offered so pleasing to her as to swallow up all painful elements in the scene just closing? "Brian is not yet at home?" he asked abruptly, unable to overcome a sudden fierce impulse of curiosity.

"No, he will not be in England before next summer. His three years in Queensland will be up then, and he hopes to get work over here." Again she spoke without blush or tremor, in a cold, perfectly matter-of-fact tone.

"And then you will be married, of course, and live happy ever after?" with a nervous laugh. "Well," giving her a cold, keen look which contrasted singularly with his impassioned one of a few moments before, "you both have my best wishes toward that desirable consummation."

Almost involuntarily Dorothy faltered, "And you?"

"I?" with an air of surprise. "Oh, I shall turn round, after the manner of the Seven Sleepers of Ephesus when disturbed, and try to drop back into the old, comfortable, slumberous conditions of the days before I made your acquaintance, as fast as I possibly can. I haven't been awake very long; so, perhaps, if I try hard enough, I may get to sleep again. What!"—in reply to her troubled look, and faint shake of the head—"you want me to keep awake? That's rather cruel of you. Something like a nurse who should take away the chloroform bottle in order that the patient may feel all the pain of the operation, and thereby learn a salutary lesson of endurance. For I presume that's the end you have in view? You think it would be for my moral benefit to suffer a little more?"

Tears started to the girl's eyes; she clasped her hands and almost wrung them in passionate distress.

"Don't talk so! I don't know what to say—but if you knew how it hurts!"

"Does it? That is curious." Her evident pain cried shame on his suspicions; but bitterness still had the mastery of his spirit. "Since you are so kind-hearted as to be pained by my remarks, I apologize for them, however. You see, it never occurred to a selfish egotist like myself that you would be likely to feel much for the ill luck of a man who is nothing to you. I beg your pardon for misjudging you. Good-by."

He touched her hand and left her; and this time it was not to look back after he had once turned away. But, had he looked back, he would not have found her, as once before, gazing earnestly after him. His good-by was scarcely spoken before she had reseated herself in her old place on the wall; and she seemed in no hurry to leave it again. Letting her hands fall into her lap, she sat staring down fixedly into the turbid water of the river making its

slow way southward through the clumps of reeds that had withered
to limp, brown, broken stalks since the moonlight night in June
when first she had brought him to the Lady's Walk, and told him
the sad legend of the place. He must have been far away on the
Donnington road before she lifted her white face, and with a quick,
sudden movement, the movement of one who is suffocating, put
up her hands to her throat, and broke into a strange little laugh.

CHAPTER XI

AT SEA—BY NIGHT

"This is life's height. . . This must end here :
It is too perfect."

THE railway station at Southampton was full of people on their
way to one or other of the Channel Islands. It was also full of a
peculiarly dense, damp, all-involving fog, which had the effect of
greatly aggravating the bustle and confusion incident, even on fair
evenings, to the despatch of the Jersey mail-boat. On this particular March night, which was certainly rather foul than fair, the
platforms, dimly illumined by dull-burning gaslights, scarcely
visible at a few paces' distance, presented a scene of noise and
hurry indescribable. Male passengers were scurrying to and fro
in search of baggage or information; anxious women clutched
frantically at the elbows of distracted porters ; here and there a
frightened child, left for a moment to itself, was whimpering pitifully; while a veritable babel of human voices, to which the
harsh, warning tones of the fog-horns and sirens in Southampton
Water supplied a monotonous ground-bass, filled the air on every
side. Lyon, who had his own private reasons for not wishing to
be hustled or otherwise roughly handled just then, looked askance
from the booking-office, where he had been taking his ticket for
Waterloo, at the vociferous, pushing crowd outside and hesitated a
moment before plunging into the whirlpool.

As he paused, irresolute, on the threshold of his temporary place
of refuge, the slim figure of a woman detached itself from the
moving mass of eager passers-by, made two or three steps in the
direction of the doorway he felt so loath to forsake, stopped, as if

to reconnoitre, advanced afresh, and then, presumably catching sight of the overcoat and hat which blocked the way, stopped once more.

"Will you be so kind as to tell me where to find the ticket-office?"

.It was a familiar voice which put the question, and all Lyon's pulses gave a leap as it fell upon his ear—a leap much too sudden and too violent to be agreeable. For an instant his breath was not only figuratively, but literally taken away.

For an instant only. It was a scarcely perceptible pause which occurred before he answered with perfect apparent composure :

"Certainly, Miss Temple. I see you don't recognize me,"—making a step forward, so that the light of the lamp over the doorway should fall more fully upon him,—"though, indeed, how should you in this darkness? Did you ever see a better imitation of a London particular?"

"It is dreadfully foggy," Dorothy replied. Even now that they were close together it was impossible for him to see her face at all clearly in such an imperfect light; besides, the tolerably thick veil she wore would at any time have sufficed to disguise a passing change or expression. But Lyon fancied that he detected a thrill of excitement in her voice. "How—how very strange that I should meet you here !"

"Seeing that I have just come over from Jersey, and you, I suppose, have done the same, not so very strange, after all, I should say. The only wonder is that we did not encounter one another on board the boat, hours ago."

"I have not come from Jersey, I am going there." Dorothy spoke stiffly ; the tone of Lyon's last speech had offended her, and she also felt taken aback at his making no movement whatever to shake hands. "I am going by the steamer which starts at eight o'clock, and I want to find the booking-office. It appears I ought to have taken a through ticket in London ; unfortunately, I didn't know that. Why, here is the booking-office !"

"Not the one you want ; that's on the other side. I'll go there with you. Are you travelling alone, by the by ?"

"Quite alone."

"Perhaps it's as well we chanced to meet, then. It's always difficult for a lady to command attention in a crowd." He stepped out on to the platform. "Keep as close to me as you can. We have some little way to go. Stay a moment ! I'll leave my bag ·

and umbrella behind this door. It's always best to go unencumbered into a crush."

He deposited the articles in question, both of which he had been holding till now in his left hand, in the rather dangerous hiding-place he had designated, and, a minute later, they were painfully making their slow way round to the opposite platform, where the " down " booking-office was to be found.

Sustained conversation *en route* was impossible ; and speech between the two soon became strictly limited to the issue of brief occasional instructions on Lyon's part, and a generally monosyllabic signification of assent on the girl's.

Lyon's height and great breadth of shoulder stood him in good stead on the present occasion, in the task of clearing a way for himself and his charge. But Dorothy might have noticed, had she been in the mood for close observation, that his movements were singularly awkward, and that he made use of his left hand where it would have been far more fitting, and to all appearance convenient, to have brought his right into play. Thus, for instance, when a momentary block occurred in the moving crowd, and he, fearing she would be separated from him, took firm hold of her elbow, he put his left arm across to reach her, although she was standing close at his right side.

In the scrimmage that followed the breaking up of the block—produced chiefly by a big, burly Yorkshireman, who, planted just behind Dorothy, pushed and shoved as vigorously on all sides of him as though he had been a frantic half-back at a North Country football match—the girl, thrown violently against her companion, caught a smothered exclamation of pain, or impatience—which was it ?—which he was not quick enough wholly to suppress.

"I beg your pardon ! " she exclaimed in her turn, looking up half alarmed. " What was it ? Have I——"

" It was nothing," he cut her short brusquely, not giving her time to complete her question.

They reached their destination at length, procured the needful ticket, and then started off afresh in quest of Dorothy's luggage. This they identified without much difficulty in the weighing-room, and took up their station beside it, waiting till their turn at the scales should arrive.

"Luckily, you have plenty of time before you," Lyon remarked.

"Yes."

"And this is not such a bad place to wait in. We can at least see each other. Till now I could hardly have sworn to you, but for your voice."

Dorothy turned aside rather sharply, and began busying herself with the lock of her travelling-bag. There was a moment's pause. Then Lyon enquired for Mr. Creighton.

"He has gone to Egypt for three months on business connected with the book. That is why I am here to-night. My uncle thought at first of leaving me at The Haulms while he was away. But he got a good offer for the house from some people he knew, so he decided to send me to Jersey instead. He has a cousin there, an old maiden lady, who will take me in for the time."

"Not very lively for you. Creighton should have taken you to Egypt with him."

Dorothy shook her head.

"I should have encumbered his movements too much; he is going a good way up the Nile. I dare say I shall like Jersey very well."

"I trust you may. At any rate, the change will be better for you than staying on alone at The Haulms."

"Do you think so?" doubtfully. "I would rather have stayed at home, if it had been possible, I think. Could you kindly give me that little hat-box over here? I forgot to strap it before starting, and I know the lock is weak. Oh!"—with a sudden change of tone, as he turned to do her bidding with his left hand, and she perceived for the first time that he carried his right arm in a sling—"you have hurt yourself!"

"A little. It's not a hurt of any consequence."

The color came into her face; in dealing with the diminutive lock of the bag she had found herself obliged to put up her veil, and her eyes grew wonderfully soft.

"Was it up at Creyke, in the riot, that you were hurt?"

"Yes," he admitted reluctantly. "I hoped," after a moment's pause, speaking in a tone which betrayed profound annoyance, "that I had at least succeeded in keeping that foolish little affair out of the London papers."

"It wasn't in a London paper that I read the account," she explained. "It was in a local paper. My uncle's parlor-maid is a North Country woman,"—this more hurriedly in answer to his look of surprised enquiry,—"and she lent me the Leeds *Argus*, but the *Argus* didn't mention your injury!"

"Probably so trifling an injury wasn't worth mentioning, from the *Argus'* point of view. If I had been seriously hurt, if I had had one of my eyes knocked out, for instance, no doubt they'd have given me a paragraph all to myself. In leaded type, very likely."

"As the riot took place more than a month ago, and your arm isn't well yet, it hardly looks as though the injury had been so *very* trifling, after all," Dorothy retorted. "How did it— happen?"

"Oh, it was the work of the missile usually most in favor on these occasions, the traditional ' 'arf a brick.' " Lyon spoke with less reserve than before. It was sweet, irresistibly sweet, to find that she could be so moved by the thought of his past peril, his present pain.

"You might have been killed!" she ejaculated in a low voice, with a barely suppressed shudder.

Lyon answered nothing. He was thinking privately that, on the whole, it was perhaps a pity the half brick had not done its work more thoroughly.

"And I never could understand how the riot arose at all," Dorothy continued, with a most appealing note of interrogation in her voice.

"It had its origin in a simple difference of opinion. I thought one public house to every sixty inhabitants an over-large provision ; the inhabitants considered it barely sufficient for their wants. Then the publicans to whom I gave notice to quit were naturally displeased, and they had plenty of friends in Creyke. Oh, the outbreak is easily accounted for ! Especially in view of my own unpopularity with the miners."

"Are you sure that you are—unpopular?"

"How should I be anything else? An absentee owner, who habitually leaves everything to a hard-fisted agent, is not likely to be much beloved."

Dorothy played nervously with the bunch of keys in her hand.

"Have things—are things going quietly at Creyke now?"

"I believe so. The pitmen threatened an attack on the workmen who are rebuilding the club-rooms. But, so far, they haven't carried their threat into effect."

"You are rebuilding your club-house, then?" Dorothy's eyes were bright now as well as soft.

"Certainly."

"It was completely wrecked, wasn't it?"

"Completely. Only the foundations remained intact."

"I was afraid——" Dorothy began irresolutely.

"Of what?"

"That you would be so annoyed—and—and disgusted with these people that you would feel inclined to wash your hands of them altogether. It's very good of you to rebuild the club-house——"

"Not in the least," he interposed. "Goodness has nothing to say in the matter, nor philanthropy either. It's a simple question of obstinacy. I have started on a certain course, and I naturally don't choose to be bullied out of it. No man likes to own himself beaten, if he can help it. Here comes that porter at last!"

The fog had deepened considerably by the time Lyon and Dorothy emerged from the weighing-room; and their short remaining journey, to the jetty where the Jersey boat was lying, had its dangers as well as its difficulties. Lyon kept silence till the quay was reached. There, close to the gangway of the *Cleopatra*, which, but for two huge lanterns held aloft on either side of it by two wharfmen in blue jerseys and slouch hats, would have been invisible in the darkness, he ventured a remonstrance.

"This is a sea-fog. You ought not to cross to-night."

"I must." Dorothy spoke very decidedly.

He argued the point with her, to no purpose. In vain did he represent how easy it would be to telegraph an explanation to Mr. Creighton's cousin; in vain did he expatiate on the respectability and quiet of a certain hotel where she might spend the night in perfect comfort and safety. For some reason or other, she was clearly determined to go to Jersey by this particular boat.

For such a simple and sufficient reason, if only he had known! But, of course, it never occurred to his masculine mind that her seeming unreasonableness might be due to the fact that she had not money about her wherewith to pay for a night's lodging.

Reluctantly he assisted her on board, and saw her to the top of the companion. Their argument had occupied some minutes, and now it was fully time for him to get on shore again, so he prepared to take his leave at once.

"I hope you may find it clearer outside," he said a little angrily, for her obstinate refusal to give any heed to his expostulations had annoyed him, "but I doubt it."

"I *must* go," Dorothy repeated for the fifth or sixth time. "Indeed, it's really impossible for me to do otherwise. And now, thank you a thousand times for all your kind help, and good-by."

She shook hands with him quickly, hardly looking at him, and disappeared down the cabin stairs, in the wake of a lady having sole charge of two small children, one in arms, a variety of bags and baskets, and a canary-bird in a cage. Before he turned away, Lyon heard Dorothy enquiring of this much-encumbered matron, " Can I help you at all ? " and caught the reply, uttered in tones of unmistakable relief and gratitude, " Oh, if you would kindly give your hand to my little girl ! "

He went back to the gangway, and, in the very act of setting his foot upon it, stopped irresolutely. Beyond the figures of the lantern-bearers at the edge of the quay, not an object was visible ; everywhere a curtain of blackness, heavy, motionless, impenetrable, met and stopped the eye. The chorus of fog-horns and sirens was growing louder and more continuous.

Lyon hesitated. The wharfmen, ready to withdraw the gang-way, called to him impatiently to come ashore.

" No, I've decided to cross."

He had no chance of rescinding this hasty decision. The gang-way swung hastily on shore ; there came a hoarse shout of " Let go ! " and next moment the *Cleopatra's* screw was beating the water, and Lyon was fairly on his way to the island he had quitted only twelve hours before.

" This is a piece of arrant folly," he said to himself, as he groped his way amidships, stumbling over sundry coils of rope and the stretchers of half a dozen deck-chairs *en route.* " It shows what a once self-respecting man may come to," with grim amusement. "That was a particularly nice bag I left behind the door, as a legacy for the first enterprising traveller who comes that way. However, the folly is at least harmless, and will never be known to *her.* Of course she will spend the night in the ladies' cabin. Besides, even if she came on deck, this fog would effectually prevent her seeing me. And if anything *should* happen, I should be at hand—though of what possible use I could be to her, Heaven only knows. Ah, there's the captain ! I'll go and ask him what he thinks of the weather."

The captain inclined to the opinion that, once in the Channel, they would get clear of the fog. And his opinion appeared to be correct. As the *Cleopatra* neared the opening of Southampton Water, the mist lifted and grew lighter ; before she had been half an hour outside Lyon could discern the stars over his head. Whereupon he retired to a seat under the bridge, calling himself an egregious fool for his pains, lit a pipe, and smoked furiously for an hour or so. At the end of that time, the air being still somewhat oppressive, and his pipe having gone out, he fell asleep.

Fell asleep and dreamed ; dreamed himself back in Queensland in a certain mountain-gorge, through which he had once helped to carry a line of railway. A huge mass of rock barred the advance of his iron road, which, in his dream, he was making over again, and he gave orders that it should be blasted with dynamite. Somebody—one of the navvies standing close to him, he supposed —cried out in his ear, " We've struck ! " and he understood that they had struck the match which was to fire the train. That was wrong, the train should have been lighted by a slow fuse ; he tried to say so, to call out, but the explosion was too quick for him, already it shook the ground, it was shattering the rock into a thousand fragments.

He awoke, springing to his feet in the very act of waking. He found himself in darkness, in a darkness which, like that in Egypt of old, "might be felt," a darkness made hideous by a confused noise of shrieks and shouts, mingling with an ominous sound of groaning timbers, and a rush as of water entering the steamer's side. She had struck upon a rock, and was filling fast.

Ten seconds sufficed to inform Lyon of what had occurred. Before half a minute had elapsed he was feeling his way along the deck in the direction of the companion, guiding himself by the roof of the saloon-cabin. He had some difficulty in keeping his feet, for the *Cleopatra* had heeled over to the port side when she struck, and to walk her decks now was much like attempting to perambulate the roof of a gabled house ; but he managed, with the help of the cabin-roof, to avoid a fall, though several times very near one. Presently he ran full tilt against a man with a lantern in his hand. The light from the lantern illumined the man's features sufficiently for Lyon to see that he was deadly white. It was the second officer.

" What has happened ? " Lyon demanded.

He knew perfectly well what had happened, as I have said. Still he put his question all the same. People on such occasions seem invariably moved to put unnecessary questions, directing them, preferentially, to persons who have no leisure to answer.

The officer did, however, pause to answer Lyon. " Run on a rock—starboard side half stove in," he replied briefly. " Hold's filling." He tried to pass on.

"Any boats?" enquired Lyon, detaining him by the shoulder.

"Two. The rest are smashed up."

The mate tore himself free, and vanished into the darkness. Lyon groped on his way, guided to a certain extent by the few lights, which, like tiny oases in a waste of gloom, still burned faintly on the funnels and in the rigging, survivors of a more numerous company that had been for the most part extinguished by the shock of the steamer's encounter with the rock which had pierced her vitals. The lamp suspended over the door leading to the companion was larger and burned rather more brightly than its fellows. By its light Lyon, when he reached the spot for which he had been making from the first, was able to distinguish the faces of the crowd of frightened women pouring up from below, half-dressed in many cases, some sobbing and vociferating terrified enquiries, others with the wide-open, fixed eyes, the blanched, silent lips of unutterable fear bearing witness to the horror of dread that had fallen upon them.

Lyon stood aside from the doorway—it was impossible to get down the staircase—scanning each face as it passed by with clenched hands and held breath. How long, how long she was in coming! Could she by any chance be so foolish, so utterly mad as to think of staying below? He was fast growing desperate in his terror for her when he heard her clear voice say in firm, decided tones, "You must put down that bird-cage!"

There was an indistinct reply, the words of which sounded choked by sobs.

"Put it down immediately!" Dorothy's voice said, yet more decidedly than before. "You can't carry the child safely with that thing in your other hand."

Apparently Dorothy's firmness won the day; for when, next moment, the lady of the bird-cage emerged, dishevelled and weeping, from the doorway, she held only her baby in her arms. After her, forced swiftly upward and along by the panic-stricken crowd behind, followed Dorothy, carrying the little girl to whom the mother had begged her to give her hand when she first came on board. She had evidently been lying down in her berth at the moment of the disaster, for she was bareheaded, one thick coil of her disordered hair loose, and hanging down into her neck, and she wore no jacket or cloak over her blue serge gown, only a little woollen shawl, which barely covered her shoulders.

"Give me the child," said Lyon, suddenly stepping forward.

Dorothy evinced not the smallest sign of surprise at his appearance. She merely answered quickly :

" You can't carry her, with that arm."

" Give her to me," Lyon reiterated. " Do as I tell you, at once ! " speaking with the testy impatience people so often display in moments of strong excitement. " At once, do you hear ? We are blocking the way."

She obeyed.

" Now, catch hold of my sleeve, and don't let go for your life ! This way ! keep hold of the rail with your other hand ; be careful you don't slip."

The crowd was moving astern. They moved with it. On every side of them were sobs, cries, loud calls for this and that child or friend missing in the darkness ; above them, the captain was shouting hoarse orders from the bridge. The sailors, little lithe Jerseymen for the most part, were getting out the two sound boats with a good deal more of chatter and gesticulation than English seamen would have indulged in under the circumstances. Already one boat was half lowered. Just above where she swung. in mid-air the crowd halted, a swaying mass; with it Lyon and Dorothy halted too, perforce.

" Will she sink—the vessel ? " asked Dorothy, speaking, save for her half dozen words of remonstrance when Lyon proposed to take the child from her, for the first time.

" I fear so."

" The first officer gives her ten minutes," put in an elderly man who stood close by, and whose face showed ghastly gray in the light of the lantern, swinging just over his head.

" Shall we——" Dorothy left her question unfinished.

" There are the boats," Lyon answered her. " We must hope."

Here the child on his arm, hitherto paralyzed with fright, began to scream lustily, and the mother turned a distracted, tear-stained face over her shoulder upon Dorothy, as if mutely beseeching her to comfort the little creature. Dorothy did her best, with soothing words and touches ; and the child's screams subsided gradually into an ordinary fit of crying.

" How is it that you are here ? " asked Dorothy all at once of her companion, looking up from her occupation of caressing the terrified baby.—" There, there ! don't cry any more, little one !— I didn't think at first ; it seemed natural. Somehow I had a sort of fancy you were on board. But you were going to London ? "

Lyon hesitated a moment. Overhead the captain was shouting fresh orders to the crew, a little farther astern a woman had gone into hysterics, and was laughing maniacally. He hesitated—why not tell her the truth? In a few minutes the sea would have closed over him and his follies alike.

"I disliked the idea of your crossing quite alone in such weather. If I were superstitious, I should say I had a presentiment."

"Man the boats!"

Then followed a wild rush to the side. The elderly man next Dorothy pushed forward with all his strength, and she heard Lyon's voice cry, "For shame! The women and children first!" Other voices echoed the cry, and the reproach. In another minute there was a general chorus of, "The women and children!" and some of these were being assisted to their places by men who knew well that the escape of their weaker companions involved their own certain death within a few minutes.

The lady whom Dorothy had befriended was one of the first to obtain a place in the boats. Putting the child she carried already on her left arm, she snatched the other from Lyon's hold with her disengaged hand, and, thus loaded, was lifted bodily over the ship's side. Dorothy looked after her with tears in her eyes. "Oh, I am glad they let her take them both!" she exclaimed.

Lyon had the second mate by the shoulder. "You must find a place for this lady."

"None left in this boat. Room in the other yet," responded the man laconically. "This way quick! or she'll lose her chance."

"Come!" said Lyon, taking Dorothy's hand.

She, intently watching the perilous descent of the woman and her two children into the boat, had heard nothing of the brief colloquy between her companion and the ship's officer.

"Come? Where?" she asked in bewilderment, as the two men forced a way for her through the crowd.

"To the other boat. They've room there for you."

"And you?" her grasp of his hand tightening suddenly.

"The women and children go first, of course. We men must take our chance——"

"Chance! You heard what that man said. Is there no other boat?"

The mate in front heard the question. "Devil a one!" he flung back savagely over his shoulder.

Dorothy stopped short. "Then I won't go."

9

"Not go? because——   What folly is this?" cried Lyon angrily. "Come, be quick!   I tell you there's no time to lose.   Your place will be taken——"

"I don't want it."

"You are off your head——"

"Not at all.   You are here because of me.   I will stay with you."

"This is simple madness!" exclaimed Lyon, nearly beside himself.   "But you shall not stay with me!   I don't want you—do you hear?   I don't choose to have you.   Here, officer! take her; she's out of her mind!"   And before Dorothy could divine, much less resist, his purpose, he had wrenched his hand from her hold, and pushed her, as easily as though she had been a small child, into the grasp of the big seaman.   "There, go, like a good child——"

She stretched out her hands to him.   "No, no!   You have not even said good-by."

"Good-by, then," hastily.   He added, with a ghost of his old cynical smile, drawing back out of her reach : "You may take comfort in remembering that drowning is an easy death ; and that, on the whole, I'm not sorry."

Denying himself, for her sake, the last poor pleasure of a final look at the woman he loved, he turned and deliberately plunged again into the crowd of those left behind.

"Cast off!" he heard the stern order shouted over his head. Then arose a tempest of despairing cries, of piteous entreaties to the departing boats to take "one more—only one more, for the love of God!" but his ear was conscious only of a confused *mêlée* of sound, from which he longed to get away.   He groped his way back to his former place under the bridge ; here at least it was comparatively quiet.   His heavy travelling-cloak, which, the night being so oppressively warm at starting, he had taken off and thrown over the end of the bench where he had finally fallen asleep, still lay where he had left it ; he recognized it by its rough texture. It was colder now, with the marrow-chilling cold of the hour that comes just before dawn, and the foggy air was saturated with moisture.   Mechanically he picked up the cloak, and threw it over his shoulders.   It did not occur to him that since his body would certainly in a few minutes' time be tossing to and fro in the waves of the Channel, cold with the rigor of death, he need not be at such special pains to guard it from mere temporary discomfort. His mind was not by any means exclusively fixed on the coming

catastrophe. This, indeed, scarcely occupied more than the background of his thoughts, which were mainly busy with the riddle of
Dorothy Temple's strange behavior. All sorts of possible explanations of her conduct suggested themselves to him in swift succession,
but only one seemed adequate to account for it. What if, after
all—— Even now the supposition fired his blood and set his pulses
throbbing.

All was now comparatively quiet on board the doomed vessel.
The useless cries for help had ceased; men talked together in low
voices; and such women as had been left perforce to perish
crouched motionless in their places, weeping silently, if at all. The
whizz of the rockets which the captain had ordered to be sent up
in the faint hope that they might attract the attention of some
passing vessel, the intermittent detonation of the distress-signals
as they were let off from minute to minute, and the monotonous
lap-lap of the water into the hold, were now the only sounds stirring the heavy air. It remained heavy and dark as ever. Pray
Heaven it grow lighter soon! Else may she, in that little open
boat, easily miss safety, after all——

"Is it—— Ah, it *is* you!"

Lyon started violently. The faint light of the lantern above his
head showed him Dorothy Temple standing in front of him;
flushed, trembling, with an expression at once timid and trium-
phant.

"What!" he exclaimed, almost stammering in his bewilderment; "what does this mean?"

"Don't be angry with me!" she pleaded. "There was a girl
who wanted my place, to go with her mother. And the mother
begged them so hard not to leave the girl behind! I felt it couldn't
be wrong to give up; it was just a question between her and me.
And she wanted to go so much, while I wanted—to come back."

"Because"—Lyon spoke almost harshly—"you had an absurd
notion that it was ungenerous to go without me?"

"No, no. Because I *wished* to be here—for my own sake."

Terrified, perhaps, at having said so much, she half turned away
from him. But he laid a detaining hand on her arm.

"Don't move," he said in a husky voice. "Since you are here,
we may as well stay together."

She stopped, shivering a little, and stood quite still. He let his
fingers slide down the arm he held till they met hers.

"Are you cold?" he asked.

"I don't know. Yes, I believe so, a little."

"Better have my cloak. See here, if you'll just help me off with it—this arm makes me so awkward——"

"No, no ; I don't want it! I won't have it! Ah, what's that ?"

The vessel, now becoming every moment more deeply water-logged, had reeled suddenly farther to the port side, with a lurch which nearly threw Dorothy off her feet. Simultaneously with her exclamation of alarm there broke out a storm of confused cries from the crowd of passengers in the stern. Lyon flung his arm round his companion.

"Let me hold you ; it will be safest so. Then I can shelter you a little, too," he said in the same husky tone, drawing her close to him, and gathering the heavy Inverness about her as best he could with his one available hand.

For an instant she seemed inclined to resist his movement; then all at once she yielded to it completely, and her cheek lay against his breast. His ear caught the sound of a stifled sob ; he bent his head over hers.

"My poor child," he murmured brokenly, "I am so sorry ! If there were anything I could do, any hope I could honestly give you——"

"You need not be sorry for me !" Her voice, if tremulous, was perfectly clear. "I am quite content—quite willing and happy——"

She had raised her face to speak ; and now for a moment he saw it distinctly in the light of the lantern ; flushed, quivering, with eyes that shone strangely behind their veil of tears.

"Dorothy !" he cried in passionate bewilderment, "Dorothy, is this thing true ?"

"Yes," Dorothy said.

He caught her closer than before to his breast, pressing her to him with the whole strength of his strong arm ; and for a moment both were as completely forgetful of their surroundings, of the terrible circumstances that had given them to each other's embrace, of the death actually yawning under their feet while they clung together, as though these things were not, and the deck of the sinking steamer had been suddenly transformed into some sheltered garden of Arcadia.

But the moment was necessarily brief. The woman was the first to awake from that oblivious ecstasy into recollection of the grim actualities of the situation.

"I suppose there is no wrong done now ?" she faltered.

· "Wrong?" Lyon repeated dreamily, kissing her eyelids in a sort of passion of tenderness. He was still so much in the seventh heaven that her question held no meaning for him. "What wrong should there be?"

"I meant wrong toward *him*—Brian."

"Oh!" indifferently. He had quite forgotten that such a person as Brian Travers existed. And, even now that he was reminded of the fact, it seemed to him a fact wholly unimportant, and totally without bearing on the present crisis.

"It is all as if I were dying—you said there was no hope. This is not to break my promise, is it?" she persisted.

Lyon had tangled his hand in her loosened hair, and was thinking how fine and silky and thick it felt. With an effort he roused himself to answer:

"No, child, no. Promises such as yours don't extend to the next world, thank Heaven! Why did you ever give that promise, Dorothy?"

"I did not dream you cared—and his mother begged me so when she was dying. You know *he* had wished it so long. And she said I should be responsible for his ruin if I cast him off."

"Then, if I hadn't hesitated and dallied——— My God, this is bitter! To see, too late, what might have been."

"Surely it doesn't matter much now!" She nestled softly against him, putting up her arms to clasp his neck.

"Not matter? A few short minutes set against a whole lifetime!"

Lyon's voice shook with a passion of longing, regret, rebellion. He felt himself thrilling with a frantic desire to live—he, who had so often pronounced life not worth living. He was fiercely athirst for the cup about to be dashed from his lips before he had well tasted its sweetness; hungry beyond words for the feast that, Barmecide-like, fate was showing him in mockery, only to sweep it beyond his reach forever.

Dorothy, recognizing in his cry of bereavement the utterance of an anguish which it was beyond her power to measure, was silent a moment. Then:

"There will be all—the other life for us," she suggested gently.

Lyon had his doubts on this point. "The other life" seemed to him a sadly shadowy and unsubstantial substitute for this flesh and blood existence he must presently forego. It had never been much more to him than a cold, unreal abstraction—a graceful, glacial hypothesis constructed to fill up the darkness and void of the Beyond. Words he had once heard quoted beat in his brain :

> " This warm, sweet world is all I know."

Yes, it was warm—warm and sweet ; he confessed it at last. It was having its revenge upon him who had so long maligned it as cold and bitter.

He had his doubts. But he would not throw the shadow of them across the sunlight of her unhesitating faith. So he only murmured, " Yes," vaguely, and kissed her again.

"So you're content ? " he asked a moment later.

" Yes."

He reflected that her love must be cold compared with his own ; else she could not be satisfied with the prospect of a merely shadowy future, in which they might be together or apart—who could tell ?

" And, do you know," Dorothy was saying in his ear, " I hardly think I could bear a whole lifetime of happiness like this. It would be too much. Indeed, I can hardly bear it for these few minutes."

" Oh, hush, hush ! " he interrupted, crushing her against his heart, the creature who had deliberately returned to die at his side, and whose pure love he had dared for a moment to belittle in his thoughts, because it could live and breathe in the spiritual air which was too rarefied for his selfish, earthly passion. " Why did you ever love me, child ? I have cost you your life, and God knows I'm not worth the sacrifice."

" What was that ? " asked Dorothy, starting.

" Nothing, nothing. Another signal gone off."

" No, it was something giving way below—under where we're standing. Is the steamer—going to pieces, do you think ? "

" I don't know—perhaps. Don't be frightened, dear ! I shall not let you go. And the pain, what there is of it—it won't be much—will be all over in a minute or two." Lyon spoke with the confidence of a person who had undergone the process of drowning several times already. He was conscious of so speaking, and even felt faintly amused at himself.

" I don't think I am very frightened," Dorothy responded. " It's strange, but I am not. Only—don't do that, please," suddenly hiding her face on his shoulder. " I can't think of anything—when you kiss me."

"I don't want you to think of anything," pressing her cheek to his.

"But I must—we ought ! In two or three minutes, perhaps, we shall be—before God."

"Well, do you suppose He wishes you to come before Him in an agony of terror? Doesn't it look rather as if my being here, when there were a thousand chances to one against it, were Heaven's way of making this *less* terrible for you, poor little thing ? "

A sob shook her. "Oh, I know God has been very good to us ! " she cried, with tears.

He was silent, stroking her bowed head gently. All was quiet around them ; a sudden ominous hush seemed to have settled down upon the *Cleopatra* and her hapless freight. The cold breath of the morning was in the air, and the fog was gradually thinning, fading from black to gray ; though the lantern overhead had flickered out, Lyon could just discern the brightness of Dorothy's hair against the rough, dark surface of his coat. For some moments she did not move ; he guessed that she was praying, and would not disturb her. At length she lifted her face of her own accord.

"They have stopped signalling."

"Yes."

"Why ?"

"Either the supply's exhausted, or "—reluctantly—" they're out of heart, and think it's useless to make any further effort."

"Then the end's near ?"

"I suppose so. Oh, my child, my child ! why did you come back ?"

Her eyes were brighter than ever. "I am so glad I came. Don't —don't be sorry for me ; indeed, there's no reason. I was so unhappy ; and my life would only have been harder to bear as time went on. Sometimes I could scarcely face the thought of it."

A loud, harsh call, differing wholly from any sound that had preceded it, rang out through the fast-thinning fog. It was answered by an unintelligible shout from the man still keeping a forlorn lookout forward, taken up in stentorian tones by the captain on the bridge, repeated and echoed with infinite variations by a hundred voices hoarse with emotion.

"What is it ?" asked Dorothy, with quivering lips and eyes.

For answer Lyon loosed his arm from her, pointing to w

the *Cleopatra's* port bow, two huge red lights shone stationary in
the mist.

" What is it ? " he repeated. " Why, it's a steamer ! a steamer
come to our rescue ! Those are her lights ; she is lying-to to help
us. We are saved, Dorothy ! saved to live for each other, and love
each other. Do you understand, my darling ? " catching her to him
anew and pressing passionate kisses on her forehead and lips. " Do
you understand ? "

If Dorothy understood, she gave no sign of rejoicing in her
knowledge. She kept silence, trembling in his arms—as she had
not trembled before.

<hr>

CHAPTER XII

ON SHORE—IN THE MORNING

"Here stand I ; I can no other ; God help me !"

It was a boat bound for St. Malo, and strayed from her course
in the fog, which now came so opportunely to the rescue of the
helpless human beings on board the *Cleopatra*.

She had not arrived a moment too soon. The last boat-load of
the shipwrecked had barely reached her side when the vessel they
had just quitted reeled over like a drunken man, and went down
almost masts-foremost into the dark, mist-enshrouded waters that
had been gaining on her with such fatal rapidity during the past few
minutes. By the time the last occupant of the boat had climbed
on board the *Marie Thérèse* the faint light of dawn, breaking
through the dispersing vapors upon a sea smooth as oil, showed
the place of the unlucky *Cleopatra's* burial, unmarked by so much
as a ripple.

The *Cleopatra*, it appeared now, had been but a few miles distant from Guernsey when she met her fate ; the captain of the St.
Malo steamer, therefore, announced his intention of landing the
rescued passengers and crew at St. Peter-Port before proceeding
on his way to the Breton coast. Doubtless, the fact that his own
vessel—a much smaller one than that which had just gone down—
was uncomfortably, and even dangerously, overcrowded by the
unexpected addition to its freight, played a large part in the cap-

tain's considerations when he decided to take a course so welcome
to his temporary guests.

"We shall be in so soon, it will be hardly worth while for you
to go below," Lyon said to Dorothy. He seemed afraid to let her
out of his sight; even now he was holding one of her hands tight,
under shelter of the fur cloak a compassionate lady-passenger of
the *Marie Thérèse* had insisted on lending her. "I'll beg, borrow,
or steal a rug for you, and you will be quite comfortable in this
sheltered corner of the deck. Besides, it is getting warmer every
moment——"

"But how about the child?" said Dorothy doubtfully, looking
down at a small girl of seven or eight years old, who was clinging
timidly to her other hand.

Travelling alone, under the care of the stewardess, sent by an
aunt in England to join her parents in Jersey, she said, this child
had been placed next Dorothy in the boat that conveyed her and
Lyon from the sinking *Cleopatra* to their present asylum; with the
result that Dorothy had, as a matter of course, assumed charge of
the forlorn, frightened little creature.

"How about the child?" she asked now. "You can see she is
quite worn out."

With difficulty Lyon choked back the impatient exclamation,
disallowing altogether the child's claim on Dorothy's attention,
which rose to his lips. "Can't she go back to the stewardess?"
he asked discontentedly. "She's supposed to look after her, isn't
she?"

"The stewardess is in no state to look after anybody, poor
woman! She is quite hysterical with fright."

"Well, if you are set on keeping her with you, we might make
her up a bed on this seat."

Dorothy accepted the suggestion, a little reluctantly it seemed
to Lyon. He was conscious that she would have preferred the
shelter of the cabin; and this consciousness disquieted him. In
her timid effort to escape from him temporarily he discerned the
first symptom of an endeavor to escape him altogether. He
clenched his hands, silently vowing that neither the one attempt
nor the other should succeed.

Meanwhile, having gained the victory in this preliminary skir-
mish, he judged it wisest to adopt a tactic of prudent reserve,
keeping back all his forces for the more serious trial of strength
foresaw looming in the near distance. During the half-hour

elapsed before the *Marie Thérèse* dropped anchor at St. Peter-Port
he scarcely proffered so much as a remark; he merely stood beside
Dorothy as she sat at the end of the bench on which her little
protégée lay sleeping soundly, overshadowing her, as it were, with
his silent presence. And yet he would have given a year of his
life to know what course her thoughts were taking.

Her face, often as he glanced at it, closely as he studied it every
now and then, told him nothing. Her features kept the set, expressionless look that great exhaustion, whether mental or physical, so frequently produces; her eyes remained, for the most part,
persistently cast down. He could not even feel sure that she was
aware of his recurrent scrutiny.

Once, however, she looked up and said abruptly, "Couldn't you
find a seat somewhere? This bench is so short, it's impossible to
make room—— But elsewhere, perhaps——"

"Thanks," he replied laconically. "I prefer standing here."

"You will be so tired!"

"I am much too happy to think of being tired," with a slight,
grave smile.

He made not the slightest movement toward her in speaking.
Nevertheless, as he spoke, she drew farther away from him, with a
shiver; and, herself, spoke no more till they were alongside the
pier, and speech became a matter of practical necessity.

In pursuance of the plan he had almost instinctively formed for
maintaining his hold over her will, he scarcely made a pretence of
consulting her as to what she chose to do on landing; rather, he
took the command as a matter of course, issuing his orders with an
air of expecting them to be implicitly obeyed. No boat would
leave for Jersey till the following morning; it was, therefore,
necessary for her to have rooms, meantime, at an hotel. He knew
the hotel she ought to go to; he would take her there at once.

"I must keep *her* with me," Dorothy interrupted, pointing to
the child.

That was as she pleased, of course. The child's parents must be
telegraphed to, and Miss Dumaresq? Very good. Lyon would
send the telegrams, and bring her the answers—there would be
answers, no doubt—when she had rested. For she must put herself,
as well as the child, to bed, and get a thorough good sleep before
noon.

"Promise me you will do that," he entreated. They were standing, by this time, in the hotel corridor, she with her hand already

on the lock of the half-open door leading into the little sitting-room he had engaged on the plea that she could not possibly take her meals downstairs in the coffee-room ; the child, her fright forgotten, had already run inside, and was eagerly exploring her new and strange quarters. . "Promise me, please! Remember, I cannot have you falling ill, on any pretext."

"I promise to go to bed at once," she answered in a flat, toneless voice.

"And you'll try to sleep ? "

"Yes. You'll bring the telegrams when they come ? "

"At twelve. I don't think you ought to get up sooner. I beg you'll observe that I am acting in a most self-denying fashion," he added, laughing nervously, but watching the effect of his words keenly, all the same.

She seemed to wince under his look ; she turned her face slightly aside. "If there should be no answers, you'll still come, at twelve? Because—I—have something to say——"

"So have I—hundreds of things ! " he returned, with resolute, but not very genuine, cheerfulness. "To begin with—— No, I won't begin ! If I did I should probably keep you talking till noon, or midnight, in this exceedingly cold passage. Good-by, then, till noon ; sleep well, my darling."

No one was in sight ; these two had the whole long, ill-lighted corridor to themselves. He made a movement as if to take her in his arms, but she eluded without seeming to see it, and slipped away from him over the threshold of the doorway. "At twelve, then," she said—and softly shut to the door.

He stood contemplating its grimy oak-grained panels for a full minute with a curious, baffled expression of countenance. Then he mechanically put on his hat, and went downstairs. Going across the hall, he found himself shivering violently ; all the blood in his veins seemed to have suddenly grown cold. Certainly that passage was very draughty. Or, perhaps he had got chilled sleeping on deck in the fog during the early part of the night. He must try to shake the sensation off by taking a walk. So he made his way briskly to the nearest post-office, and despatched his two telegrams to the addresses with which Dorothy had furnished him ; then wandered down one of the steep streets of St. Peter-Port to the sea.

The sun was now in full splendor, and had long since drunk up all lingering remnants of last night's dangerous mists. The sky in which it shone was blue and clear as a Provence sky in spring, and the blue-green expanse of the Channel looked, in its waveless smoothness, like a gigantic pond. Behind Lyon, as he stood gazing out seaward, the sunlight played deliciously upon the quaint red and brown roofs of the old town which seems to cling so desperately to the bare face of the cliff, up which it has gradually climbed to the fertile tableland above; before him it made beautiful the brown sails of a little fleet of returning fishing-boats and the white wings of a yacht or two lying just outside the harbor, and glittered bravely on the sides of dainty little Herm and Jetta rising sparkling from the calm sea. At this hour all was quiet on the quays; only a few fishermen were laying out a pile of dripping nets to dry on the strip of shingly beach below. Lyon sat down on an overturned boat, at some little distance from this busy group, and set himself to review his position seriously—to perfect and elaborate the plan of action he had already inaugurated.

He remained there a long time; and when he got up to walk back to the hotel, his face wore a look which said, plainly enough, that he did not intend to be beaten in the coming encounter.

Precisely at twelve o'clock he knocked at Dorothy's sitting-room door, and Dorothy herself admitted him. She looked worn and tired, far more so than when they parted, six hours earlier. It was clear that she had not slept.

"I'm afraid you have not kept your promise," said Lyon, taking her hand and holding it firmly.

She made no attempt to withdraw it. But there was a certain effect of shrinking in her manner as she responded quickly:

"Oh, yes, I did! I've been resting for hours."

"H'm!" doubtfully. "You don't look as if you had had much sleep."

"No; I couldn't manage that. It's—it's so difficult to sleep in the middle of the day. Have you had any replies to your telegrams?"

"To one of them. Mr. Maynard wires that he will be here by this afternoon's boat, to take his child off your hands. But there's nothing from Miss What's-her-name—Miss Dumaresq."

"Perhaps she didn't think it necessary to telegraph, as you said I should come on to-morrow. You must remember she doesn't know me yet."

"All the same she might have expended sixpence in expressing a decent satisfaction that you had not found a watery grave on your way to visit her. I am not prepossessed in favor of this elderly maiden lady of yours, Dorothy. If I don't like her looks to-morrow, I shall just bring you away again at once; so hold yourself warned!" said Lyon with deliberate audacity, and a clumsy attempt at playfulness. Nothing, he said to himself, like carrying things with a high hand from the outset. The sooner matters came to a point between him and Dorothy the better; this speech would probably bring them to a point.

It did. To a point which he, with all his prevision of some sort of resistance on her part, had hardly anticipated.

Said Dorothy, resolutely freeing her imprisoned fingers from his hold:

"Forgive me, but—that is foolish talking, Mr. Lyon. You must know quite well that you can't go on with me to Jersey."

"Why not? Because you are not provided with a duenna? Do you think Miss Dumaresq would be shocked at my escorting you?"

"Don't pretend to misunderstand—and, oh, please"—with a sudden pathetic break in her voice—" don't try to—to joke about it! You must see, as well as I, that—what happened last night goes for nothing now."

"Pardon me, I see nothing of the kind."

"Things are just as they were before we happened to meet at the station."

"Not at all; excuse my contradicting you so bluntly, but it's important you shouldn't involve yourself in a mental fog, which you are evidently striving to do. Things are on a perfectly different footing between us now to what they were twenty-four hours since. I know that you love me, remember. You have acknowledged in so many words——"

"When I believed that I—that both of us—were going to die within the next five minutes!" she interrupted eagerly.

"Which makes the acknowledgment doubly valuable. I am all the more sure of your sincerity. You can't undo last night's work, Dorothy."

"Not wholly. But——"

"But you are troubled about poor Travers? My darling child, do you suppose I didn't know the first glimpse of the *Marie Thérèse's* lights was a signal for you to begin fretting your heart out over that poor fellow? I am sorry for him, too—heartily sorry; but he has partly himself to blame for his disappointment.

You never cared for him, and he knew it. He should have had the manliness to take 'No' for an answer, and leave you in peace. Instead of this, he first tries to catch you in the snare of an indefinite promise; then sets his mother on to play upon your feelings, and worry you into a definite one at a time when you were not fit to make any serious decision——"

Lyon, in his eagerness, was actually talking fast. Dorothy put up her hand as if to stay this unusual flow of words on his part.

"Still, that makes no difference," she said. "I have given my word to him—and to her; I must keep it."

There was a quiet decision in her manner which struck coldly across the fever of Lyon's excitement. But he gave no outward sign of alarm. His answer was none the less prompt and imperious. "I will not allow you to keep it. You have given me a right——"

"No, no! I have given you no right—no right over me at all."

Lyon felt the chill of fear increasing upon him. Dorothy was revealing herself in an entirely new light. In making up his mind to silence peremptorily all attempt at opposition to his will on her part, he had never taken into consideration the possibility of her refusing to be silenced. He had thought of her as an inexperienced girl, impulsive, malleable, probably with little will of her own—though the events of last night, at least, might have taught him better; he had not reckoned on having to deal with a determined woman, resolutely bent on satisfying her conscience at all costs.

"No right?" he repeated indignantly. "I no right over you? Who should have any but I? If it's true that you love me, as you gave me to understand last night you did—— *Is* it true, by the way?"

"Yes, it is true," she answered, flushing suddenly.

"Then to talk of marrying another man is folly; and, worse still—falsehood," retorted Lyon trenchantly. "Falsehood, both to me and to him."

Dorothy pressed her hands tight together. "It was just the same—last November—when you came to Heyford," she said in a low voice.

"How, just the same? What do you mean?"

"I mean that I—cared for you just as much"—her color deepening again. "But you did not ask me, *then*, to break faith! you took it for granted that—my engagement put an end to everything."

"Because I had no idea how matters really stood at that time. There is no use trying to fence with me, Dorothy ; I tell you frankly you have no right to marry Brian Travers, and I won't let you do it."

"I must keep my promise," setting her lips together tightly.

"You talk like a romantic child. You *are* a romantic child, or you would never have consented so lightly to give yourself into lifelong bondage to a man you don't love, on the off-chance that your self-sacrifice might possibly work his reformation. That is the sort of thing a young girl imagines noble and heroic, because she reads of it in novels ; frantic self-immolation seems to be the favorite virtue of that strange creature the modern novelist," flung out Lyon. "Hush ! If you say you gave your word to please Mrs. Travers, then *I* say the motive was still more inadequate to the action ! But let that pass. You have made a great mistake ; I'll help you to retrieve it. I'll save you from the life of misery and degradation you seem so eager to enter upon. Promise ! "— lashing out angrily again. "What's a rash, ill-considered promise compared with the happiness of two lives ? "

"Happiness is not everything," said Dorothy mournfully.

"Then, for the sake of a few words spoken at random, I am to lose the only hope the world holds for me, and you are to be sold body and soul into the worst kind of slavery a woman can know ? You acknowledged that you had been miserable this last six months ; do you think you will be less miserable in the years to come as Brian Travers' wife ? You don't know what you are doing, child. Look at it coolly. A year won't see the end of your sacrifice ; nor ten years, nor twenty ; it will last as long as your life, or his. You will have to make it afresh every day—and every hour of every day ; and you will torment yourself all the time because you don't, and can't, make it perfectly ; because, for all your efforts, you cannot help sometimes remembering and regretting, and rebelling secretly against your chains. Be brave before it's too late ! Don't think of what the world will say—or your friends ; have the courage to be true to yourself ! If only women had courage to be true to themselves there would be fewer wretched marriages than one hears of nowadays, and fewer ruined lives."

"But," she said with an earnestness that was almost childlike, "I am trying to be true."

"Do you call it being true to take one man for your husband

when you are all the while in love with another ? " Lyon demauded bluntly.

" Would it be true to break one's word—to the living and the dead alike ? Oh, I am afraid, I am afraid ! "

" Yes, I know well enough that you are afraid," he responded tauntingly. " But what are you afraid of ? Of Mrs. Travers' angry ghost ? "

" No ! " Her eyes flashed sudden anger upon him—and poignant reproach.

" Of what, then ? "

" Of seeing Brian's life spoiled, utterly spoiled, as his mother feared, because of my failure to keep faith with him."

" Why should you hold yourself responsible for the spoiling of Brian's life ? "

" I have made myself responsible—in a way."

" Then, to speak plainly, you had no business to assume any such responsibility—making yourself a kind of special providence——"

" Maybe not." She sighed wearily, as if getting tired of the prolonged contest. " It's often very hard to know whether one is doing right or wrong."

" You confess you feel bewildered ? Let me judge for you, then. I'll take the sin, if there be any, of your breaking off with Travers upon my shoulders, readily enough." He held out his hand to her.

But she drew back proudly. " No. I cannot let you judge for me. I must judge for myself.

" And yet," she added, after a moment, his consciousness of having made a false step keeping him silent, " I think I could be content to let you judge for me, too. Suppose that I were in your place, and you in mine. Suppose that you were not free——"

" Well ? " uneasily.

" Suppose that you had been engaged to another girl before you ever saw me. Would you have thought yourself at liberty to break faith with her because you liked me best ? "

Lyon seemed stricken dumb for an instant. He cast about wildly for an answer that should not afford her any weapon of defence. But, with her sad, enquiring eyes fixed full upon his face, he dared not lie to her.

" That's a different matter altogether," he said at length evasively. " The cases are not on all-fours." Not very ingenious evasion this. But it was the best he could do on the spur of that difficult moment.

"Would you feel at liberty to break faith with that girl?" Dorothy persisted.

"Well—no, I suppose not. No—of course a man is bound to—to——"

"To keep his word at all costs, you mean? Yes, I know he is. And why not a woman? Why may I do that with a light heart which you would be the first to pronounce dishonorable in yourself, or any other man? A thing for which—you know it very well—a man is despised and contemned, and even *cut* by all the men of his acquaintance who have any sense of honor. Do you suppose we women have no sense of honor? that I, in particular, have none? Oh, how meanly you must think of me?" cried Dorothy passionately.

"Meanly?" he cried in his turn. "Why, I worship you! I could kiss the hem of your gown for reverence."

"And yet you urge me to do this shameful thing, knowing all the while that, if I were weak enough to let you persuade me, I should never again be the same in your eyes. Oh, you can't deny it!" in return to his vehement gesture of dissent; "I see in your face that you feel how it would be!"

Lyon could have cursed that ingrained habit of truthfulness which made it impossible for him to utter a good round lie at this crucial moment.

"You confuse things," he responded, still lamely evading a direct answer. "A woman's obligations, under such circumstances, are not so serious as a man's."

"Perhaps not, according to conventional rules. But you did not talk just now of conventional rules; you told me to be *true.*"

Ignoring this interposition: "Try to look at things from a common-sense point of view," he urged. "If a man throws a girl over—jilts her, to use an ugly word—he injures her by so doing. It's not a mere question of hurting her feelings. He injures her prospects in life, sometimes her standing in society as well. A woman who breaks with a man does him no material injury whatever."

"She doesn't spoil his chances of marrying in the future, if that's what you mean," retorted Dorothy, with a touch of scorn. "Breaking his heart, and perhaps driving him to destruction, are not material injuries, of course, so I suppose they don't count——"

"Oh, yes, they count," Lyon returned, with at least equal bitter-

10

ness of tone. " When Brian Travers is in question, that's to say.
Has it never occurred to you "—half threateningly—" that your
admirable fidelity to *him* might be the means of sending *me* a little
more completely to the dogs ? Since you are so anxious for Brian's
moral welfare, it seems rather strange you should remain indifferent
to mine."

" Ah, I am not so afraid—for you ! "

" I thank you "—sarcastically—" for your flattering opinion, but
I fear it's not very well founded. Dorothy "—his harsh tones melting suddenly into appealing softness—" I *cannot* do without you ;
you know it ! Put Brian out of your thoughts for a moment."

" I can't ! I dare not ! He has no one left now but me ; his
mother was the only other person he cared for and clung to."

" And whom have I ? " said Lyon quietly.

A look of intense distress crossed her face. " Oh, I know ! It
breaks my heart ! But think how he has waited, waited and
worked for three years. Would you have me tell him when he
comes home that all his work and waiting is to go for nothing,
because I—I—— I can't. I will not ! Surely *you* should be the
last to ask this of me, you who know what it is to—to——"

" To have a woman play me false." He completed the sentence.
" Yes; perhaps you did well to remind me of that, too. I am certainly unlucky," with a contortion of the mouth intended to pass
for a smile. " One is fickle, and another over-constant ; one has no
principle at all, and the other is principle itself incarnate. In either
case, *I* go to the wall."

She said nothing in answer to this outbreak. A little ashamed of
it, perhaps, he took a turn across the little room and came back
again.

" However, that's neither here nor there," he said in a quieter
tone. " Let us leave my interests out of the question altogether,
and consider yours. I tell you once more, you are bent on com-
mitting an act of folly. Noble folly, I acknowledge—but folly,
downright madness, for all that. You are taking up a burden
that's too heavy for you. You are making a sacrifice of which you
haven't even begun to count the cost; a sacrifice which, mark my
words ! will never achieve its aim. I know Brian Travers better
than you do. I know him as one man knows another; as no
woman—no *good* woman, even if she be his wife, ever knows any
man. And from what I know of him I foresee the failure, the
utter uselessness of this self-immolation of yours on the altar of his

selfish weakness. If he is too weak to stand alone, do you think *you* will be able to hold him up ? "

" At least I shall have done my best."

" He does not deserve——"

" Hush ! All the more reason, then, why I should try to help him."

" Shall I tell you," said Lyon, after a moment's pause, " what you are doing ? You are immolating yourself, not to Brian at all, but to your own craze after usefulness."

She grew a shade paler. " I—I don't think so," she murmured. But her eyes had a frightened look. " And, anyhow, it's my duty to think of Brian first."

" And *I* am—nothing ? "

" No ! " quickly moved by a sudden passionate impulse to the utterance of the whole truth. " You are everything—in one sense. You must be content with that."

He stood a moment, not speaking—conscious that she had uttered her last word. The very frankness of her confession witnessed to the unbroken strength of her resolution. Further argument would be worse than useless.

" I suppose I ought to feel grateful to you for saying so much," he observed, after a while. " But I'm not. You only aggravate the hurt you've done me by attempting to heal it with such transcendental balms. I'm not spiritually minded enough to appreciate them. The love that shows itself by denying itself, by obstinately refusing a man everything he asks of it, may be a very lofty kind of love perhaps. It's certainly beyond my comprehension. Well, so I am not even to have the pleasure of escorting you to Jersey ? "

" You must see yourself that—it's better not," the girl answered in a broken voice.

" Oh, I see nothing. The whole matter is very dark to me, and highly confusing. But, of course, I bow to your judgment in the matter. I had better go back to England by the six o'clock boat, I suppose—the one that is to bring Mr. Maynard. I forgot ; you will have an escort, after all, in him."

Dorothy seemed to have become all at once incapable of speech. She stood before Lyon in perfect silence, her fingers plucking nervously at one another.

" So there's no more to be said, except good-by," he resumed. Then he half put out his hand. " Strange to think that it's not yet twelve hours since that night. Such a night ! to go for nothing, after all."

"It doesn't go for nothing. It remains always." She spoke scarcely above a whisper.

His upper lip took the unlovely curve, half smile, half sneer, that had ceased to be habitual to it of late. "Hardly fair to Travers, that, is it?" he asked almost insolently; "since your main object is to be true to him."

Her eyes were ablaze with indignation. "I mean to be true to him, and with him," she retorted proudly. "I shall tell him——"

"Everything?" in the same exasperating tone.

"I shall tell him again"— commanding herself with difficulty— "what I told him before he went away : that I don't love him, that I am only fond of him—as a cousin. And I shall tell him, besides, that I know now I can never feel differently, as he hoped I should do, some time or other. If he still wishes to marry me on those terms——"

"Listen!" Lyon interrupted, his manner wholly changed. "If you say so much, he may guess more. He may ask you—— "

"No. He won't ask me anything."

"Then he must be——" Lyon pulled himself up sharply. "Any man who really cared for a woman would be eager to discover her reason for feeling certain that she must always remain indifferent to him. And no man, worthy the name, would wish to persist in marrying a woman when he knew she cared for somebody else. See here, Dorothy, you have not shown yourself very ready hitherto to listen to any appeal of mine, but don't shut your ears to this one. If Travers asks you anything, promise me to be honest with him, for God's sake."

She paused a moment before replying. His eyes pleaded for him more eloquently than his tongue had done—those mournful, tender blue eyes which contrasted so oddly with the rest of the dark, harsh face confronting her. She drew a long breath.

"If he asks me, I will tell him—all the truth."

"And, one thing more. Promise to tell *me*, too, all the truth. As soon as he comes back, write to me—yes, that much I may fairly ask for. One letter, but let it be a *true* one. Don't think, before you begin to write, of what it would be most fit and proper to say under the circumstances ; write me the truth. Whether you write to tell me to come back to you, or to say that you're going to be married next week to Travers, let me have the truth, without fear or favor!"

"I will write, since you wish it," she said, half turning away from him. "But there will be nothing to say. Oh, why don't you go?" she exclaimed suddenly, turning round again with an impatient movement. "What is the use of our talking anymore?"

His whole face gave a kind of convulsive twitch. "I beg your pardon," he said quickly. "I'll go at once."

"Oh, not like that!" Dorothy cried after him, holding out her hand—for he was moving to the door, without any attempt at farewell. "Not as—as if you were angry."

"Angry? My darling!" he said.

Perhaps it was his partial helplessness that appealed to her beyond her strength of resistance. She liked to think so afterward; to imagine that, if he had had both arms free to stretch out toward her, she might have found it in her heart to refuse his embrace.

"You must stay with me, Dorothy; I can't give you up," he whispered, his lips touching her hair.

She made no answer. Wearied out, she may have felt tempted, for a moment, to yield to his importunity.

"Have a little courage!" he urged her. "I know I'm not asking you to do what will cost you nothing—but if you love me!—Oh, it's worth your while to make this sacrifice, Dorothy! Don't reason or argue any more about the matter; it isn't a matter for reason and argument at all. You must let your heart decide. What's Brian Travers' claim beside mine? You could never be his wife in reality; you belong to me, and you will continue to belong to me, though the law and the Church together were to make you his ten times over."

"I can't think," she faltered pitifully, "why you should care for me so! I am not really fitted to be your wife. I know so little— I am so different altogether."

"Yes," he interrupted, "you are different—totally different, thank Heaven! You are everything that I am not; you have everything that I have lost. And therefore—therefore I love you with all the strength of my soul; and I am going to keep you mine, in spite of yourself."

"No." She lifted her white face resolutely; the weakness that had momentarily disabled her from resistance was already past. "No; I can't break faith—not even for you. Let me go now, please."

He loosed his hold of her at once. "It's quite true," he observed, fixing her with a hard, keen glance; "women don't know how to love. The world is always more to them than any one man in it.

Well, since it is your highest ambition to be known as a woman of
your word, by all means go and carry it out! No doubt the
unwavering esteem of East Hillshire will amply compensate you
for any little sacrifice you may have made in order to retain it."

He stopped suddenly short, smitten with compunction. Swaying
backward against the end of the mantel-piece, she faced him, white
and dumb, her wide-open eyes full of a piteous appeal to his mercy;
shivering under his bitter words as though they had been so many
blows.

"Heavens! what brutes we men are!" he exclaimed, almost
under his breath. "After last night—to taunt *you* with want of
love! How could any man be guilty of such baseness? You
may think yourself well rid of such a selfish coward."

"Hush!" she interrupted. "I know you did not mean it—
really; I sha'n't think of it again." She stopped short in her turn,
seemingly because she had no voice to go on speaking. At the
same time she put up one hand surreptitiously to the mantel-piece
to steady herself.

Lyon saw the movement. "You are trembling," he observed
abruptly. "You are worn out—and no wonder!" He moved
forward an arm-chair that stood near. "Sit down here," he said.
"You are cold, too"—just touching her hand as she mechanically
obeyed his order. "And this fire has quite gone down. Let me
see if I can mend it a little—before I go."

He knelt on the hearth-rug, coaxing the dying embers till they
blazed again, and Dorothy lay back in the big chair watching him
silently. When he got up from his knees, and faced her, she did
not turn her eyes away.

"You look better now," he observed briefly.

"I am better—thanks." She looked up at him gratefully.

"I don't ask your forgiveness for my inexcusable brutality just
now," he went on, drawing a long breath. "You must take it that
I was mad for the moment."

"I do." Her lips trembled; she made a great effort to control
them. "And you—you must try to believe that I—cannot help
myself."

"No," he responded quickly. "Being what you are, I don't
suppose you *can* help yourself. Only"—with strong emphasis—
"I wish to God I could be sure you are not making a mistake!
Good-by."

A strange darkness, such as gathers before the eyes of men in moments of unendurable physical agony, gathered before Lyon's eyes as he uttered those last words. He held Dorothy's hand for an instant—seeing her face, meanwhile, blurred and blotted as by an intervening mist ; it was by a sort of instinct only that he found the door, and, somehow or other, got himself downstairs and out into the steep street, where the sun was still shining merrily, and a pleasant air blowing in from the sea.

CHAPTER XIII

THREE MONTHS LATER

" Time has done with his one sweet word,
   The wine and leaven of lovely life."

IT was as yet early in July; but the night was heavy with a sultry heat suggestive rather of mid-August. Although eleven had struck some time since, and, despite the lateness of the hour, the three windows in the library of the rambling old Manor House at Creyke remained wide open, Lyon, sitting in his shirt-sleeves at a table drawn up close to one of the aforesaid windows, felt himself absolutely panting for air. With a sigh, born partly of physical discomfort, partly of sheer weariness and dejection of spirit, he laid down his pen, and, leaning back in his writing-chair, sat for some minutes staring stupidly at two letters which lay spread out before him, side by side, upon his blotting-book.

One of these was in his own handwriting ; the other, which had reached him only twelve hours since, bore the signature of Dorothy Temple. It was a very short letter, this of Dorothy's ; very simply expressed and, one might have fancied, easy of comprehension. Yet, even after Lyon had read it through some half dozen times, he had had difficulty in realizing the truth that it conveyed. It seemed impossible to believe that all was indeed over; that the last slender chance of happiness had slipped through his fingers. And yet from the first he had, so he supposed, schooled himself to expect nothing from Fate, less than nothing from the generosity of such a man as Brian Travers.

He knew now that, in spite of this schooling, he had, in his secret heart of hope, expected everything from one or the other.

And his illogical confidence had played him false. Fate had

not gone out of its way to work a miracle on his behalf ; neither
had Brian acted—who but a semi-lunatic would ever have dreamed
of his acting ?—in direct defiance of his natural disposition.
Things had fallen out exactly as any man endowed with ordinary
common-sense must have foreseen they would fall out, and the
Nothing which Lyon's reason had so frequently assured him
would be his portion, *was* his portion.   He might say farewell to
his absurd plans for a new life, his unsubstantial dreams of a future
which could never be realized.   From henceforward there was
only one course open to him : that of an unwilling return to the
old objectless, spiritless, purposeless existence ; the old wearisome
attempt to kill time by means of pastimes which had lost their
savor ; the old wretched inability to get up a real, hearty, honest
interest in anything ; the old bitter scorn for his fellow-creatures,
rendered doubly bitter now by a new and most sincere contempt
for himself.   Certainly the prospect before him was not a cheer-
ing one.   If his life for years past had seemed to him scarcely
worth living, what of these coming years, in which he saw himself
by anticipation growing more and more disgusted with self and
the world ?   Envious now, not only of other men's successes, but
of other men's happinesses ; tortured by the ache of unsatisfied
passion ; stung to impotent rage by the consciousness that his own
loss was another's gain—and that other, one whom he honestly
held unworthy of the prize destiny had decreed to him ?   Musing
on his prospect, which stretched itself out before his mind's eye
with such cruel clearness that he seemed to be already living in
the midst of the sandy waste he surveyed, it was small wonder if
his dark face took on its hardest and most forbidding expression,
the brows drawn close together in a painful frown, the compressed
lips tightening more and more into an unyielding straight line.

  " Well, it's a prospect that doesn't bear thinking about," he
said to himself at length, getting up and pushing back his chair.
" Fortunately, or unfortunately, one can live through anything
—with the help of regular meals and an undamaged constitution.
I see myself still cumbering the earth at eighty, preaching cheap
cynicism at my club to anyone I can induce to listen to me, and
making life a burden to my valet."

  He crossed slowly over to one of the open windows, and, resting
both arms upon the sill, leaned out into the night.   It was a dark
night, illuminated only by " the faint light of stars "; the massive outlines of a group of cedars on the left barely detached

themselves from the prevailing soft gloom. Immediately in front
of the window the ground fell rapidly into a slope, and at the end
of this slope, perhaps a quarter of a mile away, a group of
twinkling lights proclaimed the presence of the pit-village; a
presence further proclaimed by the medley of sounds which, every
now and then, disturbed the stillness of the night air: sounds of
the barking of dogs, intermingled with snatches of hoarse and
unmusical song, and a confused noise of men's voices in angry,
and apparently tipsy, dispute. Lyon listened to this unlovely
concert with a faint smile not pleasant to see.

"'You have so much to fill your life,'" he quoted to himself
from the letter lying on the table behind him. "Yes, so much
indeed, Miss Temple! I possess the inestimable privilege of
being able to shut a public-house or two against those drunken
beasts yonder—so long as I'm prepared to be stoned for my pains;
I can afford to reglaze the reading-room windows as often as my
public-spirited tenants please to break them—and that's about
once a week, on an average. No doubt I ought not to complain
—my life is a full one. I wish to Heaven I had never set foot
inside Creighton's doors!"

He lifted himself from his leaning position, and began to walk
up and down the room. "No"—pausing, after a while, in his
walk—"on reflection, that's a lie. I'm not sorry, on the whole.
Indeed, I'm not sure I regret anything. Her marrying Travers
is rank folly, and a hideous mistake; at the same time, she spoke
truly: if she had let me persuade her to break her word to him,
she would not have been the woman I took her for—and take her
for still, since she has refused to be persuaded. It's something to
keep *one* ideal unshattered. One pays for it, of course, as one
pays for everything in this world. It may be I'm paying too
much—more than the ideal's worth, intrinsically. We won't
probe that question too nicely. Having lost the substance, I may
as well try to persuade myself that I prefer a shadow."

Taking up Dorothy's letter from the table, he read it through
once more. "She is certainly very guileless," he commented
bitterly, on coming to the end. "Or very self-deceiving—which
is it? She calls him generous, because he asked no questions.
As if his asking no questions were not the most consummate proof
of shameless selfishness he could have given. If he *had* asked
questions; if he had insisted on probing the reason of her conviction that she could never care for him; if he had drawn any kind

of confession from her ; why, then, for very shame he must have
released her from her promise. He was too wary to do anything
of the kind. Instead of asking questions he settles the marriage
for September. Generous ? It is a cur's action—the action of a
man who simply wants his way and will use any means in order to
get it ; to whom *she* is nothing, her happiness nothing, apart from
his own wishes. Could not she have seen that—ought she not to
have seen it ? Well, what use if she had ? The recognition of
his baseness would only have made her sacrifice of herself more
painful. It would not have absolved her, in her own sight, from
the obligation to keep faith with him."

He laid the letter down again. "That fellow has missed a
great chance—if only he knew it. He might have been a hero in
her eyes forever. What right have I, though, to reproach him
for not acting like a hero ? My own conduct has been unheroic
enough. What have I done but add to her burden by reproaches
and entreaties which hurt her cruelly—as I intended they should
do—though she had too much strength and loyalty to let them
influence her decision ? I need not flatter myself that I shall cut
any other than a sorry figure in her memory—as the man who did
his best to make her false to his friend. No, no ; instead of casting
stones at Brian Travers, I should do better to sit down and realize
what a singularly contemptible part I have played, myself, in this
business."

His eye fell at this moment upon the second sheet of paper lying
on the blotting-book—his own reply to Dorothy's letter. Couched
in even briefer terms than the note it acknowledged, it consisted
only of half a dozen lines. His face softened a little as he re-read
these lines.

"At least, I have written nothing here which would give her
a fresh right to despise me," was his reflection. "I have ac-
quiesced in her decision—she could not expect me to rejoice in it.
And I have neither lamented nor reproached ; I have even for-
borne to warn her afresh that she is making a mistake."

He folded the letter carefully and put it into an envelope.
"And yet," he added, pausing with the envelope in his hand before closing it, "it *is* a mistake—a more awful one than she
guesses. She has undertaken more than her strength will bear—
pledged herself to more than she can possibly pay. And when
she recognizes the truth—then God help her! for she will
assuredly find no help in Brian Travers."

Part II.

CHAPTER I

AT SAN LORENZO

"The sun may shine, and we be cold."

"TAKE care of Dolly, Robin. And don't go out of sight, either of you."

"No, mummy, dear, we won't. Catch hold of my hand, Dolly. No, don't begin picking them yet; they're ever so much bigger higher up."

"They" were the white narcissus flowers with which the olive terraces leading up to San Lorenzo's rude shrine are literally carpeted in the early days of April. From her seat at the foot of a great gray olive, a patriarch among his brethren, growing half-way up the northern side of that long ridge of hill from the top of which, looking southward, the eye travels past the outlying white villas of San Remo to the blue waters of the Mediterranean, Robin's mother beheld a veritable sea of starry blossoms spreading, in climbing waves, above, below, and on every side of her, as far as her sight could reach. The all-glorifying sunshine of an Italian spring morning bathed the flower-clothed slope with a flood of light, and shimmered mysteriously between the gray-green leaves, and along the fantastically twisted boughs, and down the gnarled silvery trunks of the hoary old trees that at intervals over-shadowed it. Every now and then a tiny breeze, wafted across the hill-top from the unseen sea on the other side, would pass through the branches of the olives with a rustling sigh, and set the whole floral company clustered round their ancient roots dancing daintily for a moment.

Some women would have found it occupation enough, on such a morning, to sit idle in the olive-shade, and watch for the recurring delicate puff of air which never failed to awake so pretty a response among the trees overhead and the flowers underfoot. Not so Robin's mother. Her children had no sooner left her than she took up a book and began to read diligently. And if, now and then, her eyes wandered involuntarily from the printed page before them to the exquisite surroundings of her place of study, she never suffered them to play truant long, but recalled them almost immediately—once or twice with a movement of impatience —to more serious employment.

The voices of the little narcissus-pickers grew more and more indistinct, dwindled, and finally died away into the distance ; still the mother read on undisturbed. Apparently she imagined it unnecessary to watch her children closely ; trusting either-to a general habit of obedience on their part, or to the stability of Robin's plighted word, she seemed to take it for granted that they would not dream of transgressing her command. When, therefore, she at length closed her book and glanced round, to find that the boy and girl had alike vanished wholly from view, her surprise was as great as her alarm.

Certainly, Robin had altogether failed to keep his readily given promise. In justice to him, however, as a small boy of honorable principles, it should be said that he had given the promise in all good faith, and that his failure to keep it might fairly be accounted to him as an error rather than a crime. At seven years old, with thousands of the *Narcissus poeticus* above and around one, only waiting to be picked, those a little farther off, a little higher up, always looking larger and whiter than those quite near at hand, it would be strange indeed if one did not, after a while, forget to turn back dutifully every two minutes or so, just to make sure that the skirt of one's mother's gown was still easily visible in the distance ; poor mother ! who, strange to say, did not seem to care about picking flowers herself. Then, Robin's already divided mind was further distracted by the care of Dolly—Dolly, two years his junior, a sadly short-legged and short-winded climber, needing much assistance in her scrambles from terrace to terrace, and terribly given to dropping her own and her brother's joint spoils out of the gathered-up corners of her frock whenever Robin failed for an instant to keep a watchful eye upon them and her. Burdened thus with many cares, and lured onward a step at a time by the temptation to add finer and yet finer specimens to his store, Robin, without any intention of disobedience in his heart, found himself atop of the ridge and going down the other side—honestly unconscious of having done evil, until the sparkle of the sea revealed to him how far he had strayed from the bounds set by his mother's order.

This revelation took him considerably aback ; but he gave his dismay no voice. Indeed, his first impulse was to conceal it from Dolly—Dolly, whom he had been at immense pains to train into an attitude of unswerving respect for himself—respect which, he felt instinctively, any unguarded admission of wrong-doing or weakness on his own part must seriously affect. He merely remarked, therefore, with a finely simulated air of carelessness :

" Come, we've got enough now. We'll go back."

" Lots more," observed Dolly succinctly, emphasizing her observation by pointing with a fat forefinger to the terraces below. " Big ones."

" Yes, I see," returned masculine wisdom in a superior manner. " But it's too late to get those to-day. We can come again to-morrow. Oh, Dolly ! *do* keep your frock up ! You'll have them all out again, if you don't take care."

" Bring baskets to-morrow," interrupted Dolly, unheeding of reproaches and warnings alike. " And pick them *all*."

" I don't know if we *could* pick them all." Robin shook his head over the undertaking. " They're such a lot, you see. We might try, though "—brightening. " Perhaps, if we came *very* early, and brought our dinner in one of the baskets—— Now, hold up your frock—tight, with both hands—and I'll hold your arm——"

" Where we going now ? " Dolly enquired.

" Why, back to mummy, of course ! " Robin spoke the more boldly and confidently that he was secretly beginning to feel some uncertainty as to " mummy's " exact whereabouts. " She's down on the other side, by that funny big tree that's all empty inside—don't you 'member ? "

Dolly " 'membered " the tree in question well enough—quite as well as Robin himself. Unfortunately it turned out that with neither of them did remembrance of the giant hollow-trunked olive extend to its position among the other olives. In vain did Robin say airily, " This way," and, when " this way " proved to be the wrong one, turn undaunted in the opposite direction ; he had lost his bearings, and could not hit upon the path of return. Among ranks upon ranks of terraces, each terrace just like the other, all alike planted with olives, all carpeted alike with white narcissus, the topographical instinct of a tourist of seven may easily become hopelessly bewildered. In less than ten minutes the dreadful truth that he and his sister were *lost* had dawned upon Robin's youthful mind.

Before the contemplation of this overwhelming catastrophe even Robin's regard for his dignity momentarily gave way. His confession of the dismal truth to Dolly was made to an accompaniment of unmanly sobs; with the natural result that Dolly, though really much less impressed by the perils of their position—not being as yet promoted, like her brother, to fairy-tales in two syllables, and thus made perfectly aware of the awful dangers to which lost children are invariably exposed—began to cry lustily for company. At the sound of her loud wailing Robin made a generous effort to pull himself together.

" Don't cry, Doll," he adjured her valiantly, rubbing away his own tears manfully with his knuckles. " P'r'aps they'll find us before—before we die. And I s'pose there aren't any wild beasts in this wood ; 'cos if there were, mother wouldn't let us come here at all. Only those boys in the Sunday book used to play on the edge of a forest that had lions in it, and the lions didn't hurt them unless they went too far in. I wonder if we're far in ? "

" Would the lions eat us ? " enquired Dolly in an awestruck, tremulous whisper.

" Of course they would. I haven't got a spear to fight them with, you see, like the boy in the book. But I'll tell you what, Doll—if the robber-captain comes, I'll fight *him* for you——"

" Will he be sure to come ? "

" I don't know. There's a man coming up the hill now—but he doesn't look quite like him. He's got such ord'n'y clothes on," observed Robin in a depreciatory tone, " and a hat just like father's. Oh, how fast he does walk ! " clutching Dolly's arm in a paroxysm of mingled terror and admiration. " Just look ! he'll be up here in a minute——"

In truth, the newcomer on the scene, a big, broad-shouldered, strongly built man, prosaically arrayed in the short tweed coat, knickerbockers, and comfortable, if unbecoming, straw hat which together constitute the ordinary livery of the actively disposed Briton on his summer travels, was mounting the series of terraces which still lay between him and the bent and crooked old olive under which the two children had stopped short when Robin first began to expound the true nature of their situation to his

sister, at a rate which not only spoke well for the strength of his
wind and limb, but was calculated to strike the mind of an aspir-
ing athlete in his eighth year with absolute awe. In the interest
of watching the magnificent length and ease of the stranger's
ascending strides, Robin forgot to think of his possibly sinister
character and evil purposes toward himself and Dolly; and
Dolly, faithful to her *rôle* of copyist, dried her eyes also, and for
a while imitated Robin by staring at the active tourist with all
her might. However, when, as presently happened, he gained
the topmost terrace, and, passing close to the two children,
glanced at them enquiringly for a moment, Dolly's alarms renewed
themselves, and she shrank fearfully behind her brother.

"What are you afraid of, you silly little thing?" demanded
Robin in a low voice—contemptuously, indeed, but yet not unkindly. He was quite aware that one cannot expect a girl to
face danger in the unmoved manner peculiar to his own sex.
"Can't you see it's just a gentleman?"

"He had such a big stick," whimpered Dolly in self-excuse.

"Well, don't all grown-up men have big sticks, stupid? I
wish," quoth Robin, growing very brave indeed—"I wish I'd
spoken to him, and asked him to help us find mummy. He looked
rather cross, but I'm sure he was an English gentleman. I've a
great mind to run after him now; I could catch him if I ran very
fast. And I *can* run very fast when I'm without you——"

But here Dolly, terrified at the idea of being left for a time
alone, lifted up so vehement a voice of protest against the daring
plan that Robin was forced to abandon it. Perhaps he was not
altogether sorry to be precluded from displaying his heroism in so
extreme a fashion.

Meanwhile the big Englishman continued his rapid road downhill, wholly unconscious of the admiration he had excited, and
without the smallest inkling of the distressing position in which
he had left his diminutive admirers. The children's good looks—
Robin was a singularly handsome boy, while little Dolly, if she
could not boast very regular features, had been well-endowed by
nature in the matter of pink cheeks and yellow locks—had
attracted his notice for an instant; then he passed on, and
thought no more about them. The fact of their being alone made
no impression, no particular impression whatever, upon his
mind; and, even had it done so, such impression would at once
have been neutralized by the very natural following reflection that

a guardian of some kind—mother, nurse, or governess—must undoubtedly be in the near neighborhood. Under no circumstances, therefore, short of receiving a direct appeal for assistance, would he have dreamed that it could be incumbent upon him, as a benevolent passer-by, to proceed to the succor of these modern babes in the wood.

Very soon, thanks to his active movements, he found himself half-way down the long slope. Here, where two paths struck off in opposite directions into the woods, he paused suddenly ; and, having first looked about him irresolutely for a minute or two with the air of a man reconnoitring unknown ground, took out a small pocket-map and consulted it with attention. The result of his consultation was that he presently took the path to his left, and resumed his course, still a downward one, at an even increased rate of speed.

The path on which he had entered, guided by his map, scarcely merited so respectable a name, being little more than a mule-track of the roughest description, full of huge rolling stones brought down by a winter torrent. It was tortuous as well as steep, with innumerable sharp turns and corners ; corners so sharp that our pedestrian, swinging rapidly round one of them, narrowly escaped knocking over a lady who, coming from the opposite direction, was ascending the hill at nearly as great a pace as he himself was descending it. But for the aid of the formidable stick which had struck so deep a terror into Dolly's timid little soul, he could hardly have stopped himself in time to avert this catastrophe. Even as it was the lady, startled, and already out of breath by reason of her own previous haste, staggered back a pace or two, and must have completely lost her balance—an accident which, seeing the path ran alongside the brink of a deep ravine, might have been attended with very serious consequences— had not he had the presence of mind to catch her by the arm.

" I beg your pardon ! I beg ten thousand pardons ! " he exclaimed, hastily releasing her as she regained her equilibrium. " I should have looked better where I was going ; but one grows careless in these lonely places. Pray allow me to apologize most sincerely——"

He broke off suddenly and completely in the midst of his vigorous expressions of regret ; a light of recognition, that for an instant seemed *glad* recognition, flashed over his strong, sombre face with the effect of sheet-lightning playing upon a mass of dark rock, and was gone. Then he spoke again, in a slightly altered voice :

"I am the more sorry, now I see—I beg your pardon for not recognizing you at once—Mrs. Travers." He hesitated perceptibly before uttering this name, as though it had cost him some effort of memory to recall it. "Excuse my stupidity— my double stupidity. This is such an unexpected—pleasure." Again he seemed to have been searching for the right word ; and this time, to judge from the dissatisfied and thoroughly unjoyous tone in which he uttered that he finally elected to use, he had been baulked in his search. "I hope you are quite well ?" And he half extended his hand.

"Quite, thank you." Robin's mother was very pale. She did not seem to observe the hand half offered her, and its owner therefore prudently proceeded to withdraw it.

"I am afraid I have been unfortunate enough to frighten you," he observed, as he did so, in a tone quite remarkable for its frigidity. "It was abominably careless of me ; one has no business to rush round corners in that heedless fashion."

"Oh, that was nothing !" she averred eagerly. "It did not matter—pray don't trouble yourself."

"One is naturally annoyed to know that one has startled a lady half out of her wits."

"I am not so easily startled out of my wits, I hope," she retorted, in something of her old quick fashion. "I *am* frightened—but that's for another reason altogether. I am in great distress about my children—my two little children. I can't find them anywhere."

"You cannot find—your children ?" He said the words slowly ; they refused to come trippingly from his tongue.

"No. They were picking flowers while I read, and somehow they wandered out of sight without my noticing it. I shall never forgive myself ! I have called to them again and again ; I can't make them hear me. I don't know what to do—where to go. Mr. Lyon, you will help me to look for them ?"

"With pleasure," Lyon answered politely. "But it seems to me you are alarming yourself unnecessarily," eying her white face and quivering lips with what she felt to be a coldly disapproving look. "Remember, they are not likely to come to any harm in these olive-gardens. And finding them can only be a question of time."

11

"But Dolly is such a little thing, and so easily frightened! She is particularly afraid of dogs—the sight of a big dog nearly frightens her into a fit—and. most of the caretakers in these gardens keep such savage ones. And Robin is very rash and adventurous; he may lead her into all sorts of places—most dangerous places." A thrill of terror was in Dorothy's voice, and her mouth worked convulsively.

But here, luckily, Lyon bethought himself of the small couple he had passed on the hill-top so short a time before.

" *Two* children, I think you said ? Boy and girl ? the girl the younger of the two ? That's all right ! I've not a doubt I met them just now—not more than five minutes ago."

" Where ? " Dorothy enquired breathlessly.

" Up yonder ; just on the crest of the ridge," he signed over his shoulder. " Was the girl dressed in white, with a kind of sun-bonnet thing on her head, and light hair ? "

"Yes, yes ; that's Dolly ! And Robin had on a sailor suit."

" The same, then. I'll go and fetch them down. You can sit here and rest till they arrive. No, really, you had better not come any farther yourself ; this path is excessively rough. I will tell—your children "—again that scarcely perceptible pause —" that you have commanded me to recall them, and they shall be with you in a very few moments. Only don't move away from this spot, I beg. Because, if .you do move, you will certainly reduce us to the necessity of searching for you."

He turned away, and, without heeding either her thanks or her protestations, shot up the path he had just come down at a pace it would assuredly have been impossible for her, even though spurred by maternal anxiety, to emulate. A curious smile flitted about the corners of his lips as he went.

" Well, Fate does certainly seem to take a malicious pleasure in baulking all our forecasts ! " was his inward reflection. " I fancied I had exhausted in imagination all the circumstances that could possibly attend such a *rencontre* as this. It appears I was mistaken. Of course, after eight years, one is, or should be, prepared for anything. I was equally prepared to find her annoyed by my reappearance, or civilly indifferent to it. But—too pre-occupied even to go through the formality of shaking hands ! and, at the same time, quite ready to make use of me as a runner of errands on behalf of Brian's children—that's a conjunction I did not anticipate. Ah, here are the youngsters ! They have had the good sense not to extend their wanderings farther."

They had not, in fact, moved from the shelter of the tree under which Lyon had seen them first. Reassured, perhaps, by the metamorphosis of the supposed robber-captain into a peaceable tourist, they had apparently resolved to await the course of events, and in the meanwhile to get what fun they could out of their perplexing situation. So they had settled down in the shade of the crooked olive ; and while Dolly, seated on its roots, engaged in some mysterious game with the flowers in her lap, Robin, with a broken-off bough, which he had carefully stripped of its leaves, poised on his shoulder to represent a rifle, was stalking up and down in front of her, keeping sentry.

Perceiving Lyon's massive figure emerging once more from among the olives, the boy stopped short in his martial walk and faced the returning intruder with an outward and assumed calmness, much at variance with the inward misgivings which the stranger's unexpected reappearance aroused in his mind.

Lyon's first utterance was not calculated to lay these misgivings to rest. Unused to deal with children, he failed. to see that the case was one for cautious advances, and proceeded to deliver himself bluntly of his commission.

" You're young Travers, I suppose ? " he said interrogatively. Robin nodded, grasping his olive-bough very tightly in his small clammy hand. " I've been sent to fetch you and your sister."

Here Dolly rose precipitately to her feet, tumbling every narcissus in her lap to the ground. But for once Robin took no heed of her misdemeanors. His great dark eyes were fixed, in mingled curiosity and apprehension, upon his formidable-looking interlocutor, whose mode of address was so suspiciously suggestive of the robber-captain, if his garments could not be said to dress the part appropriately. But then robber-captains have been known to disguise themselves before now !

Being a plucky little fellow at heart, however, Robin resolved not to yield without a struggle to the perfidious foe. " Where do you want to take us ? " he demanded suspiciously.

" Down the hill to your mother. Do you know that she has been looking everywhere for you. You have frightened her to death by running off in this fashion," said Lyon severely, having a vague idea that it was his duty to improve the occasion by administering some kind of reproof.

Robin let the reproof pass.   But he still continued to eye Lyon
with distrust.   Vague recollections of blood-curdling histories of
children lured to enchanted castles by means of false messages
stirred uncomfortably in his small brain.   " What's your name ? "
he asked.

" My name is Lyon," gravely returned the owner of that
patronymic, beginning to understand something of the humor of
the situation.

" And are you a friend of mummy's ? "

Lyon paused an instant before replying " Yes."

" I never saw you before," was Master Travers' comment.

" I dare say not.   I never saw *you* before, either.   It's many
years since I saw your mother—or your father."

" Did you know mummy when she was a little girl like me ? "
interrupted Dolly, who had suddenly become much interested in
the conversation.

" She was rather older than you.   Come," said Lyon, who felt
that he had answered questions enough, and that further catechis-
ing might become inconvenient.   " We mustn't keep her waiting
any longer.   Pick up your flowers and let us go."

Robin, reassured as to the stranger's good intentions—it seemed
impossible to suspect evil of a person who had known " mummy "
when she was a little girl—and overawed by his imperious
manner, made no further attempt to create delay.   The floral
treasure which Dolly had scattered abroad, by this time growing
somewhat the worse for wear, was once more collected, and the
trio were soon on their way downhill.

" How came you to stray away like this ? " Mr. Lyon enquired presently, chiefly with the object of making conversation,
an object which he fully attained by his well-chosen question, for
Robin's voluble explanations had hardly come to an end before
that sharp turn of the path which Lyon had rounded so unthinkingly twenty minutes before, to find so great a surprise awaiting
him beyond, brought the little party within sight of Mrs. Travers.

She stood, leaning against the trunk of an olive, her hands knit
together in front of her, looking up the path for the first sign of
the children's approach, her whole attitude curiously expressive
of the constraint she was putting upon herself in remaining
stationary.   Seeing her, Robin broke into a subdued whoop of
delight.

" There she is !   I must run ! " he exclaimed.   " Take care of

Dolly, please, Mr. Lyon. She can't walk very well on big stones." And he flew down the rough path, agile and sure-footed as a young roe, straight into Dorothy's waiting arms.

The meeting between mother and son made a pretty picture enough ; and so, perhaps, Mr. Lyon thought, for he stood a moment contemplating it, quite oblivious of his small companion's presence, until he felt a pull at his sleeve and heard a grave little voice saying :

" I take your hand, please."

A baby Dorothy, with Dorothy Temple's eyes, hair, features, —stood looking up into his face in placid, confident appeal. He gave a slight, involuntary start—it was the first time he had observed the child with any particular attention, most of his notice having been necessarily given to the dark-eyed, talkative boy, whose every feature and gesture proclaimed him Brian Travers' son—then he stooped down and said in a carefully softened voice :

" Suppose I carry you ? How would that be ? "

" No, thank you," replied Dolly with much dignity. " I don't like being carried. Take my hand, please."

So, hand in hand, the oddly assorted pair stepped on together, and reached Dorothy's side without mishap.

" I don't know how to thank you properly ! " Mrs. Travers exclaimed, turning at last to Lyon, who, quietly observant, had stood by with a perfectly impassive countenance while little Dolly received her share of glad caresses. " It was so good of you—so very, very kind ! And, really, I must apologize for my behavior just now—when I first met you. I was quite distracted. I believe I hardly said so much as ' How do you do ? ' "

" No one would have expected you to observe such formalities under the circumstances," Lyon returned in his old level, noncommittal tone.

Dorothy glanced at him quickly—perhaps suspecting a covert sarcasm. But her suspicions found no confirmation in his expression, which connoted nothing beyond grave attention.

" Are you staying in San Remo ? " she asked.

" For a short time—yes. And you ? "

" We have been here some weeks already. I don't know exactly how much longer we may remain."

" Your first visit to the Riviera ? "

" Oh, no ! We come to San Remo every year for our annual

seaside outing. Living in Italy, as we have done for the last five years—— Perhaps you heard that Brian was appointed, five years ago, to be surveyor of the Bussana railway—that new line they are carrying through the Romagna? No? I thought—Jem might——"

"Jem is a wretched correspondent, Mrs. Travers, as you doubtless know, by this time. He has not written to me for years. So I had heard nothing. But I'm glad to hear now. Surveyor of the Bussana line, I think you said? That must be a pleasant berth for Brian. I hope he likes it?"

"Oh, yes! He was delighted when he found he had been elected. We hardly hoped the directors would be prevailed upon to give it to an Englishman."

"No; in this land of engineers one would have expected a foreigner to have small chance of getting any post of the kind. All the more gratifying for Brian. The only drawback to such an appointment is the expatriation it involves. But perhaps you don't object to that? You like Italy?"

"I love it," Dorothy answered warmly. "I am so sorry to think we must leave it very soon. The line is all but completed now," she explained, "and I don't suppose my husband is likely to find fresh work in this country."

"You dislike the idea of going back to England?"

"I am afraid we shall have to go a good deal farther afield than England." Lyon noticed that she left his question really without an answer, though she seemed to reply to it. "The market there is so terribly overstocked. Hush, darling! in a moment" —this to Dolly, who was pulling at her mother's hand, and suggesting in an audible tone that they should " go home and have dinner." "They get such appetites, living this open-air life," she added apologetically to Lyon. "You must ex-cuse——"

"Hurrah!" struck in Robin from the summit of the bank bordering the path on the right-hand side, to which he had laboriously climbed while the foregoing conversation was in progress. "I think I see the top of father's hat—a long, long way off—quite low down among the trees. May I run and meet him, mummy?"

"Better not, dear. You don't know which path he may take. He promised to meet us somewhere about this time"—turning again to Lyon. "He has been out all the morning, taking photographs. Perhaps, if you are not in a hurry, you will wait a moment and see him? I know he would be so glad."

"Thanks; I should like to meet him again. So he has caught the fashionable photography-fever? Has he taken it very badly?"

"Did you ever know anyone take it mildly?" returned Dorothy, smiling. "Yes, my Dolly, we are going home directly, as soon as father comes."

"Is Mr. Lyon coming with us?" Robin enquired eagerly—so eagerly that his mother launched an anxious look in his direction. But to her surprise Lyon's rejoinder—"Perhaps I may walk part of the way back with you, if your mother has no objection"—was met by an enthusiastic ejaculation of "That's jolly!" on Robin's part, which quite drowned her own modestly murmured, "Of course I shall be very glad."

"I feel extremely flattered," observed Lyon, with an odd, fleeting smile which Robin did not half like, and which caused him, for a moment, to hesitate in making the request already on his lips. Rallying his courage, however, he swung himself down the bank, and, sidling close up to his new acquaintance, asked in a highly confidential tone :

"You *will* show me how to get up the terraces as fast as you do, won't you? If we ran on in front a little way, we could practise all the way home. Mother always walks so slow, because of Dolly."

"Robin!" interposed Dorothy, catching the whisper, and flushing distressfully. "You must not ask Mr. Lyon to run about with you. I dare say he is tired."

"Oh, he can't be tired! Why, he ran ever so quick when he came to fetch us!" was Robin's confident rejoinder.

"That's the very reason for his being tired now. Remember, he had to climb quite a long hill in search of you two naughty little lost children, and climbing hills in a hurry is very tiring. Isn't it, Mr. Lyon?"

"The excuse will serve, thank you. I am not very happy in children's society," Lyon added, speaking more hurriedly than was usual with him. He felt that his deliberate churlishness needed some apology; at the same time he was quite determined to show Mrs. Travers that he had no mind to let himself be turned into a playmate for her spoiled imps. "I don't pretend to understand them, and I never know what to say to them. I don't

believe I could play with a child to save my life! I'm afraid
you'll have to wait a good many years before you can get up the
terraces as quickly as I do, my man," he concluded, turning to
Robin, who was still looking up at him with pleading eyes.
"It's a question between long legs and short ones, you see."

Considerably crestfallen, and uncomfortably conscious that he
had received a snub, Robin withdrew to a little distance. A
moment's silence ensued. Perhaps Mrs. Travers, too, felt chilled
and thrown back upon herself. A puzzled expression crossed her
face; perhaps she was asking herself what she had done or said to
excite Mr. Lyon's displeasure. Lyon interrupted her self-ques-
tionings by asking abruptly :

"And your brother-in-law? Where and how is he?"

"Jem is in India. He has been there for—let me see—over
six years now. Ever since his father's death."

"Doing the barefooted friar business?"

"He has joined the Brotherhood of St. Philip—yes," returned
Mrs. Travers. "You know, that was always the desire of his
heart."

Lyon nodded. "I remember. Well, I hope he finds the de-
lights of itinerant missionary life, in sandals, all his fancy
painted them. You look as if you felt some doubt on that score.
Has Jem betrayed any disappointment?"

"No; I have no right to say he is not thoroughly satisfied.
Only now and then the tone of his letters has led me to think——"

"That the desire of his heart has turned out—not so very
desirable, after all? Poor Travers! But he might have foreseen
his fate. If there's one thing more foolish than cherishing high-
minded plans for benefiting one's fellow-creatures, it's attempting
to put them into practice. In what part of India does his work
lie?"

"At first he had his headquarters in Calcutta, and only made
journeys in Bengal. But latterly they have moved him about a
good deal. He rather hoped to have been sent to the Northwest
last year; but the Superior decided otherwise. Just now he is
in Tinnevelly, I believe."

"He has never worked in the Northwest?"

"No."

"Ah, that accounts for our paths having failed to cross! I am
fresh from India myself," Lyon explained, in answer to Dorothy's
enquiring look. "But most of my time there—I may say all of

it—was spent in the Northwest. Here comes Brian, evidently !
Not much altered, after all these years. Though I see he has
taken to wearing a beard.''

Before he could finish his sentence Brian was actually upon
them, talking, laughing, uttering eager exclamations of pleasure.
Lyon, whose natural reserve and hatred of emotional scenes was
that of the ordinary Englishman of his age and class tenfold inten-
sified, found his old school-fellow's enthusiastic greetings a little
too exuberant for his personal taste. He was even inclined to suspect that such extravagant expressions of delight—for extravagant
they seemed to him—must necessarily be insincere ; by which
unkind suspicion he quite wronged poor Brian, whose whole
offence really consisted in the fact that he had, during his five
years' residence in Italy, unconsciously caught something of the
excitable manner and gestures of the men who were his daily colleagues. His volubility and animation on the present occasion
were in no way assumed ; they were the legitimate result of a feeling of genuine satisfaction. He was honestly glad to see Lyon ;
he was even better pleased that Lyon should see him in the new
and agreeable position of a successful man. Lyon had known him
in his humiliation ; it was well that Lyon should know him also in
his triumph. Brian was one of those persons who habitually give
magnificent names to the events of their lives.

He stood, therefore, wreathed in smiles—his teeth were as fine
and white as ever—pouring forth ejaculations, asking friendly
questions, and nearly wringing Lyon's hand off ; while that
taciturn and inexpansive person returned brief and business-like
replies to his numerous eager enquiries. As Lyon had perceived
at once, a whole decade had wrought but little change in his outward man. His good looks were almost as remarkable now as they
had been when he was ten years younger. If the square-cut Italian
beard, by partially concealing the fine oval of his face, detracted
a little from its classic beauty, it added to it, on the other hand, a
much-needed suggestion of strength—the one thing formerly lack-
ing to its cameo-like perfection.

"Who would have thought of meeting you here ! " he ejaculated joyously, contemplating Lyon with pleased eyes. "Where
did you drop from ? and how long have you been in these parts ? "

"I only arrived from Brindisi last night."

"Curious, our coming across each other at once ! A great
stroke of luck ! "

"It was, indeed, a stroke of luck, my meeting Mr. Lyon when I did," Dorothy said. And she explained the manner of that meeting, and gave an account of Lyon's subsequent services. "Yes, it was very lucky. For I had not the remotest idea what direction the children had taken. They had been gone some time."

"And you were fast approaching the verge of lunacy, I doubt not," her husband put in good-naturedly. "You chose the moment of your appearance well, Lyon, if you wanted an effusive welcome. But how did you manage to identify each other? Surely you've never——"

"Oh, yes, you forget!" Dorothy did not give her husband time to finish his sentence. "Mr. Lyon came to Heyford one summer, while you were in Queensland—don't you remember?—and stayed at The Haulms."

"Ah, I do remember hearing something about it, now you remind me. The summer of my poor mother's death, wasn't it? Well, I'm glad you two don't meet as strangers. Always supposing"—Brian added, with his old bright laugh—"that both of you have pleasant recollections of your former acquaintance. Did he snub you systematically, Dorothy? Because, if I recollect right, that was his ordinary fashion of dealing with young women in those days."

"I think Mrs. Travers will acquit me of anything so deliberately unamiable as systematic snubbing," Lyon said, before Dorothy's reply was quite ready. "I may add that it wasn't very easy to snub her. Of course I made myself highly disagreeable to her now and then, I've no doubt. Constituted as I am, it's hardly possible I should have failed to do *that*."

"But, on the whole, you were good friends? That's satisfactory. You don't find Dorothy much altered? She does the Italian climate credit, doesn't she?"

"Mrs. Travers certainly looks very well."

"I am very well," Dorothy said.

To all appearance, her boast was justified. She had lost something, perhaps, of her early bright bloom, but her fair complexion still retained the smooth clearness of perfect health; her hair, under her pretty spring hat, seemed as abundant as ever; her figure, if it had grown a little fuller, was still slight and firm and supple, upright in carriage, and active in all its movements; and, as regards actual beauty, she was certainly prettier at thirty than she had been at twenty-two. She had gained besides in grace, in charm, in distinction—in all those indefinable qualities which go far to make a passably good-looking woman into a positively pretty one ; and she was singularly well dressed. It was easy to see that she had acquired a habit of taking pains with herself, of studying the becoming, and giving serious thought to her clothes. Her morning costume, simple and entirely appropriate to the rustic occasion though it was, had not been adopted haphazard, for mere comfort or convenience' sake ; it bore unmistakable traces of careful design.

"I am perfectly well," she said, smiling, and her smile, like her new prettiness of face and new daintiness of dress, roused a sense of vague irritation in Lyon ; it was so unlike Dorothy Temple's smile as he remembered it. "So is Brian ; so are the children. We are a singularly robust party."

"Yes, we are all so extraordinarily, prosaically healthy," her husband chimed in, "that now and then we feel out of place in a health resort. It seems as if we lacked all justification for coming here so often. Well, I needn't enquire after your health, Lyon, I presume ? "

"No, thanks ; I'm very fit."

"You don't look a day older than when I last saw you in Half-Moon Street ! What is it, Dorothy ? Must we be moving already ? Why, there's heaps of time; only a quarter to one "—looking at his watch. "You haven't ordered luncheon at any particular hour, have you ? "

"Not for ourselves. But the children's dinner was ordered for one, and they are both hungry, and Dolly is tired."

"Oh, the children ! " cried Brian in mock exasperation. "Never were such tyrants as those youngsters, I assure you, Lyon ; my wife and I lead the life of bondslaves to their claims. Want your dinner, Robin, my boy ? All right, you shall have it ! *En route* with you ! We'll follow."

Nothing loath, Robin led the way into the valley, Lyon and Travers, at Dorothy's request, going next, while she brought up the rear with Dolly.

"And what have you been doing with yourself these ten years ? " Brian demanded presently of his friend. "We shall expect a full, true, and particular account of your adventures."

"My adventures have been few, and singularly uninteresting, I'm sorry to say. They'll keep, I assure you. From what Mrs.

Travers was telling me just now, yours seem to have been of a more gratifying nature. That appointment, for instance."

"Yes, I've found the berth a very pleasant one. And, of course, my being a foreigner made the election something of a special compliment. The worst of it is," said Brian, swinging his Kodak thoughtfully to and fro as he walked, "that my term will be up in June. Then I shall be on the stream again."

"You don't think of applying for a renewal? I understood that a branch line to Santa Anna was in contemplation ; and, as a leading member of the old staff, surely you——"

"No, no ; no chance in that quarter ! They want the post for one of their own men," Brian interjected quickly, with a half-uneasy glance backward, apparently to see whether Dorothy, who had stopped a moment before to tie the strings of Dolly's sun-bonnet, and was now quickening her pace in order to regain lost ground, were yet within ear-shot. "Fair enough ; I've had my turn. No, I shall have to look out for work elsewhere—probably in one of our own colonies. I shouldn't have disliked India, myself, and I think I could get an opening there, perhaps. But my wife is absolutely against India—so that's out of the question."

Half-involuntarily, Lyon looked back at Mrs. Travers, who was now close behind him, with an interrogative expression.

"I could not take the children to India," she said.

The words were very quietly and simply spoken. But he understood, nevertheless, that this question of taking or leaving her children was a matter of life and death to the speaker.

"Clearly, in her estimation, 'the children' are first and foremost," he drew his conclusion. "They have made up for everything, filled every void. It's always the way. A woman who cares for her children never seems to have room left for any other feeling. Natural, I suppose—and certainly satisfactory. In the present case, most decidedly satisfactory. Even you," quoth Lyon, contemptuously addressing himself—"even *you*, I hope, are not quite such an ill-conditioned brute as to wish things were otherwise."

CHAPTER II

A PARTIE CARRÉE

"Men study women as they do the barometer; but they do not understand until the day after."

IT was not during the walk just chronicled that Lyon formulated these sage reflections. All the way to San Remo, Brian, fluent and talkative as of old, gave him no chance of indulging in any reflection whatsoever, and, San Remo being reached, not only insisted on accompanying him as far as his hotel—situated a quarter of a mile beyond that in which the Traverses had taken up their temporary abode—but on entering it along with him, in order to renew acquaintance with his travelling-companion, another old school-fellow, now an officer of Engineers, invalided home from India. Thus some time elapsed before any space for meditation was accorded Lyon. Only after Brian had at length taken leave, and a late luncheon had been discussed by himself and Captain Sebright, was he free to establish himself with his pipe under the shade of the biggest pepper-tree in the hotel-garden, alone—for Sebright, who was suffering from the effects of a recent sunstroke, found a darkened room his best refuge from the glare of the southern sun at this hour—and there pass the events of the morning in review.

So at last he had encountered Brian Travers' wife ! Well, the encounter, if it could not be said to have given him pleasure, might have its salutary effects.

"Nothing," he reflected philosophically, "like a renewal of long-interrupted acquaintanceship for dispelling lingering sentiment ! One imagines—knowing all the while that one is a self-deceiving fool, one persists in the imagination—that one's ideal woman must have remained unchanged and unchanging, till one comes across her unexpectedly, 'ripe and real,' with a mind become limited to babies, frocks, and the exigencies of society. In most cases, the ideal is found to have grown fat. Mrs. Travers has failed to carry out the general rule in this respect ; but in all others she fulfils it admirably. I dare say many people would find

her 'improved'; to me her improvement has simply stripped her
of every charm she once had.   I had not been five minutes in her
company this morning before I felt myself on the way to recover
of all long-standing delusions concerning her ; a few more such
meetings would make a sane and healthy-minded man of me for
the rest of my life.   I really don't know why I should have been
so absurdly annoyed with Sebright for blurting out the fact that
we had taken our rooms here for three weeks, in his usual open-
mouthed fashion ! nor yet why I should have perpetrated that perfectly unnecessary lie about a non-existent engagement for to-night
when Travers asked me to dinner.   Well,"—knocking the ashes
out of his pipe against the low wall on which he sat with a vigor
most incautious, seeing that the pipe in question was a valuable
meerschaum, colored to perfection,—" if he renews the invitation
to-morrow, I'll accept it."   He struck a match with a slight smile,
that went very near to degenerating into a sneer, on his lips.   " In
the hope of completing my cure, of course.   What pitiful hypo-
crites we are !   Do I really want to be well ?   It strikes me, on
the whole, that this process of getting well is about the most
painful part of the whole business."

Of course, Brian, being full of hospitable instincts and a prince
of good fellows, did renew his invitation the following morning ;
and the invitation, this time, included Sebright as well as Lyon.
So it was a party of four which assembled at eight o'clock the
same evening round one of the dozen little tables in the restaurant
of the big hotel on the hill overlooking the promenade and the sea,
and spent a couple of hours more or less pleasantly in company.
Sebright, like his host, was a fluent talker who loved to hear his
own voice, and he and Brian, between them, claimed the lion's
share of the conversation, though Dorothy played her part in it
readily and gracefully enough.   Lyon fell back on his old *rôle* of
listener—a *rôle* which served the double purpose of saving him
the trouble of talking, and affording him leisure in which to study
his entertainers comparatively at his ease.

Such observations as he was able to make only confirmed his first
impressions : that the past eight years had wrought but little change
in Brian Travers, while they had had a positively transforming
effect upon Brian's wife.   Dorothy, to Lyon's view, had suffered
a metamorphosis of her whole individuality ; in looks, dress, manner, speech alike, she had become another woman.   She assumed
no distant or frigid airs, she showed no inclination to stand on

the defensive with her quondam lover—whom she addressed,
every now and then, with just as much of cordial ease and
absence of all embarrassed consciousness as though he had never
been more to her than any other passing summer visitor at Heyford ; yet every tone of her voice rang unfamiliarly in Lyon's ear,
every fearless meeting of her eyes with his seemed to thrust him
further back upon himself, and fill him with a deeper sense of loss
and disappointment. He resented less her absolute self-command,
her perfect coolness where he himself was concerned—though he
did secretly resent these, even while he acknowledged in his heart
that a less impassive demeanor would have lowered her indefinitely
in his estimation—than her display of qualities and characteristics
which, by their newness, made him feel an utter stranger to her.
Dorothy Travers' flow of small talk, her ready acquiescence in
other people's opinions, her conventional smiles, her little scraps
of worldly wisdom and hints of an enlarged experience of men and
things interlarding the cautious expression of her views : all these
things, like her Parisian gown and elaborately dressed hair, were
distasteful to Lyon, by so much as they were at variance with his
memories of Dorothy Temple. "Superficial ! shallow ! conventional ! unreal !" such were, time after time, his unspoken comments on her contributions to the talk circling about the little
round table. "She takes as little real, hearty interest in these
things for which she professes enthusiasm as—as I do." Lyon felt
thoroughly aggrieved by this failure on Dorothy's part to fulfil
the promise of her girlhood. Somehow the possibility of her failing to fulfil it had never presented itself to his mind. A pronounced sceptic as regards the rest of the human race, he had continued for eight years to cherish an illogical and illimitable belief
in one woman. He told himself that he was justly punished for his
irrational credulity.

It was easy, or so at least he thought, to understand Mr. and
Mrs. Travers, taken singly; considered together, they offered a
somewhat more perplexing subject for speculation. What they
were, severally, in themselves, Lyon felt himself qualified to determine out of hand ; what they were in their relations to each other
was less strikingly apparent. At the very end of the evening their
guest had got no further than the fact that husband and wife
seemed to be good friends ; that Brian's manner to Dorothy, if no
longer lover-like, was at any rate unfailingly courteous and good-
humored, while Dorothy, on her side, showed a laudable desire to

follow the lead of her lord and master in her choice or avoidance of topics of conversation.

Both Travers and Sebright had so much to tell each other of their several experiences during the past decade that Lyon began to hope he should be spared all question on the subject of his own insignificant personal affairs. His hope, however, was foredoomed to disappointment. Some chance reference of Sebright to the length of time during which his present travelling companion had been, "in an Indian sense, his next-door neighbor," aroused Brian's curiosity at once.

"Three years!" he exclaimed. "You don't mean to say you've been three years in India, Lyon?"

"Twice three, I believe," Captain Sebright answered, speaking before Lyon had time to open his mouth. "He came out in—'82 —wasn't it, Lyon?"

"End of '81. I've had all but seven years of it."

"But what on earth induced you to expatriate yourself for such a length of time?" enquired Travers in astonishment.

"Beggars can't be choosers—more especially in this era of competitive examinations. I got an offer of work out there; so, naturally, I went."

"Work? But—but surely——" Brian, for once, was at a loss for words.

"You weren't aware I had rejoined the noble army of those who eat their bread in the sweat of their brows? You never heard of the romantic reappearance of my cousin from Australia?"

Brian shook his head. "Never a word."

"Perhaps you didn't even know my late uncle once had a son who was supposed to have died in North Queensland? Well, he didn't die, after all. It had simply pleased him, for certain private reasons of his own, to disappear for a while. When he heard that I was usurping his patrimony, he very naturally thought it time to reappear and bid the base intruder forth of his family halls."

"My dear Lyon!" Brian's tone was a mixture of sympathy and indignation. "What a very unpleasant surprise for you! You had no warning?"

"None whatever. I simply got a letter from his solicitors announcing that he was not dead, but very much alive—and in London."

"Still I don't quite understand." Brian knitted his handsome eyebrows in perplexity. "If there were no proofs of this man's death, how did you ever get possession at all ?"

"But there were proofs of his death, proofs in plenty. It was his interest, as I told you just now, to disappear wholly for a time, and he had friends who helped him to carry out his plan. Their devotion even went the length of providing certificates to show that he was actually dead and buried. Those certificates were rather a nuisance to him when he wanted to revive," added Lyon. "He had made the proof of his own death so very complete that he had some trouble in convincing the lawyers of his identity with the man supposed to have been put safely under ground in the bush ten years before. A pity you didn't see the story in the papers"—turning to Dorothy ; "it really read like a romance. Don't you think a novelist might make something of such materials, Mrs. Travers ?"   •

"If he were a novelist worth his salt, he ought to make a very good three-volume novel out of it," was the answer. "Only, if I were the novelist, I should want to alter the *dénoûement*. In my version, the returning cousin would be no real cousin at all, but a false claimant, whom you should triumphantly unmask." She smiled.

"Thank you," Lyon responded briefly. But there was no answering smile on his lips.

"A much more satisfactory ending to the play," remarked Brian, "to you and to us. I can't tell you how sorry I am, Lyon. You've no doubt, I suppose, in your own mind, that this cousin *is* a genuine article ?"

"None whatever. I never had any—after I had once set eyes upon him, that's to say. For which reason I declined to waste any money or time in defending my perfectly rotten title to his inheritance."

"You gave in without a struggle ? At once ?"

"I waited to see if he could bring the necessary proofs of his identity first, of course. But I made no attempt to fight his claim. It was too clearly a sound one."

"Well, I hope he behaved considerately himself in return for your forbearance ?"

"Really, there was no forbearance in the matter. It was simply a question of the wrongful possessor giving way to the rightful one, without making a useless, and very expensive, fuss first. I acted out of regard for my own pocket."

12

"All of which means, I presume, that the gentleman has *not* shown himself considerate?"

"I don't very well see how a perfect stranger can show consideration under such circumstances," returned Lyon brusquely. "Nor yet how one could avail one's self of the consideration, if he did. So long as a man behaves justly and fairly, he does all that can possibly be expected of him, in my opinion."

"Depend upon it," said Brian Travers to his wife, half an hour later, when—their two guests having meantime taken leave—he was free to comment on Lyon's story in the privacy of Dorothy's little *salon*, "depend upon it, that curmudgeon of a cousin has made him refund all he spent during his two years of possession."

"Don't you think Mr. Lyon is the kind of man who would have insisted on doing that, in any case?"

"I don't know, I'm sure. Old Lyon is proud, of course. But he hates work. And he must have had to work like a black to pay off such a debt, and live at the same time."

"Did he tell you, after I went upstairs, what sort of work he had been doing in the Northwest Provinces?" enquired Dorothy, taking a muslin pinafore she was embroidering for Dolly from her work-basket and beginning to sew upon it.

"Road-making, chiefly, he said. Lately, he's had something to do on the frontier railway, I think. You know he had a lot of experience in Australia, especially with regard to mountain lines; and, though he's not a brilliant engineer, I dare say he makes a very useful underling. Then he has the bump of authority strongly developed; he'd keep his coolies in good order, I've no doubt."

"Does he intend going back to India when his holiday is over?"

"Yes, he's going back; I asked him. But not to the North-west this time. I gathered, from the little he would let out—it was always like drawing teeth to get Lyon to talk about himself—that he has secured a better berth, somewhere in Oudh. I'm glad the old chap is doing so well," Brian said with a magnificent air of patronage. "It was awfully rough on him, that cousin turning up." He walked to the window and leaned out for a moment; then, turning back into the room, observed tentatively, "I suppose you wouldn't care to come out for a stroll?"

The interrogative note in Mr. Travers' enquiry sounded but faintly. The form of his question showed that he had little or no expectation of obtaining a favorable answer from Dorothy; its tone, to the cynical bystander, might have conveyed the notion that he was not specially eager to obtain one. If he had counted on a negative, he was not disappointed. Nothing could have been 'more prompt and decided than Dorothy's :

"No, thanks. You know I always like to be within call of the children while Jane is at her supper."

Brian took his hat and stick. "Well, don't wait up for me ; I may be a little late. It's really sinful to come in early in such weather. By the way, what do you say to Monte Carlo to-morrow ? "

"I don't see how I could be away the whole day." Dorothy spoke in a doubting tone.

"Ah, I expected you would say that ! " Brian's tone was quite easy and unruffled. "I must go by myself, then, I suppose ; unless I find someone inclined to join forces with me. Sebright, per-haps "—thoughtfully. "If I could only feel sure Sebright wouldn't involve Lyon ! "

"I thought you liked Mr. Lyon ? "

"So I do—on appropriate occasions. But one should suit one's company to one's surroundings. At Monte Carlo one feels the need of a companion not above frivolling a little in season. I have it ! I might ask Sebright to go with me to-morrow, and engage Lyon for a hill-expedition on Friday or Saturday. That wouldn't be a bad plan, eh ? "

"A very good one, I should say," Dorothy answered a little absently.

CHAPTER III

UNDER THE OLIVES

"Was wir selbst erwählen, das müssen wir auch selbst durchführen."

CAPTAIN SEBRIGHT proved perfectly willing to bear his quondam school-fellow company to Monte Carlo ; from which delectable spot he returned in the highest possible spirits, and unable to say enough in praise of the charms of Travers' society. So warm was his eulogium of that pleasant gentleman at breakfast the following morning that Lyon cynically decided it must have been Brian's advice which had induced his panegyrist to stake his money on the winning number overnight.

"Travers is really a most amusing fellow"—thus Sebright returned to the charge later on in the reading-room, of which apartment he and his friend chanced to have sole possession for the time. "So much *verve* and go about him. He was the life of our luncheon-party at the Paris yesterday."

"Travers always had a pretty wit," responded Lyon from behind the open sheets of the *Times*.

"His wit certainly hasn't grown rusty during the past ten years. By Jove! it was good fun to hear him and Mrs. M'Allan together!" Sebright chuckled at the recollection.

"Mrs.——"

"M'Allan. A very pretty and lively American widow, who sat by him at table, and drew him out—and on—as only a clever Yankee knows how. On second thoughts, though, not a widow— or only a grass one; I'm pretty sure I caught something about a husband in Philadelphia. A fascinating little woman all round. She and Travers seemed to be great allies. By the way, how does his wife strike you?"

"I knew her before." Lyon's tone had a decided curtness, which would have effectually checked a less irrepressible talker than Sebright. Sebright, however, was not easily snubbed into silence.

"Is she an intimate friend of yours?" he asked.

"Mrs. Travers? No." ("That's *not* a lie," Lyon added in an aside to himself. "I know no one with whom I feel myself more utterly a stranger.")

"Then I suppose I may venture to say she strikes me as hardly the sort of woman one would have expected Travers to have married. And I understand there's little or no money in the case, so his motives can't have been mercenary."

"What kind of woman should you have expected Travers to marry?" enquired Lyon suddenly.

"Well, I should have thought he would have looked out either for beauty or gifts of some kind. Now Mrs. Travers is barely pretty, and—if you'll excuse my saying so—just a little bit dull."

"Oh, I hold no brief on behalf of Mrs. Travers' looks or intellect, I assure you! So you found her dull? I thought she seemed to have plenty to say for herself at dinner on Wednesday evening."

" She talked ' an infinite deal of nothing '; she never said a single thing worth remembering."

" How many people's ' things ' are worth remembering ? "

" Mrs. Travers' sole ambition is apparently to say just what would be expected of her on every occasion. What can be more tiresome in a woman ? "

" I'll tell you," replied Lyon, carefully turning his newspaper inside out. " A fancy for saying the totally unexpected thing—or trying to say it. A woman with a wild desire after originality is the most exasperating creature breathing. She keeps one's feeble intellect always on the stretch ; there is never any knowing at what place she may break out next, and put one to open shame before one's assembled acquaintance. No, no ! of the two, give me the conventional woman ! At least one knows where one is with her —and she doesn't get upon one's nerves."

" I give you Mrs. Travers willingly. She doesn't attract me at all." And Captain Sebright returned with a yawn to his novel, happily unconscious of a yearning desire on Lyon's part to knock him backward out of the French window in the embrasure of which he was lolling comfortably, book in hand.

Lyon saw but little of the Traverses during the ensuing week. The hill-excursion, for which Brian had pronounced him a fitting companion, hung fire in an unaccountable manner; Brian excusing himself for putting it off from day to day by vague pleas of " business " and " engagements which took him out of the place." Whither these engagements took him he did not explicitly reveal ; presumably not to Monte Carlo, since he never again renewed his invitation to Sebright to be his fellow-excursionist—somewhat to the chagrin of that ingenuous young rifleman. But whenever Lyon came across Travers, whether in the streets of the town, or on the pretty palm-bordered promenade connecting it with the West Bay, he always appeared to be more or less in a hurry, and his hurry was generally leading him in the direction of the railway station.

These brief chance meetings, and two or three equally brief encounters with Mrs. Travers and her children apart, nothing occurred to bring Lyon into contact either with Brian or his wife for the six or seven days following the evening of the little dinner at the Hôtel d'Angleterre. He had, of course, as in duty bound, called upon Dorothy ; but she being out at the time of his visit, this had resolved itself into the mere formality of leaving a card for her with the *concierge*. He congratulated himself on having at once recognized the absurdity of the impulse that had urged him to antedate his departure from San Remo when first he became aware of the Traverses' presence in the place ; to have yielded to it would have been to proclaim himself indeed one of those fools who can be frightened by a shadow. As things had turned out, he had seen next to nothing of Mrs. Travers ; and all he had seen had only contributed to his growing disillusionment concerning her.

At the end of ten days Brian's engagements finally permitted him to fix a date for the long-deferred expedition to Baiardo. The following morning was the time chosen by himself, and agreed to by Lyon ; and it was further settled between the two that—the Hôtel d'Angleterre being on their outward line of route —Lyon, whose hotel was situated in the town, should call for his companion.

Great, therefore, were his surprise and indignation, when, having climbed the long flights of steps that form the approach to the Hôtel d'Angleterre, and presented himself at the appointed hour of ten within its great glass doors, he was informed that Brian had left it an hour before, having—so the *concierge* positively asserted— gone down to the station in the hotel omnibus, intending to take the nine o'clock train.

Lyon's expression, on receipt of this information, became decidedly forbidding. Some instinct to which he gave no name—a fair-minded outsider might have called it an instinct of generosity —had prompted him to endeavor to think as well as he could of Brian Travers, and to be especially watchful against any tendency to over-sensitiveness where that young man's conduct was concerned. But Brian's present behavior struck him, even from the severely impartial standpoint from which he forced himself to regard it, as a trifle cavalier.

" Mr. Travers left no message for me ? "

In so far as the *concierge* was aware—none. But it was possible that madame—— Perhaps monsieur would like to see Mme. Travers ?

Lyon only hesitated a second before replying in the affirmative. Then a waiter was sent upstairs, and returned with the information that Mrs. Travers was in the garden. Would monsieur go to her there ? Yes, he would.

As Lyon threaded his way along the narrow shingly paths, between the rows of orange and lemon trees, in the wake of the diminutive Italian *garçon* with his shock of well-oiled black hair and ill-fitting black coat, grown shiny at the shoulders with long use, he was irresistibly reminded of the autumn afternoon, now nearly nine years since, when, amid very different surroundings, and in a strangely different mood, he had gone out into the garden of The Haulms in search of Dorothy Temple. As far as his own feelings were concerned, not nine years only, but ninety, might have elapsed since that November day ; so unreal, so like the recollections of a vivid dream, or of something that had happened in another state of existence, did his reminiscences, all clear-cut and unfaded though they yet were, appear, as he viewed them afresh in the light of present circumstance.

Curiously enough, his first sight of Dorothy—when at last he came within sight of her she had crossed the boundaries of the garden proper into the olive-grove beyond it, and had there established herself under a tree, book in hand, a work-basket beside her—did much to dispel this sense of unreality, and to give a new life to his devitalized memories. For the first time since his meeting with her a fortnight ago, she reminded him forcibly of her old self. Perhaps it was the absence of the children which led to this thought, or fancy, on his part ; or it may have been induced by the fact that she was more plainly dressed, her hair arranged with less of elaborate care than usual, and that her appearance had thus regained something of its former air of simplicity. Certainly much of the quick impetuosity of her girlish days was in her manner as, on perceiving him, she sprang up and came forward, not waiting for the servant's announcement.

"You didn't get my note, then ? Oh, I am so sorry ! Brian had no time to write; he was obliged to hurry off, directly the post came in, almost without his breakfast. But I wrote at once, and sent down the note by nurse and the children. I'm afraid Jane has loitered on the way—perhaps the shops were too much for her, poor thing ! But it's most annoying that you should have had your climb up here for nothing !"

"Pray don't trouble yourself to be annoyed ; it's of no consequence, for I had nothing else to do," Lyon returned magnanimously. Then the two shook hands, and Mrs. Travers said, with an embarrassed glance on either side of her :

"I wish I could ask you to sit down ; but——"

"I see you have no chair to offer me," put in her visitor coolly, to the relief of her embarrassment. "Never mind. I'll take the terrace instead, if you'll allow me, for a minute or two. Mother Earth affords a very safe seat in these regions," he added, proceeding to carry out his proposition—"even for a rheumatically inclined individual, like myself."

"Excuse me, but—you hardly look the character," Dorothy said, with a pretty, civil smile, for which Lyon felt inclined to hate her.

"My looks belie me, then—in that matter."

"Then it *was* on account of health that you came here, after all?" Dorothy's smile had faded, and she spoke with her old sudden directness of interrogation.

"Partly."

"You have been ill, then?"

"Oh, I had a sharp touch of rheumatic fever last rainy season. That's all."

"And more than enough"—relapsing into the smile once more. "You certainly ought to be very careful for some time to come."

"I am, I assure you. Being laid by the heels for four months on end isn't so charming an experience that I should care to provoke a repetition of it." ("Why on earth do I tell her all this?" Lyon asked himself, with secret self-contempt. "My misfortunes can't possibly interest her; and I've no right to wish that they should.") "So Travers has been called away suddenly? No bad news, I hope?"

"Oh, no! only some business matter. He had to go over to Savona for the day."

"Rather hard on him—in the midst of his holiday."

"Very hard, I think. He asked me to tell you how sorry he was to have to put off Baiardo once more. There seems a fate against that expedition coming off."

"There does. All the more reason why we should insist on carrying out the plan. I don't approve of giving way to destiny."

"Perhaps you don't believe in destiny?"

"Oh, yes, I do! I should be a stiff-necked infidel indeed if I didn't. Destiny has beaten me so often that I was long ago forced to believe in her—and to respect her, too. But it's always well to fight her as long as one can. How's my young friend Robin?"

"He's very well, thank you; and so is Dolly. They will soon

be home from their walk, if you—— But I forgot!" Dorothy interrupted herself. "You don't like children."

"I never said so, Mrs. Travers."

"Something very like it, Mr. Lyon."

"I beg your pardon! I said I didn't *understand* children—quite a different thing. Understanding and liking are not synonymous terms, believe me. Some of the grown people I like best have always remained more or less of a sealed book to my understanding. And in other cases—where I have succeeded in breaking the seals—I am sorry to say ' better knowledge ' has not by any means invariably conduced to ' dearer love.' Again armed with a book, I see!"—abruptly changing the subject, after a scarcely perceptible pause. "You seem to have become a great reader."

"I was always fond of reading," Dorothy said. "But I didn't always prefer it to every other occupation."

"And now—you do?"

"Decidedly. There is nothing in the world—at least, so I find as I get older—that takes one so completely and satisfactorily out of one's self."

There was a momentary flash of intelligence and sympathy—or was it satisfaction?—in Lyon's eyes. Then he dropped his eyelids in the old fashion, and observed lazily:

"It's always an advantage to get rid of one's own company, even for an hour or two. But you must be singularly fortunate in your choice of books if you often find one that will do so much for you. I think I shall beg the favor of a copy of your old library lists! May I ask what you are engaged upon just now?"

She handed him the volume she had been reading when he came; a copy of "Amiel's Journal," in the original French.

Lyon frowned thoughtfully at the title-page.

"Do you care greatly for this book?" he enquired, with one of his startling direct looks straight into her face.

"I can hardly tell you, as yet. I only began it this morning; I don't suppose I have read much more than a dozen pages——"

"Would you think me very impertinent if I advised you to stop short here—not to go beyond the dozen pages?"

"Not at all. But why——" with a touch of hesitation.

"For this reason. You'll not be any the happier for reading what follows."

"Is the book so—harmful, then?"

"Not in the ordinary acceptation of the term. It doesn't inculcate immoral doctrines, that's to say—unless the doctrine that nothing in life is worth while may be considered immoral."

"What do *you* think ?" Dorothy asked.

"I ? I'm no authority. No man is fit to pronounce on the morality of a principle he holds himself, especially if he in any sort acts up to it. But this I will say : Knowing the fruits of that faith by experience, I don't wish to see it making fresh converts among my friends. One may believe a creed to be perfectly sound—and yet be quite without desire to propagate it."

"I see," replied Dorothy, putting "Amiel" aside, and taking a small half-knitted sock from her work-basket. "I see also," she added after a minute, when she had brought her needles into play, "that you still retain your old fancy for painting yourself and your opinions as black as possible. In that respect you have not changed at all——"

"However much in others ?" Lyon put in, as she stopped short, becoming suddenly conscious that her half-completed phrase was susceptible of an uncivil interpretation. "Ah !" he went on, with a lightness that did honor to his powers of dissimulation, seeing that never in his life had he felt less inclined for levity than at that moment ; "Travers was a little too hasty with his compliments the other day at San Lorenzo ! Poor fellow ! I saw it was a dreadful shock to him the first time he beheld my uncovered head. Nothing like a hat—especially a straw hat "—touching the article in question, which he was carefully balancing on his knee —"for giving one a spurious appearance of juvenility !"

"The Indian climate——" Mrs. Travers suggested.

"Thanks. It's very nice of you to put it in that way." Lyon drew his hand though his half-grizzled locks—the top of his head was certainly getting very gray—with a mock sigh. "The Indian climate is doubtless chiefly responsible for the transformation. And then, I believe mine is the kind of hair that always 'turns early'—at least I am in the habit of laying that flattering unction to the soul of my wounded vanity. Hark ! don't I hear your young people's voices ? That is surely Master Robin's pipe——"

Dorothy's knitting-needles dropped into her lap ; with them went her company manner, her conventional smile. Her whole face changed, brightened, became gradually illuminated with a radiancy of expectation. "How she worships these children !"

thought the man watching her, with a throb of unreasoning jealousy.

She had not long to wait and listen. A moment, and Robin burst, as it appeared, out of the heart of a clump of oranges, flew up the steep bank to his mother's side, and began to pant out :

" Oh, mother, will you please come——"

" Gently, sonnie ! " Dorothy interrupted him. " Don't you see Mr. Lyon ? Say ' how do you do ' to him before you tell me any-thing. And, Robin, dear, you should try to remember that the padrone does not like you to rush about among his orange-trees in that wild way."

" I'm very sorry, mummy, dear—I forgot. How do you do, Mr. Lyon ? " And Robin, having hastily extended a small hot hand to the visitor, returned once more to his mother's side. " May I tell now, mother ? "

" Yes, boy; certainly."

" Well, you know you gave me some money to spend at Naldi's. But we met a little beggar girl, quite in rags, and without any shoes, and she said her mother was blind, and Dolly hadn't any money, of course, and Jane hadn't any, either—and I was so sorry for her, so I gave her all my *soldi*——"

" That was quite right, dear," Dorothy said encouragingly, as the young narrator paused for want of breath.

" But we've been talking to Carlo, the porter, since we came in, and we told him about the little girl, and he says he knows her quite well, and she isn't a nice little girl at all, and her mother isn't blind a bit ! And I want my *soldi* back, and Jane won't ask the little girl for them. Won't you come and ask her for them, mummy, dear ? She's only out in the road, just at the bottom of the steps. Do come, please ! "

Dorothy's face had grown grave. " No, Robin, I can't ask for your *soldi*. Nobody ought ever to ask for things back they have once given away. It would not be right—and it would be very unkind to this poor little girl——"

" But Carlo says she is a very naughty little girl ! "

" All the more reason why you should try to help her, perhaps."

This was much too profound philosophy for Robin, who stood for a moment silent, leaning on the back of his mother's chair, and swinging one foot to and fro, with a puzzled expression of counte-nance. Then he burst out hotly :

"It was all Dolly's fault—she wanted me to give my pennies to the little girl. I wish I'd kept them, and bought those lead soldiers in Naldi's window. I only gave up because I thought her mother was blind. They're *lovely* soldiers. Or I might have got a new knife."

"If I were you," Mr. Lyon remarked, "I'd try to put soldiers and knives out of my head—till I had some more *soldi*."

"But why can't I have those *soldi* back?" Robin demanded with passion. "I *want* them back. Mummy, do come and speak to the little girl, and make her give me my money, please!"

"No, Robin; certainly not." Dorothy's tone was almost severe. She had flushed deeply during the last minute or two; she looked both annoyed and distressed. "I should not think of doing such a thing. It was your own choice giving this money away; you know I never ask you to give your money to poor people. But it's a very shameful thing to give money, and then want to take it back again. Let me hear no more of this. Run away to Jane, I see her in the garden with Dolly, and don't talk any more about it."

"Poor little chap!" ejaculated Lyon compassionately, as the boy went slowly and sulkily down the incline he had run up so eagerly a few minutes earlier.

"He is a very impulsive child," she responded—and there was an undertone of sadness in her voice. "And his impulses are mostly generous. Only, unfortunately, as you see, they don't last."

"You can't expect seven years old to reckon the cost of its sacrifices very accurately beforehand. For the matter of that, older people than my friend Robin have been known to sacrifice their lead soldiers to the calls of benevolence in a fit of short-lived enthusiasm—and then clamor to have them back again. Personally, I believe there's nothing mankind is so prone to regret as its virtuous actions. Especially when they fail to bear any ostensible fruit."

"I dare say you are right," Dorothy answered, in a rather subdued voice.

Something in her fashion of uttering the commonplace phrase caused Lyon to glance at her swiftly, from under his eyelashes. Was she convinced that *her* sacrifice had been a fruitless one? had she arrived at the point of acknowledging the correctness of those predictions of failure with which he had threatened her in Guernsey nine years before ? Her face gave him no clear and unmistakable answer to these questions. But, like her tone, it sent a sudden pang of suspicion into his soul ; it pierced him with a sharp doubt of his first hasty judgment. What if this woman's serenity were, in truth, quite artificial ? or, at best, merely skin-deep ? What if all Dorothy Temple's old capacity for feeling and suffering lay, not by any means extinguished, but simply hidden away under the Parisian gowns and smooth, self-possessed manners of Mrs. Brian Travers ? The idea was one which he felt it unwise to pursue under his companion's eye. He returned, with an effort, to the subject of Robin.

"Now, I should like to know, as a matter of curiosity," he said interrogatively, "whether you would consider it an immoral proceeding to replace those *soldi?* or devise some other means by which your son might have his lead soldiers in spite of all ? "

Dorothy laughed. "I should call it misleading rather than immoral."

"And how misleading ? "

"Isn't it to mislead a child to let him think he can go back upon his actions ? or wipe out their consequences, as he would wipe out a figure on his slate ? "

"I had no idea"—Lyon's tone was slightly sarcastic—"that your philosophy of life was of so stern a character."

"Do you believe in the wiping-out process, then ? " enquired Dorothy, with her prettiest—and least expressive—smile.

"No, I don't," replied Lyon bluntly, with a touch of irritation in his manner—getting up and putting on his hat as he spoke. "On the contrary, I believe that, once set down a wrong figure in your sum, it remains a factor of the sum to the end of time. You may introduce other modifying factors, you may add to the figure, or subtract from it, but you'll never succeed in wholly neutralizing it, and its effect will always appear in your final result. Oh, I don't for a moment impugn the correctness of your theory. If there's one truth experience establishes before all others, it is this—that every man must bear the burden of his own mistakes. Only it seems to me—if you'll excuse my saying so—a little early to begin impressing that sort of truth upon your son."

"Don't the copy-books tell us that ' truth cannot be learned too early ' ? " gayly retorted Dorothy. "Are you going ? " for her visitor was holding out a sun-burned hand. "Shall you attempt Baiardo alone ? "

"No; I think I shall give up Baiardo for to-day, and content myself with something less ambitious by way of a walk—something within Sebright's marching powers. That is to say, if I get back to the hotel in time to catch him before he goes off on some expedition of his own devising."

CHAPTER IV

IN A DESERTED GARDEN

"They told me she was sad that day
(Though wherefore tell what love's sooth say
Sooner than they did register ?)
And my heart leapt and wept to her,
And yet I did not speak nor stir."

LYON did not succeed in his attempt to "catch" Captain Sebright. When he got back to his own hotel it was to find his friend flown to Monte Carlo ; from which alluring scene of dissipation the young man returned only toward dinner-time—with an empty purse and a torturing headache.

"Serves you right," growled Lyon unfeelingly, when he had shut the *persiennes* of their common sitting-room, and supplied his suffering companion, who had thrown himself down miserably on the one sofa adorning that modest apartment, with a sufficiency of pillows. "How could you be such a madman as to expose that head of yours to this glaring sun ? to say nothing of the abominable heat of those stifling rooms. You may think yourself precious lucky if you haven't got a fresh stroke. At best, you are bound to have stirred up all the old mischief."

"Don't be too down on a fellow. I *was* a fool for going, I know. I knew it before I'd spent an hour in the confounded place. But one doesn't like to own one's self so easily beaten ; it's humiliating," said Sebright, closing his eyes with a stifled groan.

"So you held on till you couldn't stand any longer, I suppose ? "

"Well, I was pretty bad before I beat a retreat. I was so blind and dizzy I couldn't walk straight. I'm certain the officials at the Casino thought I was drunk, and were in two minds about arresting me, and I hardly know how I should have got away at all but for Brian Travers."

"Brian Travers?" ejaculated Lyon. "Was *he* at Monte Carlo to-day?"

"Luckily for me—yes. What a good-natured fellow it is! He even forsook his American charmer—by the way, there's a lively flirtation going on in that quarter; I advise your friend Mrs. Travers to keep her eye on the volatile Brian—he actually left his lady temporarily in the lurch to see me safely into my train. By the way, I got to Ventimiglia——"

"Was Travers playing?" asked Lyon, interrupting Sebright's narrative without ceremony.

"I saw him staking a few five-franc pieces early in the day—no more. He seemed too much absorbed in the other game to take any serious interest in roulette. She's an uncommonly pretty woman, let me tell you, that Mrs. M'Allan. Don't know when I've seen such coloring. By the way, didn't Travers give you the slip to-day? Weren't you to have done a tramp together?"

"Yes, to Baiardo. I understood he had been called to Savona on business," returned Lyon, whose countenance had gathered considerable blackness while Sebright was speaking.

"So, apparently, did his wife." Sebright laughed a little faintly. "I'm afraid Master Brian is not so straightforward as he might be. All the same, I am sorry my incautious remarks should be the means of involving him in domestic unpleasantness—as will be the case, I fear. And yet I put my foot in it so innocently! I honestly thought to make myself agreeable to the lady by dilating on her lord's good-nature."

"You met Mrs. Travers just now?" Lyon interrupted again.

"On my way up here from the station, worse luck!"

"And you told her you had met Travers at Monte Carlo? What a blockhead you are, Sebright!"

Sebright looked considerably surprised, and a trifle offended, by this outspoken expression of opinion on his companion's part. "No doubt," he returned rather dryly. "Still, a wiser man, you yourself even, might, under the same circumstances, have committed the same blunder. How the dickens was I to guess that Travers had been giving his wife a false address for this particular afternoon? I repeat that I'm sorry to have been the means of getting him into trouble. No doubt Mrs. Travers will have an effective scene ready rehearsed for his return to-night; but, if you consider the matter impartially, he really has only himself to blame in the matter. Men shouldn't tell lies—especially to their wives

—unless they want to be found out, sooner or later. That's all I have to say," concluded Sebright, closing his eyes once more with an injured air.

He need not have regretted his involuntary betrayal of Brian even thus much—at least as far as that gentleman himself was concerned. No "scene" awaited Mr. Travers on his return to the domestic hearth ; indeed, several days elapsed before Dorothy made any allusion at all to the revelation which Sebright's fluent gratitude had been the means of making to her. Perhaps she remained silent in the hope that her husband might involuntarily confess the truth, and so spare her the humiliation of accusing him; perhaps, the situation being one with which she was already unhappily familiar, it was sheer despairing disgust that forbade her to utter either an enquiry or a reproach. Strictly as she had trained herself, for some years past, not only to suppress every outward sign of strong feeling, but to strangle every secret movement toward it, steadily as she had forced herself to live upon the surface of things, scarcely ever venturing out of the safe shallows of an artificial existence into the deep, dangerous sea of genuine thought and emotion, there were, even now, moments when the old nature within her would persist in reasserting itself in fierce indignation, passionate discontent, and a sickening sense of unendurable shame.

Possibly she might never have referred to the deception practised upon her at all had not Brian himself provoked her to the reference. But when he spoke vaguely, one evening after dinner, of a call that would take him away from San Remo on the morrow, it was hardly in human nature, certainly not in feminine and wifely human nature, to refrain from the obvious retort :

" To Monte Carlo, I suppose ? "

She spoke very quietly—albeit conscious of a horrible tightening of her throat as she forced out the words.

Brian gave a slight, irrepressible start. " Well, yes; it's to Monte Carlo I—thought of going. But why did you jump to that conclusion ? "

Before she could reply to the question he realized that he had been a fool for putting it. He realized the painful truth even more fully when her reply came, measured and deliberate :

" Probably because I was informed that you were there last Wednesday, when I believed you to be at Savona." Up to this moment Dorothy had continued to draw her needle in and out of the work in her hand ; now she laid both down upon her knee, and turned her face, which was a good deal paler than usual, toward her husband. "I can't quite make out, Brian, why you should have wished to deceive me in this matter. And I think, if you reflect a little, you'll recognize that it's hardly seemly outsiders should learn that you keep me purposely in the dark as to your movements."

"I am sure I don't know why I didn't tell you I might perhaps go to Monte Carlo instead of Savona on Wednesday," responded Brian, speaking even more quickly than usual, to cover his embarrassment. "I supppose because I fancied you would take it into your head that I went to Monte Carlo to gamble—which is not the case. I don't care a brass farthing for play; I've never staked more than a napoleon or two at the tables in my life. I run over to the place simply because it's bright and amusing, and a place where one feels certain of meeting people one knows. It's not my fault that I go there alone. I should be only too glad to take you with me. But you are always tied hand and foot to the children."

"You would not like me to neglect the children ?" Dorothy was conscious of defending herself feebly. But this sudden turning of the tables upon her by her husband had, metaphorically speaking, taken away her breath.

"Certainly not. I merely protest against your devoting your whole time and thoughts to them. A man naturally looks for a little of his wife's society—even when she happens to have two children."

Dorothy bent her head once more over her work, saying nothing. She was no fool. If not a clever woman, she was at least a clear-sighted one ; she had never felt for her husband that overwhelming love which can blind the most intense keenness of insight ; and eight years of married life had furnished her with abundant proofs that his ease- and pleasure-loving nature would stoop to any ignoble shift or sham with the utmost readiness rather than face even the passing breath of a domestic storm : therefore she knew in her heart that Brian's main object in his counter-complaint was to create a diversion in his own favor, and that he was not in reality so anxious for her company as he affected to be for the moment. At the same time, her conscience, very tender where he was concerned, would not allow her to dispute altogether the justice of his grievance. It was true that, while still loyally endeavoring to make his home pleasant to him, she

18

had, of late years, gradually excused herself more and more, on the plea of the children's need of her, from accompanying him in any pleasure-seeking expedition outside it. Had she failed in her duty in so doing?

She turned the question over in her mind for the next two hours. Lonely hours they were, for Brian, finding, to his great relief, that she had no apparent intention of pursuing the subject previously in hand, presently took himself off for the remainder of the evening to the smoking-room, bearing with him the comfortable consciousness of having had the last word. When he came upstairs again, toward midnight, he was surprised to find her still sitting at work in the same place.

"Yes, I waited on purpose; I wanted to speak to you," was her rejoinder to his half-uttered exclamation of astonishment. She began rolling up her embroidery as she spoke, and her manner showed a mixture of nervousness and determination. "I have been thinking over what you said just after dinner."

"Oh! Well, I hope you see now that I didn't speak quite without reason," responded Brian, judging that he would probably do wisely to maintain the *rôle* of the injured party a little longer.

The undertone of unreality which, to her ear, was audible in this speech, jarred upon Dorothy, but she managed by an effort to control her irritation.

"I believe you are right in saying that I give up too much time to the children," she resumed steadily. "I am afraid I have seemed inconsiderate for you—and I am sorry. For the future you'll find me ready to do differently. I will consider your convenience more, and go about with you as much as you please."

"That will be famous!" Brian responded. He strove to speak with the utmost heartiness; but he could not quite keep down a note of uneasiness in his voice. "It will be quite like old times, won't it? And some gadding would do you good; it's a shame you should waste all your pretty looks and pretty frocks on an admiring audience of one—though you'll get no more sincere admirer out of doors," giving her shoulder a caressing pat. "I wish I could ask you to begin turning over the new leaf to-morrow; but I suppose that would hardly do, as the party is to be such a small one, and you don't know the people yet."

"Who are the people?" enquired Dorothy, gently releasing her shoulder from her husband's hand.

"Oh, those Americans I've often talked to you about! I don't

you remember? Their name's Warrener—most amusing people.
Strictly speaking, this dinner is given by Mrs. M'Allan, Mrs.
Warrener's sister—but they're all travelling together, as one
party. I must introduce you to them at the earliest opportunity;
I know you'd like them immensely. And Mrs. M'Allan was saying, only the other day, how much she wished to make your
acquaintance."

Nevertheless, Mrs. M'Allan did not send Dorothy any invitation
by her husband the following night; and, though Brian made
several further flying excursions to Monte Carlo in the course of
the next ten days, he continued to make them alone. Sometimes
he told his wife where he was going, sometimes he did not—
according to circumstances—and the new leaf remained unturned.

Lyon, meeting Mrs. Travers from time to time in the streets of
the town, or on the Berigo road, and noting the look of anxiety
that was becoming habitual to her eyes, the hardening of all the
lines of her mouth, when, in answer to his easy—" Brian's off for
the day, I think?" she would reply briefly, "Yes, he has gone
over to Monte Carlo," wondered whether any hint of the gossip
current in San Remo concerning Brian's growing infatuation for
the fascinating American "grass-widow" could have reached her
ears? It might be that some officious female friend had held it
her duty to report the flying rumors to Brian's wife; it might be
that her own clear-sightedness had, unassisted, given her insight
into the true character of the attraction which drew her husband so
often across the French frontier. That she had some inkling of
the actual state of affairs Lyon felt convinced.

The limit originally fixed for his stay in San Remo was now
close at hand, and he found himself, somewhat to his disgust,
regretting the fact. He was conscious of an ignoble longing to
linger on a little while—if only in order to witness the further
development of the domestic drama which had excited his interest.
He recognized the existence of this, his discreditable desire, and,
with his usual cynical frankness, made full acknowledgment of its
unworthiness to himself; but he did not carry his cynicism so far
as to propose to yield to it. When Sebright observed interrogatively, "I suppose you'll be ready to move on Thursday?" he
assented with apparent nonchalance. And if he did not join with
any particular animation in the discussion which his companion
subsequently initiated, on the comparative merits of the various
stopping-places at which they might conveniently halt on their

homeward journey, he at least allowed Sebright to thrash the
subject out without interrupting him.

It having been finally agreed that the pair should travel straight
through to Paris, and put up there for the next ten days, Sebright, who was getting eager to remove to an atmosphere more
lively than that of San Remo, and felt it prudent to strike while
the iron was hot—for he had anticipated some objection on Lyon's
part to his Parisian plan, and feared that, were that gentleman
left to reflect upon it for any length of time, he might even now
back out of his acquiescence—offered to write at once and engage
rooms; and Lyon accepted his offer. Then he lighted a cigar,
strolled out of the hotel garden filled with a laughing, chattering,
flirting crowd, for it was the hour after dinner, and so mild a
night that scarce a soul had remained within doors, and, taking a
rough path that led upward through an olive plantation, presently
emerged upon the Berigo road. There he turned his face westward, following the road in its windings round the face of the
hill downward to the sea.

For some time he tramped steadily on, encountering no living
soul by the way. Now and then he would pass a white villa with
closed *persiennes* showing black in the moonlight—for the moon
was in its first quarter, and shed a steady flood of illumination on
his surroundings ; or the palisades of a garden, screened for the
most part from sight by graceful pepper-trees or drooping boughs
of the eucalyptus, but within which he would perhaps catch a
passing glimpse of some young active figure flitting ghost-like
among the orange and lemon bushes, while a child's voice would
ring out momentarily on the quiet air. But at length even these
evidences of human life were left behind, and the way lay
between close-serried ranks of olives and pines on the one hand,
and a deep, lonely, and thickly wooded ravine on the other. To
the extreme right, beyond and far above the ravine, rose a long
hog-backed hill, tree-clothed from base to summit, crowned by a
little group of twinkling lights marking the tiny hill town of
Colla ; in front, some hundreds of feet below, the moonbeams
shimmered on the pale purple expanse of the Mediterranean. A
great calm was over sea and land ; not a ripple stirred on the
placid waters, not a leaf rustled in the silent woods—which per-
fumed all the quiet air with a subtle bouquet of spring odors, a compound fragrance to which pine, violet, narcissus, and a score of other
sweet and pungent-smelling things had all contributed ingredients.

Presently a new, delicious scent, at once more overpoweringly
sweet and less complex in its sweetness than the subtle essence of
spring which had accompanied him for half a mile, assailed Lyon's
nostrils—assailed them so strongly that he stopped and looked
about him curiously to see whence it came. His curiosity was
quickly gratified. He had, a moment before, come abreast of a
lonely, unoccupied villa, perched, far away from all its fellows, on
the left of the road ; a small, low-roofed, one-storied building,
scarcely bigger than a cottage, covered with flowering creepers,
and surrounded by a garden of some size—it was from this garden
that the scent, which he now recognized as the scent of heliotrope, was proceeding. He remembered having noticed, in some
previous daylight walk past the place, that heliotrope grew in its
neglected flower-beds like a weed.

" Pity so much sweetness should waste itself wholly on the desert
air ! " he thought to himself. " I have more than half a mind to
a little petty larceny."

He pushed the already half-open gate a little farther back on its
rusty hinges, and went in. The heliotrope was everywhere ;
clothing the posts of the veranda which ran round two sides of
the house, and straggling over its roof, looking in at the French
windows of the ground-floor rooms, lying across the weed-grown
paths, half-choking the rose-bushes which filled the borders—a
wealth of unclaimed sweetness most alluring to the predatory
instinct of the passer-by. Lyon, though he professed to care but
little for flowers, felt his predatory instinct so strongly aroused
by the sight that without hesitation he put out his hand to take of
the profusion surrounding him. But he very quickly drew it back
again, empty of spoil. Like the hero of a moral story-book, he
perceived that his intended crime would not go unwitnessed.

Sitting under the veranda, a child at her feet, was a woman—
presumably the wife of the caretaker or proprietor of the villa.
Lyon, made fearful by an accusing conscience, and anxious to
disarm suspicion, hastily summoned his scanty stock of Italian to
his aid, and, politely lifting his hat to the lady, wished her good-
evening—adding a would-be careless remark on the fineness of the
night.

For answer, a familiar little figure in a white sun-bonnet jumped
up and ran toward him, crying, " Mr. Lyon ! Mr. Lyon ! "—and
Dorothy Travers rose to her feet under the veranda, saying,
" How do you do ? You see, we are trespassing, like yourself."

Shaking off, as well as he could, all signs of the somewhat unreasonable amazement he felt at her sudden apparition, he went forward and shook hands with her. Her hand felt strangely cold ; her face was very pale, and wore a look of intense weariness. But she made shift to summon her usual smile as she observed, " Isn't this a charming wilderness ? "

" Most charming. I doubt, though, if you are wise in enjoying its charms at such a late hour. If you sit here much longer, you will probably take a chill—always supposing you have not taken one already."

" Oh, I never take chills ! " was Dorothy's confident answer. " I am immensely strong."

" H'm !—you don't look so strikingly robust at this moment. Indeed, if· you were anyone else, I should say you looked ill. But since your absolute hardiness is an article of faith with you, I suppose I mustn't venture that."

" I am not ill, truly ! " Dorothy interposed earnestly. " I confess, though, that I am tired, very tired." She sank down into her former seat as though she were, indeed, too weary to stand a single moment longer. " A party of people from Monte Carlo— some friends of my husband's—have been spending the day with us, and of course I had to show them all the lions; and it was so hot ! I own I felt a good deal inclined to collapse befòre the day was over."

Lyon guessed what had happened. Brian's American charmer —moved, perhaps, by a not unnatural curiosity concerning the personality of the woman she was doing her best to rob ; perhaps by a baser desire to triumph over the wife by exhibiting to her her rightful property yoked to her rival's conquering car—had expressed a sudden fancy to spend a day at San Remo in Mrs. Travers' company ; and Brian had been too weak or too infatuated to resist her caprice. Thence, as a natural result, long hours of galling humiliation for Dorothy, and of bold assertion of her empire on Mrs. M'Allan's part. Lyon had heard enough, during the past fortnight, from various impartial witnesses touching Mrs. M'Allan, a lady whose main ambition seemed to be, not so much the actual acquisition of power over the stronger sex, as the display of this power, when gained, to an admiring world, to credit her with any amount of audacity and cruelty in such circumstances. The estimate he had formed of her on report had been a decidedly unfavorable one ; the mere fact of her visit to

Travers' wife confirmed him in his unflattering opinion. As to his present estimate of Brian Travers—well, it was one he would have found it difficult to express in polite language.

No one, however, could have suspected that he had divined a painful secret behind Dorothy's commonplace words, or that every fibre of his body was tingling with a passion of indignation, as he rejoined, in the coolest and most indifferent manner possible :

" Lionizing strangers is galley-slaves' work ; I know nothing so exhausting. Never, while I live, shall I forget an experience I enjoyed as showman in Benares. A distant cousin of mine, gifted with a Herculean physique and an enquiring intellect, came to visit me. He was twenty-five years old ; he had read an immense number of books on the history of India ; he had studied Oriental archæology; he took an interest in irrigation works: and he wanted to know why about everything he saw. He was all but the death of me ; but then he stayed a fortnight. You are less severely tried—I conclude your visitors have already departed ? "

" Yes. They left by the eight o'clock train." Dorothy, who, for the last moment or two, had been pulling at a loose spray of heliotrope which hung down from the roof of the veranda, here broke the spray off and crushed it in her hand. " How sweet this smells, doesn't it ? " she said, abruptly leaving the subject of her visitors.

" It was the scent that drew me inside the gate—with half-formed intentions of plunder," Lyon confessed. " Do you want a bit ? "—to Dolly, who, reseated at her mother's feet, was putting up imploring fat hands for the treasure just visible between Dorothy's fingers. " Here you are, then ! " breaking off a cluster the size of a small branch, and dropping it into the child's lap. " Don't disturb yourself "—to Dorothy, who had made an involuntary movement of remonstrance. " No moral harm done, I assure you. At that age one isn't troubled with ideas about the rights of property. What delicious stuff it is ! "—recklessly pulling down another cluster. " The only pleasant thing I can remember in that God-forsaken place Creyke was the climbing heliotrope in the conservatory. The house and gardens were capable of improvement, though. I hear John Lewin has improved them out of all knowledge."

" Will he carry on your improvements ; the reforms you had set on foot in the village ? "

"It would be more correct if you were to say the reforms I vainly attempted to set on foot. No, I hardly think my cousin will be likely to repeat my mistakes; he is too practical a man. I am told that he expressed unqualified disapproval from the first of my cottage-building scheme."

"That must have made it hard to yield your place to him—for you had grown interested in your miners, hadn't you?" Dorothy spoke with a touch of genuine eagerness.

"Yes," Lyon admitted reluctantly; "I must confess that, once we were engaged in a stand-up fight, I began to feel a certain interest in those chaps—they fought so pluckily. And then my credit was concerned in the matter; one doesn't like being beaten by one's own *employés*. So, the more bent they showed themselves on taking their own way, the more anxious I became to persuade them to go mine. I fancy obstinacy survives all other vices—in the majority of mankind."

"I believe," Dorothy said after a moment, ignoring the half-contemptuous self-criticism of her companion's concluding sentence—"I believe I have never yet said how sorry I was to—to find you——"

"Playing the part of the *Disinherited?* Thanks—though I don't know that there's much to be sorry for. It's generally agreed—isn't it ?—that a man is really the better off for having to work for his living. Not that I profess any enthusiastic personal faith in the doctrine," Lyon added. "Personally, I hate work—the work I live by, that's to say."

"And that is——"

"Engineering, of course. I know no other trade."

"And your other work ? You spoke as if there were some other—which you did *not* hate ?"

"Merely play-work, so far—whether it ever takes on a more serious complexion remains yet to be seen. More cherry-pie, Miss Dolly ? All the first helping gone already ? Well, here you are again ; but try to be moderate—we must leave something for the poor proprietor, I suppose."

"But this play-work of yours, as you call it ?" Dorothy seemed to have been suddenly attacked by a severe fit of curiosity. "Perhaps, though," she added quickly, "I ought not to ask—I beg your pardon."

"Pray, don't ! The thing is not of such importance that I should make any mystery about it," responded Lyon, with a shade of annoyance in his tone, nevertheless. "I've merely taken it into my head to add one more to the heap of would-be instructive tomes under which the reading world is already groaning. If ever I can find time to write it, that's to say."

"A book on India?"

"Oh, of course! Every man who goes to India makes some highly important and perfectly novel discovery in relation to that remarkable country; generally, within six months of landing at Bombay, he has formulated an able and ingenious theory for its government on quite new and original lines. I am no better than my fellows. I have made my discovery and formulated my theory, and now I thirst to lay my exposition of both before an intelligent British public," Lyon concluded, with a queer little smile.

Again Dorothy ignored his note of self-mockery. "I believe you are heartily in earnest about the writing of this book," was her grave answering remark, uttered in a tone which seemed to rebuke and challenge him at once.

He replied to the challenge with complete frankness. "Strange to say, I believe I am. I caught myself, only yesterday, to my own profound astonishment, formulating a wish that I might live to finish it."

"Why, have you any fear—any expectation——"

Lyon struck in deftly: "Of quitting this mortal scene at an early date? By no means. But, seeing that I can only afford to write in play-hours—there being at present no very keen competition between the principal publishing-houses for the honor of bringing out this great work when completed—it's likely to be a good while on the stocks, you perceive."

"That is a pity."

"Ah, I don't know! The pleasure of writing it is prolonged for me—and the pain of trying to read it is deferred for the public; not a bad arrangement, on the whole."

"How long has it been on the stocks already?"

"A matter of three or four years."

"And when you go back to India—— I suppose the book is the great argument for your going back at all, isn't it?"

"Hardly. I've got together all the material I know how to make use of; I could easily finish putting it into shape over here —supposing that I were at the same time sure of getting bread and cheese. But in Europe I should be pretty sure of *not* getting them, so I can't stay in Europe. Not that I particularly want to stay. In many ways, India isn't at all a bad country to live in."

There was a moment's silence. Dorothy thoughtfully caressed Dolly's yellow head, which the child—who had been singularly quiet for some moments past—was resting sleepily against her mother's knee.

"Have you ever talked much about India to Brian—to my husband?" she asked abruptly.

"No," answered Lyon, evidently a trifle surprised by the unexpected question. "Not that I remember."

"You haven't said much to him in praise of the life out there?"

"As far as I can recollect, not a single word. You mustn't suppose that I am so deeply enamored of the country as to be always sounding its praises," Lyon added, suddenly guessing the motive that had prompted her enquiries. "I could find plenty to say in its disparagement—if you prefer that Brian should hear it disparaged. You think he has still some hankering after an Indian appointment? But I understood from himself that, in deference to your wishes, he had quite abandoned the idea."

"I know! I know!" she responded hurriedly. "And he thought—he still thinks—he has given up the notion. But sometimes he—he works round again to plans he has discarded—you know he is impulsive by nature. So I am always afraid he might change his mind again. And then I should either have to leave the children behind with strangers, or let him go out by himself for the first few years."

Lyon's reply was unexpectedly prompt and to the point. "Disagreeable alternatives. But you would choose the first, no doubt, if ever you had to choose at all?"

He saw her face harden visibly in the moonlight. "I cannot say," she answered, with a little catch in her breath. "The children need me so very much at present. Brian could do without me for a while better than they."

"I rather doubt that, Mrs. Travers—if you'll excuse my rudeness in contradicting you. You don't know India—or Indian life. There's no place in the world—I speak advisedly—where a man stands so much in need of his wife, and of all the help his wife can give him."

Lyon spoke almost harshly. Doubtless the constraint he was

putting upon himself at the moment helped to make his manner of speech unusually stern. Perhaps he was conscious of having assumed a somewhat unwarrantable tone, for he immediately added, at once much more kindly and less seriously, "But I hope you'll never have any choice of the kind to make. You may trust me to paint the entire Peninsula in the blackest possible hues to Brian the very next time I chance to meet him."

"Thank you"—mechanically. "I believe"—shaking off the abstraction which had fallen upon her during the last two or three minutes—"we ought to be going home; it must be very late. I ought not to have kept this child out so long; see, she is more than half asleep! Come, Dolly, my pet! wake up, and come home."

"You will let me see you safely back?" Lyon suggested. "I believe the Berigo is not absolutely safe after nightfall; and, as you are alone——"

"Thanks, I am not going back by the Berigo," she interrupted him quickly. "If the road had been our only way home, I shouldn't have felt justified in lingering here so late. But there's a path through our padrone's olive-garden, which starts from that wicket"—pointing to a rude gate in the hedge bounding the farther side of the garden—"and leads straight to the back door of the hotel. So you see we run no risks. Thanks very much, all the same. Good-night. Dolly, say good-night to Mr. Lyon."

Dolly, now thoroughly awake and ready for action, obeyed; then she suffered herself to be led off without resistance. For a while after she and her mother, leaving the moonlit garden of sweet scents and Mr. Lyon, standing with the wicket-gate in his hand, behind them, had passed into the dusky shadow of the olive-grove, where the moonbeams shimmered mysteriously between motionless leaves on gnarled trunks and fantastically contorted branches, she held fast to Dorothy's hand, a little overawed, no doubt, by the semi-darkness and strange unfamiliarity of her surroundings. But her awe was not long-lived. Soon, reassured, she began to prattle volubly of one thing and another; and, at length, catching sight of a colony of glow-worms a few yards in advance, pulled her small fingers with a cry of delight from Dorothy's hold, and scampered eagerly forward. Her mother instantly hurried after and recaptured her.

"Don't run away to-night, my sweet," she said coaxingly. "Keep close to mother, and hold her hand all the while, there's a good little child.   It's so dark, little Dolly, so very, very dark——"

Dolly yielded to this appeal—there had been far more of appeal than of command in Dorothy's tone—without demur, and, replacing her hand in her mother's, walked soberly beside her the rest of the way.   That there had been something strange in this appeal, or in her mother's manner of making it, would seem, however, to have impressed itself upon her childish mind, for she presently looked up and demanded, with a seriousness which showed that she had been inwardly revolving the question for some minutes :

" Mummy, are you 'fraid of the dark ?   'Cause I'm not 'fraid, you know ; and I'll take care of you."

Dorothy stooped and kissed her suddenly.   But she made no reply.

" *Are* you 'fraid ? " persisted the child.   " *Do* you want me to take care of you ? "

Dorothy's hand closed more tightly upon the little fingers clinging to hers.   " Yes," she said, almost under her breath.   " I think I am a little afraid, Dolly—just a little.   And I want you to take care of me, very much."

CHAPTER V

NIGHT AND MORNING

"When I can forget—then ask me to forgive."

LYON did not, after all, leave San Remo on the Thursday originally fixed for his departure—for the simple reason that, until the Monday following, no rooms were to be had in the over-full Paris hotels, crowded even beyond their wont in this early May-time.   The circumstance gave him no pleasure, however.   Now that he was perforce constrained to put off his journey, he chafed against the necessity for delay, as he had previously, in secret, chafed against Sebright's unreasonable eagerness to get to the French capital at as early a date as possible.   He felt keenly that there was something contemptible, something weakly feminine, in this illogical change of mental attitude on his own part, but he remained none the less anxious to be gone.

He had some excuse for finding the last days of his sojourn on the Riviera wearisome. All his books and manuscripts had, in view of an earlier start, been packed at the beginning of the week ; it was hardly worth while to unpack them again, yet their entombment left him almost wholly without resources. He had made no friends among the English at San Remo; he had already exhausted every excursion which the neighborhood afforded ; and Monte Carlo, the ordinary refuge of the bored Briton under his circumstances, held no attractions for him, who could neither afford to play himself, nor cared to watch others engaged, hour after hour, in a game which, however exciting it may prove to the players, is notoriously uninteresting to the mere spectator destitute of five-franc pieces. So he could only while away his time by means of solitary rambles among the olives—solitary, for Sebright, who, unlike himself, had made friends innumerable, was fully occupied during these last days in paying farewell visits and figuring at farewell picnics—varying this somewhat tame amusement by much reading of newspapers three days old. Small wonder that the end of the week found his never too-placid temper decidedly more irritable than usual.

On Saturday night, after dinner, he went down to the town— partly for the sake of a stroll in the evening air, partly in order to execute some trifling commissions of his travelling-companion, who was dining out, and had found no time during the day in which to attend to such sordid matters as the repair of portmanteaus or the purchase of extra straps. Glancing up, as he passed below it, at the square white mass of the Hôtel d'Angleterre halfway up the slope of the hill on his left hand, Lyon took occasion to remind himself that he, too, had one farewell visit at least to pay. By every rule of courtesy, he was bound to call on Mrs. Travers before he left.

Since the evening of his conversation with her in the garden of the deserted villa he had not so much as caught a glimpse of her figure in the distance ; and Brian, for the population of San Remo, had remained equally invisible. But his non-appearance, unlike his wife's, which had afforded Lyon some food for speculation, was easily accounted for : he now went to Monte Carlo every day.

Lyon did his errand at the saddler's ; then turned in at the open

door of the English chemist with the object of renewing his stock
of quinine—a remedy which his seven years' residence in India,
and a practical acquaintance with the numerous forms of malarial
fever prevailing in certain districts of that interesting country,
had taught him the prudence of keeping always easily at hand.
The shop was dimly lighted, and, doubtless owing to the lateness
of the hour, there was no one behind the counter but a young
assistant, so occupied for the moment with a lady, who stood talking to him across it, that he did not notice the entry of a new
customer.

"There is Dr. Spini," this young man was saying in a doubtful
tone, as Lyon crossed the threshold. "I'm not sure if we have
his address, but I can get it for you in a few minutes—if you
wish."

"But is he a good doctor—a *safe* doctor?" was the eager
response. The speaker's back was toward Lyon, and in the imperfect light he could scarcely discern the outline of her figure. The
voice, however, was unmistakably the voice of Dorothy Travers—
and it rang sharp with anxiety.

The assistant shrugged his shoulders—the gesture seemed oddly
out of keeping with his sturdy, square-built Saxon figure—and
answered hesitatingly :

"That is more than I can quite say. I believe he attends a
good many of the townspeople."

"I wish I knew what to do!" escaped painfully from Dorothy's
lips. She leaned against the counter, looking down—her brows
closely knit, her lips trembling visibly in the light of the lamp
which, by her change of posture, now fell full upon her pale face.

Lyon stepped forward.

"Good-evening, Mrs. Travers. Didn't I hear you asking for
medical credentials? That means, I'm afraid, that you have an
invalid at home. Nothing serious, I hope?"

She gave a little pathetic shake of the head. "Robin is very
ill," she answered in an uncertain, wavering voice. "He is
suffering terribly—and then he has so much fever."

"What is wrong with him?"

"I don't know. Yesterday I thought it was only a feverish
cold, but he became much worse early this morning, and he has
been growing steadily worse all day. And I sent for Dr. Molyneux early, before nine o'clock, and he has never been, though I
waited all day for him. So I had to come out myself, though I

couldn't bear to leave Robin—he is so restless, and cries out for me every moment." She stopped involuntarily, her voice breaking for a moment.

"But I can't understand Molyneux's non-arrival!" Lyon said; "it seems inexplicable. Your messenger must have played you false, surely."

Dorothy's face suddenly became hard and set as a stone. "Yes," she returned briefly, and her voice was as hard as her face, "he did."

"Abominable!" Lyon ejaculated. "He ought to suffer severely for such carelessness. You sent by one of the hotel servants, I suppose?"

"No," Dorothy answered in the same short, hard tone; "I sent by my husband. He promised to call at the doctor's house on his way to the station. No doubt he forgot all about the matter."

Lyon murmured, "Some mistake;" and then suggested vaguely, "May not the Molyneux man or maid be to blame?" He felt fairly appalled by Dorothy's expression—so unlike in its cold anger, its absolute pitilessness, to any expression he had ever seen upon that gentle face of hers before.

"No!"—she repudiated his suggestion with inflexible frankness. "I have just been to Dr. Molyneux's villa on my way down here. And I met Comaro besides—the man who always drives my husband to the railway. He said Brian stopped nowhere this morning; he drove straight to the station door, and went in."

"It is—very unfortunate." Lyon was at no time a particularly fluent conversationalist, but never before in his life had he found himself so utterly at a loss for a remark. "But can't Molyneux come to you now?"

"No. He went to Cannes by the four o'clock train for a consultation; he is not coming back to-night. We have lost him altogether"—compressing her quivering lips. "And the other English doctor is down with influenza; and the principal Italian one is out of the town, too—attending his mother's funeral at Alassio. No one seems able to tell me anything about the others, and I don't know whether they are reliable or not. I am at my wits' end, and I have none to take counsel with in this strange place. What would you advise me to do?"

Lyon told himself, with a touch of bitterness, that he need not feel flattered by this appeal; it was so plain that Mrs. Travers would never have constituted him her counsellor had any other

been within her reach.   He put all personal feeling aside, however, as he replied gravely :

" I'm afraid I'm hardly fitted to advise you.   But it seems to
me that if the child is at all seriously ill it might be dangerous to
delay.   In urgent cases it's often better to take the rougher help
which is actually at hand, than to wait for the more skilful.
Suppose you were to call in this Italian, just for the moment, and
at the same time——   There's an English doctor at Mentone, of
course ?   Well, telegraph for him at once."

" The wire is broken, unluckily," put in the chemist's assistant.
" There was an electric storm last night."

" You see"—Dorothy lifted eyes full of anguish to Lyon's face
—" everything is against him."

" No, no; don't think that ! " Lyon returned quite eagerly.
" The man can be got over just the same—almost as quickly as by
wiring.   There's a good train starting in about twenty minutes'
time ; I can easily catch it, and be back with him here before midnight."

" There's the delay at the frontier," the shopman suggested.

" I should drive from Ventimiglia, of course, so as to waste no
time," Lyon said, looking at Dorothy.   " You would like to
have this man—what's his name ?—Graham ?—fetched, wouldn't
you ? "

" Indeed I would.   And shall I send for Dr. Spini in the meantime ? "

" I would, I think, if I were you ; it seems the safest plan.   Keep
him with you, if possible, till the Englishman arrives.   He may
like to hear exactly what his brother medico has been doing.   And
—and don't be down-hearted, Mrs. Travers ; children are wonderfully elastic.   I dare say the little chap 'll be all right again in a
day or two.   Why, I remember——"

" Are you sure you will have time to catch that train ? "
Dorothy interposed unceremoniously, her eyes fixed anxiously on
the clock above her companion's head.

" Ample time.   However, I'll risk nothing, and be off at once.
You may look for Graham confidently before twelve," Lyon added
over his shoulder, as he disappeared into the twilit street.

He was as good as his word.   The town clocks were only chim-
ing the quarter before midnight when a light carriage drawn by
a pair of smoking horses stopped before the door of the Hôtel
d'Angleterre, and set down the small, spare figure of the English

physician—whose foreign colleague stood awaiting him just within the hall, bowing and smiling, with a sleepy *concierge* looking over his shoulder. Lyon, following Dr. Graham over the threshold, discerned no good report of his patient in the Italian's olive-tinted face. So ominous, indeed, did its expression seem to him that—having first ascertained from the *concierge* that Brian had not yet returned from Monte Carlo—he abandoned his previously formed intention of retiring at once to his own hotel, and betook himself to the gravel walk outside, there to pace up and down, awaiting the issue of the medical consultation. It seemed barbarous to go away, unknowing; and she might need help, besides—" such help as a trustworthy errand-boy can give; I am capable at least of carrying a message faithfully," he said to himself, with an odd twist of his mouth which was scarcely a smile.

It was a clear, cool night; the moon had set, but the stars shone overhead with extraordinary brilliancy; a delicate breeze blew in from the sea, stirring the drooping branches of the pepper-trees in the hotel garden, and shaking, now and then, an over-ripe orange to the ground. Lyon walked slowly to and fro, looking neither above nor around him, fully occupied with his own reflections. To him, little Robin's illness was only a single element, and that, perhaps, the least painful one, in a very complex and anxious situation, the final development of which it was impossible to foresee. The domestic drama whose course he had been following for weeks past with a fitful interest had clearly touched its crisis; would its final act be one of catastrophe? Recalling Dorothy's face and voice in the chemist's shop to his remembrance, Lyon felt the presage of such an ending press strongly on his mind. Yet he forgot, for the moment, to triumph in the fulfilment of his own prophecies. Rather was he—for an unblushing egotist somewhat curiously—absorbed in the devising of means by which such a final result of Dorothy's self-willed experiment might yet be averted.

Presently, after the lapse of half an hour or so, the Italian doctor came out alone and went rapidly down the hill. Involuntarily Lyon started forward to intercept and question him; but drew back again, remembering that Dr. Graham, in the course of the drive from Mentone, had stated positively that Spini could neither speak nor understand any language save Italian—a language of which his own knowledge was limited to about a dozen

14

words. A moment later he heard Dorothy's voice in the hall, of which the door still stood half open.

She was evidently pleading with the *concierge.* "Of course I understand that you can't leave your post," were the first words that met Lyon's ear; "but couldn't you call up one of the porters? My nurse is afraid to go down to the town so late alone; besides, she cannot speak any French. And the child is so very ill."

"Can I be of any use?" demanded Lyon, striding forward into the doorway.

Dorothy uttered a faint exclamation of surprise. "I thought—I didn't know you were still here."

"I stayed just to see if—if you wanted anything; prescriptions to be taken to the chemist's, or—or anything of that kind," Lyon said a little awkwardly. "I thought, Travers being away, you might perhaps want a messenger, at this hour."

It was in no spirit of malice, but with the simple desire to excuse and explain his lingering at her doors,'that he made reference to her husband's inopportune absence. No sooner, however, were the words off his lips than he would have given much to recall them. For, at his ill-judged allusion, Dorothy's white face took on instantly the look that had so appalled him four hours earlier, and her voice rang sharp with scorn as she answered icily:

"It is hardly fair to put Brian's neglected duties upon you."

"One is glad to be of use—and the night is delicious. I assure you it's no trouble at all," Lyon asseverated, with what, for him, was something like vehemence. "If you will just tell me what you want——"

"I will write a list," she said. She gave him no word of thanks for his offer of service. He understood quite clearly that he scarcely existed for her at the moment, save in his capacity of messenger.

Crossing swiftly to the other side of the wide hall, where, against the wall, stood a little table covered with writing materials, she began, still standing, to jot down her requirements on a half sheet of paper. Lyon followed her more slowly, and stood a few steps from the bottom of the table, facing her as she wrote. The *concierge,* meanwhile, glad of the intervention which had excused him from the ungrateful task of climbing to the top of the house and arousing a fellow-servant from his first sleep, retired into his little office near the outer door, and paid no further heed to either of them.

"There is a prescription, too," Dorothy said, as she wrote, without lifting her eyes. "Will you ask them to make it up as quickly as possible?"

"I'll see they do that. I'll wait for the medicine and bring it up," Lyon answered.

She went on writing. She had taken it for granted all along that he would wait.

"Graham stays here the night?" he adventured after a moment.

"Yes."

"He seems a sensible fellow. I hope"—nervously—"he has encouraged you?"

"He gives no definite opinion; he says it's impossible to give one at present. The attack must run its course—now. If it had been taken in time, he thinks it might have been arrested. Now it's too late." She looked up from the paper she was folding, not at Lyon, but at the wall opposite her, and pressed her lips hard together. "Twelve hours lost have made all the difference," she said in a low voice, as if half to herself. "All because Brian —forgot. If Robin dies, I shall always feel that Brian killed him!"

Involuntarily Lyon drew back a step. He did not know her in this mood—a mood of which he had never suspected her gentle nature capable. And he had supposed her to have grown shallow, artificial; to have lost all capacity for deep feeling! Here was more than feeling; here was passion—and passion of the purely elemental, even semi-savage, kind. He was so startled that he actually stammered a deprecating rejoinder.

"No, no! That would be to take too harsh a view. An unlucky lapse of memory——"

"If he had cared anything for Robin," she returned, with the same quiet but perfectly inflexible bitterness which had given terrible point to her last utterance, "he would not have forgotten."

This was unanswerable; Lyon felt it to be so. Still something within him, he could not have told whether it were an impulse of generosity impelling him to the defence of a man he disliked, or a movement of sheer perversity urging him to fling himself uselessly against the rock of Dorothy's fixed resentment, drove him to persist in his *rôle* of apologist.

"Men are proverbially stupid where illness is concerned," he pleaded. "I dare say Travers didn't take in how serious the matter really was. By the way, the telegraph office here is open all night; hadn't I better wire to him on my way home?"

"No."

"Not?" Lyon, surprised altogether out of his impassibility for the moment, stared at her almost open-mouthed.

"No; I beg you will do nothing of the kind."

"Are not you"—his voice was a little unsteady, and he spoke with manifest effort—"forgive me, I know I've no right to say anything, but aren't you punishing him too severely for—for——" He failed to find a fitting conclusion for his half-spoken question.

She looked at him coldly, with a sort of offended astonishment, but quite calmly. "There is no question of punishment," she said. "But you don't expect me to justify myself to you, I presume?"

"No," he answered helplessly. So might a queen have looked upon, so might she have addressed, a too-forward courtier. There seemed to be no end to the revelations in store for Lyon that night concerning the nature of this woman, whom he had supposed himself able to read through and through at a glance. "I—I beg your pardon," he faltered, and held out his hand for the folded paper. "That is all?" he asked, when she had given it to him.

"That is all. You will be as quick as you can? Dr. Graham says it is so important."

"You may rely on me."

Her face haunted him all the way to the town and back again; it hovered before his eyes during the remainder of the short night. He had seen that in it which terrified him; a fixity of resentment bordering hard on actual hate. He could hardly have explained why it seemed to him so unutterable a catastrophe that Dorothy Travers should hate her husband; but, as a matter of fact, he would have done almost anything, made any personal sacrifice within his power, rather than that things should have come to such a pass with her. That she should be unhappy in her marriage was an endurable thought; indeed, he had found her apparent content with her lot, at the time of their first accidental meeting and renewal of acquaintance, a trifle disappointing, and even irritating to his self-esteem; but that she should be warped by it into an unlovely bitterness, that it should ever have the effect of lowering her nature or hardening her heart, was an issue he had never contemplated, and from which he shrank in dismay now that it presented itself to him as a menacing probability.

Directly after dawn he abandoned all further attempt to sleep, dressed himself, and started for a tramp along the Bordighera road, hoping to walk off his unquiet visions. They persisted in accompanying him, however; and he returned to breakfast in no more tranquil humor than he had set out. What irritated him above all was the bitter sense of his own helplessness in the matter. Something ought to be done; and he could do nothing. It was as though he had seen her caught in the current of a dangerous river, drifting past him to the rapids which must sweep her to destruction, while he stood on the bank, destitute of boat or rope that might have aided her, incapable of swimming, without so much as a voice to call anyone else to her rescue.

Some letters had been brought to him on the breakfast-tray; one bore the Monte Carlo postmark. He opened it carelessly, read a few words, uttered a little exclamation of dismay; then his face cleared suddenly. "Unlucky for him," he muttered; "but for her—well, it may be salvation. It will soften her as nothing else could do."

He ran hastily over the remainder of the letter; then caught up his hat and sallied forth. Ten minutes later he was standing in the hall of the Hôtel d'Angleterre asking for Dorothy.

It was some time before she appeared, and then it was with a face which showed that she considered his visit ill-timed. Indeed, she had at first excused herself from seeing him at all; and it was only on his sending up a second and more urgent message to the effect that he would not detain her for more than two minutes, and that his business was of extreme importance, that she reluctantly consented to come down.

"I have come——" he began, when she had given him her hand in a perfunctory fashion, and then broke off to enquire, "How is the boy this morning?"

"Just the same. He has had a very restless night. I hardly like leaving him, even for a moment." Her look and tone seemed to add, "Why have you called me away?"

"The things—from the chemist's—last night were all right, I hope?" Now that Lyon actually stood in Dorothy's presence, he rather shrank from entering upon the matter that had brought him there. Else—especially after the very plain hint she had just given him of her anxiety to be gone—he would hardly have wasted any more time in putting unnecessary questions.

"Quite, thanks"—with manifest impatience. "Is that all? because——" She was already preparing to turn away.

"No," he interposed; "that's not all, I am sorry to say. I—I have come here to—to break some rather serious news to you."

Her face was already pale; it became ashen. "Dolly?" she gasped. "What has happened?"

"No, no; don't be frightened! There's nothing amiss with Dolly. I saw her, from a distance, going into the Public Gardens with her nurse, on my way up here. No, it's—your husband. He has met with an accident."

"An accident?" She asked the question calmly; her excitement was suddenly gone, and her face had grown expressionless.

"Yes. Trying to stop a restive carriage-horse which was doing its best to bolt, he somehow got knocked down and hurt— rather badly, I'm afraid; at least he has some ribs broken. I had a letter from him this morning—or, rather, from the manager of the Paris, where he is. He didn't wish to alarm you by writing or wiring direct."

Dorothy's face retained its inscrutable look. "Of course he has had a doctor to see him?"

"Oh, yes! Both the English doctors in the place have examined him, the manager says; and they think he'll pull through all right. Happily, there don't seem to be any complications— just the broken bones. You mustn't disquiet yourself too much; only I'm afraid it 'll be a longish business. And it's specially unlucky that such a mishap should have occurred just now, when you have already so much on your hands and thoughts."

To these well-meant condolences Dorothy responded nothing; neither did her set expression vary in the least.

"I was thinking," went on Lyon, almost timidly—for her demeanor was not calculated to set him at ease—"that, as, of course, it's impossible for you to leave the little chap just at present——"

He spoke half-interrogatively, and paused for an answer. She made an assenting motion of her head.

"I was thinking," he resumed, speaking more hurriedly, "that —that under the circumstances perhaps you would like—perhaps I might as well run over to Monte Carlo?"

"It would be very kind of you." Her tone was civil, but

severely unenthusiastic. " But—I thought you had made your
plans to go to Paris to-morrow ? "

" They are easily unmade. Travers must need some looking
after ; and if my going would set your mind more at ease about
him——"

" I have no doubt he will be delighted to see you, and feel
most grateful to you for coming."   •

He noticed that she made no profession of personal gratitude
in the matter.

" Then, if you approve, I'll get off by the midday train. Is
there anything you would like to send ? "

" I dare say Brian would be glad of some of his things. I will
tell Jane to pack a portmanteau, and have it sent down to you by
half-past eleven. Now I must go back to Robin. Good-by."

He took her proffered hand, feeling himself utterly baffled.
" Don't be over-anxious about either of them. I shall hope to
send you a good report of Travers in a few hours' time ; I will
write as soon as I have seen him."

" Thank you."

" And you will let us know how *your* patient goes on—from
time to time ? By the way, while I think of it, it might not,
perhaps, be wise to make too much of the boy's illness to Travers
just now. Of course, a good deal depends on the condition in
which I find him. Supposing, however, he seems to be seriously
shaken, and I am ordered, as very likely I shall be, to keep him
quiet, difficulties may arise. What should I say to him in that
case ? "

" What you please." Her tone expressed a most perfect
indifference to the question. And again she turned toward the
staircase.

" No, but "—he interrupted her with an eagerness most unusual
in him—" you are putting too great a responsibility upon me. I
must have your authority."

" My authority ? " she echoed, with a curious, bitter smile.
" Well, my authority, such as it is, I delegate to you. You
have my full permission to act according to your own judgment."
She had her foot actually on the first stair, when he intercepted
her again.

" Mrs. Travers," he said appealingly, and never before, not
even when the tide of his personal passion had been at its highest,
and he had pleaded with her most recklessly for his personal

happiness, had she seen his dark, heavy face so transformed by strong emotion, "one moment, please. Have you no message for your husband?"

In sheer surprise she hesitated for an instant before replying. Then her reply came, low, swift, determined:

"No. None."

There followed a moment of dead silence. She stood, one hand resting on the balustrade of the staircase, facing him; her head slightly thrown back, her breath coming quickly from between her parted lips, her eyes hard, set, uncompromising. He, standing a step lower, looked up into her face with a gaze, more fixed than he was aware of, full of mingled wonder and distress. A moment she endured his scrutiny, silent and motionless, seemingly too proud to attempt to escape from it. Then, suddenly, and without warning, she turned upon him with the mien of an outraged princess.

"Why do you look at me like that?" she cried under her breath. "I will not bear it! no, I will not bear it! What right have you to sit in judgment on me? What do you know? No!"—as he made a deprecating gesture—"you need not try to explain away your looks—I can read their meaning well enough! Because for once in my false, artificial life I venture to speak and act truthfully, you are horrified, disgusted! No wonder! What business has any woman ever to show herself as she is? Hypocrisy is her first duty—Heaven knows if I have made it mine or not, for years past! But I warn you, and all others kind enough to interest themselves in my moral welfare"—with a harsh little laugh—"that I am tired of being a hypocrite, and don't mean ever to be a hypocrite any more. I decline to be false to myself at your orders, simply to satisfy your prejudices. I will not be goaded into playing a part I am sick of to the end of time, in order that my friends' tastes may not be offended—though I am sorry to offend them. I don't want to hurt anybody's feelings—I only ask to be allowed to go my way without remonstrance. It's not much to ask, surely. You are all free to condemn me as much as you please, in your hearts and among yourselves—and you will doubtless do it. Only don't think to terrify me back into my former good behavior by passing sentence on me; for I deny your jurisdiction, and I care less than nothing for the pains and penalties you can inflict!"

She waited for a moment, as if giving him an opportunity to

answer ; then, as he merely bent his head without a word, she turned and went slowly upstairs, leaving him to consider the result of his well-meant interference at his leisure.

CHAPTER VI

AT THE THRESHOLD

"I stood . . .
And spake to the Lord God, and said, 'O Lord,
Am *I* the man ?' And the Lord answered me,
'Thou art the man, and all the more the man.'"

"LYON !"

"Well ? " Lyon responded from behind the open sheets of the *Times*.

"How about that post ? "

"It's in. Came in half an hour ago."

"Any letters for me ? "

"No."

Brian Travers, who had raised his head from his pillows while putting the foregoing questions, now let it fall back into its original position and lay for a while silent, plucking restlessly at the sheet with hot, nervous fingers. Then he spoke again.

"Lyon !"

"Well ? "

"You—you've not had any letter yourself ? From Dorothy, I mean ? "

"No."

"Not even a post-card ? "

"No. I have not heard from Mrs. Travers at all."

Brian made an impatient movement to turn over on his side ; a movement which proved futile, ending only in a stifled groan. Not so thoroughly stifled, however, but that it caught his companion's ear. Lyon laid down his paper, and came to the bedside.

"Feeling uncomfortable ? " he enquired laconically.

"How the deuce should I feel otherwise ? " was the somewhat ungracious response.

"You've been lying rather a long time in that position," Lyon went on imperturbably. " Like to be shifted a bit ? "

"No; one position's as easy, or rather uneasy, as another. I say, Lyon!"—fretfully—"how abominably dark you keep this room."

"Seeing that the thermometer stands at 92° in the shade out of doors, and your temperature last night was 103°, it seemed the part of a prudent friend to shut the *persiennes*. However, I'll open the farther window, if you specially desire it. Only don't blame me if the sun sends your fever up again." And Lyon recrossed the room toward the window in question.

But before he could lay hand upon it Brian's querulous voice checked his action. "Never mind, then—leave the confounded thing alone, for Heaven's sake! Leave it alone, I tell you!"

"My good fellow, I am leaving it alone," Lyon retorted calmly, relapsing into his chair and his newspaper. "I assure you I'm not at all eager to let in more tropical glare than is absolutely necessary. An oven is always a trying place of residence. But, to my mind, it's a needless aggravation of the suffering of being baked alive, to insist on seeing the fire during the whole process; I prefer grilling in the dark, since grill I must."

Lyon had not proceeded far with his renewed perusal of the *Times* leading article before his studies were again interrupted. At the end of a very few moments Brian—after muttering half aloud to himself, "Extraordinary! quite extraordinary!" once or twice—suddenly raised his voice and once more addressed his companion.

"Lyon!"

"Well?" queried Lyon for the third time.

"Doesn't it strike you as—as singular that there should be no letter, no message at all, from San Remo?"

"This is Friday. Mrs. Travers wrote on Tuesday last. And she has rarely written oftener than once in three days," was Lyon's diplomatic answer. "I really don't see any reason for your feeling uneasy."

"Don't you, indeed?" sarcastically.

"No," ignoring the sarcasm. "The boy is quite out of danger now."

"He's been out of danger these ten days past," Brian said bitterly. "I am not troubling my head about *him*—he'll do well enough. No; the question is, now that he's getting well, and could safely be left to the nurse for a time, why doesn't my wife come over here? Why doesn't she at least write, and propose to come?"

Lyon did not feel called upon to offer any solution of this puzzle.

"I suppose the truth is," Brian went on irritably, "the truth is, you've kept her in ignorance of the real state of affairs. You've made the best of things in your letters, and never allowed her to know what a touch-and-go business it's been with me. That was all very well at first, while she had the boy ill on her hands. But there was no need to go on keeping up the fiction to the end."

"I haven't kept it up."

"What! You've told her? Do you mean——"

"I mean that for a fortnight past I've neither underrated your sufferings, in writing to Mrs. Travers, nor pretended to her that your condition was invariably satisfactory. In short, I have been telling her the truth for some time past."

"And yet she's never, in her answers—never once spoken of coming here? Never hinted at such a thing? Never said she *wished* to come?"

"No."

"For the true vindictive spirit," quoth Brian, with increased bitterness, "commend me to a good woman. And yet," he added, after a moment, during which his companion offered no comment on his exclamation, "I don't understand. Dorothy was never the implacable sort."

Lyon got up and laid down his paper. "If she shows herself implacable now," he observed, walking slowly over to the chimney-piece as he spoke, "doesn't it occur to you that *you* may be to blame for the change in her? When a woman gives the lie, in any important point, to her own nature, it's usually some man's fault."

"I don't pretend to have been an immaculate husband," was Brian's rejoinder. "I dare say she thinks she has cause of complaint against me. Clearly she has taken all this nonsense of the last few weeks most absurdly to heart. But if she could overlook things before, when there was, perhaps, more reason for her being offended, why not now?"

Lyon paused an instant before replying, his back toward the bed, his arms resting on the mantle-shelf before him. "I take it," he said at last, when he had sufficiently mastered himself to be able to speak, "that, in the present case, it's your forgetfulness—about the child—which has turned the scale against you. All the rest your wife might have consented to forgive; mind I say 'might' only, I don't feel sure about it."

"But, good Heavens, man! there's nothing else for her to forgive! The whole affair with Mrs. M'Allan has been a piece of pure folly on my part, nothing more. Of course I regret having allowed myself to be led into it—and I dare say it may have annoyed Dorothy—but her making it the reason for a serious breach between us is ridiculous."

"From your point of view—very likely. Mrs. Travers probably regards the matter with wholly different eyes—as it is only natural she should do."

"If I could only see her, and tell her the truth of things!" ejaculated Brian. "Of course"—with a very genuine and rather hopeless sigh—"she might not believe me. Probably she would not."

"Why?" enquired Lyon, looking round sharply for a moment. Oh, I see!"—turning slowly away again. "You think she would argue from the certainties of the past to the probabilities of the present?"

"You don't put things over-pleasantly," Brian said. "However—I may as well acknowledge it frankly—you're not so far out. Three years ago—to my shame be it spoken; I hate the very recollection of the business—I did get involved to some extent in a foolish affair at Milan; and unluckily it came to my wife's ears. The woman was an Italian singer: wonderfully pretty and fascinating, and at the same time perfectly unscrupulous; I should think the most absolutely unscrupulous human being I ever came across. Well, I completely lost my head for a time. When I recovered it, I—saw things in their true light, and hated myself for the fool I'd been. Dorothy knew that, and she consented to let bygones be bygones. But I'm afraid her recollections of that miserable episode—as you know, women never forget such things —may have made her rather inclined to—to imagine—to take too serious a view. You understand?"

"I quite understand," was the reply. "And I appreciate Mrs. Travers' position."

"Now, look here, Lyon!" the sick man cried, in a louder voice, raising himself on his elbow; "what does that mean? Do you doubt my word? I tell you, on my honor, between man and man, there's no question here of anything but a meaningless flirtation. Do you suppose I should lie to you?"

" You might feel bound to," was the cool retort. " Not that I imply for a moment you are speaking anything but unvarnished truth. But I was trying to look at the matter from Mrs. Travers' standpoint, as I conjecture it. And if I may tender a little friendly advice, I should recommend you to repeat to her, without delay, what you've just told me about your relations with the American lady."

" Your advice is admirable, but not very easy to follow. Seeing that I am helpless to do anything except lie here like a log— and my wife declines to come near me—— All things considered, Lyon, I think you might have suggested the propriety of her coming last week, when I was at my worst. To herself, I mean."

Lyon made a prolonged silent examination of the various ornaments adorning the chimney-piece before he answered in a constrained voice :

" I did suggest it—in a fashion."

" How did she reply to your suggestion ? "

" She didn't reply to it at all, never alluded to it by a word. When she wrote, two days after receiving my letter, it was merely to send her usual bulletin about the boy."

" Then I may go to the dogs as soon as I please, I suppose ! " cried Brian, with something like a sob. " Since she throws me overboard—— Lyon, you don't guess what she is to me ! I've acted like a fool, I know, more than once. But—if she would only believe it—through all, and above all, I've cared for her with my whole soul. Indeed, in the real sense of the word, I've never cared, at any time, for any other woman—if only she would believe it."

" You've hardly gone the right way to make her believe it," observed Lyon dryly.

" What a candid brute you are, Lyon ! Yes, that's true enough. But I must get her to believe it. I must have her back ! " Brian's weak voice, rising to a cry, sounded almost hysterical. " I can't do without her any longer. She must come —it's her duty to come, her plain duty ! "

" Obviously, according to those social laws which enjoin resentment upon the man, and forbid it to the woman. Unfortunately, even women occasionally fail to fulfil their plain duties."

" She can't have changed so utterly," Brian muttered ; he had scarcely heard Lyon's retort, and paid it no heed whatever. " Not that women are to be counted upon. They will profess the greatest regard for you one day, and the next exhibit the most perfect indifference to the question of your life or death." Brian's reference was too clear to be misunderstood, and Lyon, who had his own private reasons for finding his patient's wrath against Mrs. M'Allan amusing, smiled somewhat grimly to himself. " But my wife—Dorothy is different from other women— always was. If she gives me up, I may account myself a hopeless bad lot indeed. But she's no right to give me up now. If only I could see her, I might be able to convince her of that. And I must see her ! I can't stand lying here, knowing she's hardening herself against me for no cause. The thought drives me wild. Something must be done, Lyon—or I shall go mad."

" No, you won't," returned Lyon gruffly. " I don't see precisely what's to be 'done,'" he added, before the outraged Travers had time to speak. " But I'll think matters over, and see if I can hit upon any plan. In the meantime, you had better take your sedative and try to sleep for a bit. I'm going for a tramp."

Lyon did not start immediately on his tramp, unless the exercise of pacing up and down his own room for half an hour, to the extreme annoyance and indignation of the old lady domiciled below, might be supposed to fall under the head of tramping. And, the half hour at an end, instead of setting off into the country, he strode down the hill to the station, and took a return ticket for San Remo.

Ten minutes later he was speeding toward the Italian frontier, looking wearily out of the railway-carriage window at a prospect of dazzling blue sea and sky, and telling himself, with merciless plainness, what a fool he was for setting out on such an expedition. Surely his last interview with Dorothy, now three weeks old, might have taught him, once for all, how powerless he was to influence her! Why, therefore, court a repetition of that scene? Why bring upon himself certain fresh mortification, and a deepened sense of failure—all to no purpose? Was it indeed worth while?

Something within him answered, " Yes. If I try again, I shall fail again, no doubt. So be it! I shall at least have done what in me lies to save her life from shipwreck."

Hard on that consoling reflection followed the enquiry: " Am I the man for this task? Am I strong enough for it ? "

With all a self-reliant man's natural distaste to acknowledgment of his own weakness, even to himself, Lyon, in making up his mind to his present course of action, had resolutely silenced the voice of self-distrust within him. Now, in this hour of enforced idleness and keen expectancy, when, with brain throbbing with excitement and nerves strung to the highest pitch of tension, he was constrained to sit with folded hands, measuring the difficulties of the enterprise before him, it refused to keep silence any longer at his bidding. Fear, that fear of himself of which he had hitherto so obstinately refused to recognize the very existence, came upon him in an overwhelming flood. He began to doubt, to analyze; to analyze the situation, to doubt his own motives in creating it, till the very impulse which had driven him to venturesome action almost died out in the process. By the time he reached Ventimiglia he was beginning to think seriously of turning back.

He had three-quarters of an hour to wait while the passengers' luggage was being examined and the usual frontier formalities were complied with: he spent it in walking up and down the platform, in a frame of mind absolutely new to his experience—one of tormenting irresolution. The fresh train that was to carry him into Italy had actually begun to get up steam for departure, and still he had taken no decision.

At length he walked rapidly away from the crowd of intending travellers, to the comparative solitude of a siding adjoining the main platform, and there, stopping short, considered the choice before him for the last time. "It's a poor chance," he reflected. "But it's her only chance. If *I* draw back from the forlorn hope, it's quite certain no one else will offer to take my place. The real question is, am I sufficiently sure of myself? It's a hard case," he mused bitterly. "Why should I, of all men, have been forced into this position—I? Somehow I daren't back out of it. And yet, how unfit I am for it, only Heaven knows. Ah, God, God help me!"

The prayer—I think I am justified in calling it one—rose to his lips with a naturalness and an earnestness which at any other time would have surprised himself. But in this crucial moment of his life, full as it was of stress and perplexity of another kind, he forgot the perplexities which, of late years at least, had made any strong movement of faith in the Unseen an impossibility to him. Alone with the sense of his own weakness, there had arisen in him not merely a craving for some strength which should supplement it, but an inexplicable belief, real if transitory, in the existence of this help, somewhere. With a voiceless cry of supplication he flung himself out into the void, seeking for it, groping after it. And he was heard in that he feared. There came to him a strange, overpowering consciousness of touching a helping hand, in the very grasp of which lay a promise of infinite security.

Without further hesitation he turned round, walked down the platform, and got into the train.

For the remainder of the way he found employment in preparing for the interview that lay before him; in devising an effective statement of the case he had to plead, in elaborating his arguments, and sharpening his rhetorical weapons of assault—a preparation which, if it served the useful purpose of occupying his mind, certainly served no other, since not a word of it survived in his memory the first sight of the woman he went to see.

Dorothy received him alone in her little sitting-room. The strain and fatigue of the last three weeks had not been without their effect upon her appearance; and Lyon was forced to acknowledge to himself that he had never seen her look less pretty. Pallor and weariness become few women: they were necessarily fatal in the case of a woman no longer quite in her first youth, whose complexion and expression were her best points. Mrs. Travers' movements, too, had lost much of their light, quick grace. She advanced to meet her visitor with the sedate, measured step of a middle-aged woman.

As to her manner, it was civilly inscrutable: impossible for Lyon to ascertain from it whether his unexpected visit were welcome or unwelcome to his hostess. But he perceived a watchful expression in her eyes, as though she divined a special purpose in his coming, and were putting herself on her guard against it.

She talked freely of Robin, who was now fairly convalescent, she said, and had been twice permitted to go out for an hour; then, after a moment of hesitation, she enquired for her husband.

. "Brian is really much better, isn't he ? "

" Yes, he is better. But he's still almost entirely helpless. And he suffers a good deal—more particularly at night," Lyon said.

" But he is quite out of danger now ? "

" The doctor hopes so. He has been much more encouraging since Monday. Last week, for twenty-four hours or so, he was rather anxious, by his own confession. But I wrote you all about that."

"I remember. You have been most kind in that matter—sending me such full reports every day."

A moment's silence. Lyon felt uncomfortably conscious that he was not getting on ; that he had not, so far, advanced by one inch toward the attainment of the object he had in view.

"Mrs. Travers"—he broke the silence desperately, convinced that no alternative was left him but to conduct his attack directly, without disguise or circumlocution—"I dare say you were surprised to see me to-day. The truth is, I came to—to make an appeal to you. Travers can't write himself, you know, and I dare say I've expressed myself badly in my letters ; I was always a bad hand at written explanations. Well, your husband is, naturally, very anxious to see you." He paused.

"Yes ? "

"Would you—may I take him some promise—some hope that you will gratify his wish before very long ? I am sure such a message would help forward his recovery. I think, perhaps, you hardly conceive *how* anxious he is on this point—how your absence preys upon his mind." Again Lyon stopped short.

Dorothy seemed to be considering his words. She was silent for a few seconds, playing nervously, meanwhile, with the cover of a book lying on the table at her elbow. "Can my husband read his own letters ? " she asked presently.

"Sometimes."

"I think the best way will be for me to write to him. You can give him the letter when you think fittest," she said slowly.
"Yes, that will be best—decidedly best."

"Do I understand—— You will send a letter by me, then ? "

"No, I won't detain you while I write. I'll send the letter by to-night's post."

Lyon could not ignore the fact that he had received his dismissal. He stood up.

"Before you go," his companion said, "I should like to ask you one question. Did my husband send you to me, or did you come here to-day of your own accord ? "

"I came of my own accord. Your husband knew nothing of my intention."

For the first time during the interview Dorothy's face changed a little. But Lyon found himself unable to construe the meaning of the new expression which it took on.

"I see," she said with a touch of irony. "I am much obliged

15

to you. Good-by. Oh, there's one thing more! If my husband
should—should be again in any danger, you will please telegraph
to me at once."

Lyon put his hat, which he had just taken up, down again upon
the table.

"Mrs. Travers," he said, "you informed me the other day that
you had done, for the future, with the conventional shams and
hypocrisies of society. I presume you allow your friends the same
liberty you accord to yourself in the matter? Have I your leave
to tell you the truth ?"

She seemed to blench slightly under his direct gaze; her eyes
faltered and fell before his. But only for a moment. She raised
them again, and looked him full in the face as she answered :

"Certainly."

"Thank you. I conclude—if I am wrong, you'll correct me,
but from what you have just said I can't help drawing the infer-
ence—that you intend to refuse the—appeal I ventured to make
just now ?"

"I do." Her tone was quietly inflexible.

"Doesn't it occur to you that you may be making a great mistake in refusing ?"

"What kind of mistake ?"

"A threefold one. In the first place, I think you misjudge
Travers. He is honestly unhappy, though you may not believe it.
Secondly, you overrate his offence. He doesn't deny himself that
he has offended you deeply ; but he had hoped you would be mer-
ciful—that you wouldn't treat an inconsiderate folly as though it
were an unpardonable sin."

"A folly which made him careless whether his child lived or
died !" Dorothy retorted with white lips.

"You put things very harshly, Mrs. Travers. Your husband
has not forgotten to reproach himself for that unlucky piece of
forgetfulness, I assure you."

"I am glad to hear it."

"Well !" Lyon exclaimed impatiently, "misjudge him as you
will—I see you will accept no excuses for him—only don't misjudge
yourself, for Heaven's sake ! Do what you please about forgiving
Travers ; but don't so outrage all your own best instincts that you
find it impossible hereafter to forgive yourself ! You *know* you
are outraging them at this moment ; and you know what the consequences of your present action are certain to be. Take your

revenge—and Travers will take his. Give him up now, fling him overboard at this particular moment, and you can guess, with a man of his temperament, what results are likely to follow. And then, when they have followed, you will be the most miserable woman on God's earth. That's the third part of your mistake, and the most fatal. You are giving yourself the lie."

"Certainly you take full advantage of my permission," Dorothy said, her voice trembling for the first time. "Your words are plain enough. I don't know"—and she moved restlessly—"why you should think you have a right to speak to me about my husband, and my conduct to him. To begin with, you speak in utter ignorance of facts. You know nothing—you can know nothing——"

"Pardon me. He has told me—pretty much the whole truth, I fancy. You need not despise him for that," he added quickly, answering the contemptuous expression that crossed her face. "The confession came out of his weakness and misery—and longing for you. It may sound paradoxical to say so, but if he had been less frank, I should not have come here to-day."

"I cannot conceive," she said, with a sudden irrepressible outburst of anger, "why you should have come, in any case. I ask you again, what possible right——"

"None," he answered huskily. "I have no right—I know that well enough. But I didn't want you to make shipwreck of your life. When it's a case of life and death, one feels compelled to interfere—even at the risk of getting soundly rebuked for one's presumption."

"It was out of regard for me, rather than for Brian, then, that you came here with your—proposal?" she demanded.

"Yes."

"You have—what's the correct phrase?—my 'happiness at heart,' then? or you believe you have?"

"I am very sure of it." He spoke with difficulty. Her irony hurt him as her anger had not done.

Her eyes blazed indignation; she caught her breath audibly, laying her hand on the table to steady herself.

"And you—you would have me put on again the fetters I had shaken off? go back to the old hopeless, useless, insincere servitude? You, of all men!"

Lyon flushed to his temples, a dark, scorching flush. For a moment the earth reeled beneath him, and the southern sunlight was blotted out, and words which it would have been madness and shame, and yet delight unspeakable, to have uttered, rose to his lips in a flood. He hardly knew how he contrived to choke them back unspoken.

" Yes, I ! " he answered, with harsh, deliberate emphasis. "I—because I know, better than anyone else, perhaps, the spirit in which you entered on your present life. You chose to make yourself responsible for Travers. Is *this* fulfilling your responsibility—to desert him at the very moment when he needs you most ? "

The light, the color died out of her face ; she passed her hand quickly over her eyes. " Are you so sure he does need me ? " she asked in an altered tone. " If *I* could feel sure—perhaps——"

" Come and see," he returned.

Again her hand went nervously across her face. " Very well," she said, with a touch of defiance, as she let it drop once more to her side ; " I will go. That is to say, if you accept all responsibility in the matter."

" I ? "

" Why not? You are evidently persuaded that a return to my duty must infallibly make a better woman of me. I have my doubts on that point. If I do this thing at your bidding—well, you are responsible for the after results."

"You put a heavy burden upon me," he said hoarsely.

" Do you decline it ? "

He considered a moment. " No. Since there is no other way—I accept it."

Perhaps she had hardly expected so laconically decided an answer. She stood an instant perfectly still, as if taken aback ; then she roused herself to say :

" That is settled, then. I suppose I had better go back with you—this afternoon. There is a train in an hour's time, isn't there ? Very well—I will meet you at the station in time for it ; I can easily be ready."

Lyon left her, and went down to the station to wait out the hour.

She was punctual to her tryst ; five minutes before the time appointed for the train's departure she appeared on the platform. Lyon put her at once into an empty first-class compartment, and himself, with a few words of slightly incoherent apology, took refuge in a smoking carriage. He would not have her think that he was in any sort attempting to keep guard over her. Perhaps, also, he may have had unacknowledged personal reasons for avoiding the further ordeal of a *tête-à-tête* railway journey.

At Ventimiglia, from which place they took a carriage for the remainder of the way, he perceived a great change in his companion's demeanor. Her defiant mood had spent itself, and clearly she found it impossible to resume her former show of impassibility. She kept her head steadily averted from Lyon, as he sat beside her, looking persistently out to sea, so that he learned nothing from her eyes. But he saw that the color in the cheek half turned from him was constantly varying, and noted a hundred signs of nervousness in her every movement. Even the frequent mechanical clasping and unclasping of her hands in her lap was to him eloquent of an inward restlessness too strong to be denied expression.

She remained silent until she had actually got down from the carriage, and was entering the Hôtel de Paris. Then she turned brusquely to Lyon.

" On which floor ? " she asked.

" The second. Will you come up at once, or——"

" I will come up. But you had better go in first, and prepare him for seeing me. It never answers to startle sick people. I'll wait outside in the passage."

Lyon nodded gravely, and, after a few words of explanation to the manager, who was hovering near, led the way upstairs and along a corridor, stopping finally before a closed door.

" This is his room," he said in a low voice, as he knocked cautiously. " Perhaps he may be asleep. He——"

But Brian's voice interrupted him, crying in very wide-awake tones :

" Come in ! "

Lyon responded to the invitation and passed into the room, leaving the door open at his back.

" Well, you're a nice sort of chap ! " grumbled his patient by way of welcome. " Do you know how long that walk of yours has lasted? Four mortal hours and a half! I've had one of those agreeable spasms since you went, too; I feel torn to pieces. Altogether, I've spent a lively afternoon."

" I dare say. I haven't been walking," Lyon responded bluntly. " I've been over to San Remo."

" To San Remo ! " repeated the other in evident amazement. Then, his tone changing to one of intense eagerness: " Not—not to see——"

"Your wife? Yes. I'm a wretched hand at letter writing, and I thought Mrs. Travers might be glad of a verbal report; so I caught the midday train, and went—and found her at home. She—she made up her mind—after hearing—— To cut the matter short, she has come back with me."

"She—has—come back?" Brian made shift to raise himself a little on one elbow, looking past Lyon at the open door, with feverishly bright eyes. "Where—why—is she here? Come in, come in! Oh, Dorothy, my darling! Dorothy! Dorothy!"

Dorothy swept by Lyon like a whirlwind—certainly not heeding, perhaps hardly even seeing, him; seeing and heeding nothing save the changed, haggard face turned toward her from its pillow of pain, the wasted, trembling hands held out to her in passionate entreaty. A second more and she was on her knees by the bedside, her face bent down to her husband's, her arms clasping his neck.

"Oh, Brian, my poor boy, can you ever forgive me? I didn't know, dear—I didn't guess—— But I might have known—I have been cruel and wicked—Brian——"

Lyon, already across the threshold, softly shut to the door, and went slowly away.

CHAPTER VII

ON SERVICE

"And what am I to you? A steadfast hand
To hold—a steadfast heart to trust withal:
Merely a man who loves you, and will stand
By you, whate'er befall."

AND now Lyon's work might have been supposed done. Not so, however. He had indeed succeeded in bringing Dorothy Travers back to her husband. But this was not sufficient. He had yet to make sure that the influence which had already once separated Brian from his wife should not again be exerted to divide him from her.

Summoning all his courage, he went boldly to Mrs. Warrener's villa, and enquired for her sister. Mrs. M'Allan was, most unfortunately, not at home, and, a greater misfortune still, no hope was held out of her being within reach for at least a week to come. She had that very morning started for a cruise of seven days in a friend's yacht.

Lyon's hastily conceived plan of an appeal to her generosity must therefore remain in abeyance for the present. This was tantalizing for him. But it was even more tantalizing that the lady's coasting trip should extend itself from a week to ten days, and from ten days to a fortnight. By the end of this time he had carefully matured every detail of his scheme, and had grown both proud and fond of it ; should adverse circumstances prevent him from ever putting it into execution at all, he felt that Fate would indeed be using him hardly.

Such hard usage would, however, undoubtedly have been his portion but for Brian Travers' obstinate refusal to accept the services of any hired nurse. Had his presence been unnecessary to the sick man, Lyon told himself that he could not, with any countenance, have continued to stay on at the Hôtel de Paris. But, as it happened, his presence there was very necessary indeed to Brian—and even to Brian's wife. The former, on his doctor representing to him the inadequacy of Mrs. Travers' strength, or of any woman's strength, to the sole care of a case requiring constant watchfulness by day and night alike, had solved the difficulty by asserting easily, " Oh, Lyon will help her. You'll stay and see us through this business, won't you, old fellow ? " And when Lyon had answered, " Certainly," Brian—with a passing " Thanks no end ! "—dismissed the subject as finally settled, and never afterward referred to the possibility of Lyon's departure.

So Lyon stayed. Whether his staying were quite as agreeable to his patient's wife as it undoubtedly was to his patient, he could not determine. His doubts on this point made his position in some respects a little uneasy. Mrs. Travers had not, indeed, expostulated with him on what she might well suppose an act of self-denying friendship on his part ; but neither had she thanked him for his kindness in remaining. And, on the rare and brief occasions of conversation between them that took place during the ensuing fortnight—dividing, as they did, the care of the invalid, their opportunities of actual intercourse were few in number, one generally leaving Brian's room as the other entered it—on these occasions Lyon fancied he detected a constraint and self-conscious-ness in Dorothy's manner toward him, which seemed to hint that, while she never, by word or look, betrayed any recollection of their singular interview at San Remo, that recollection was nevertheless often uncomfortably present to her mind.

By the time Mrs. M'Allan had returned to Monte Carlo—for she did return at last—Brian was not only out of all danger, but a long way on the road to complete recovery. Lyon, starting once more for Mrs. Warrener's villa, where he knew her sister to have arrived the night before, left his patient sitting in an arm-chair by an open window, reading a newspaper, a very hopeful and hope-inspiring convalescent indeed.

This time Mrs. M'Allan was at home, and her visitor, feeling a good deal more nervous and ill at ease than he would have cared to allow, speedily found himself face to face with her in a small sitting-room on the ground floor of the villa ; a room which from the nature of its adornments—consisting chiefly of flowers so costly that they proclaimed themselves at once to be devotional offerings, interspersed with photographs of presumable devotees, past and present : personable young men of various ages and nationalities—he judged to be her own peculiar shrine and sanctum.

His first sensation, on seeing her rise from her chair at his entrance, was one of surprise. On the two previous occasions of their meeting she had been in walking dress ; and then he had confidently pronounced her no more than pretty. Now, as she stood before him in an attitude of expectation, her uncovered golden head bending gracefully, her delicately modelled features no longer overshadowed by the exaggerated brim of an over-trimmed hat, he was constrained to acknowledge that he had done her less than justice. She was undoubtedly a beautiful woman. He recognized the fact with regret, even with dismay, but he did not attempt to blink it. It was, indeed, a fact compelling recognition.

" Mr. Lyon ? " murmured the fair American doubtfully, glancing from the card on the table beside her to the advancing intruder. " I beg your pardon most sincerely"—with a charming, if enquiring smile. " I ought to remember, no doubt—but my memory doesn't serve me for the moment ? "

She paused interrogatively ; and Lyon said to himself, " What is the meaning of this ? Why does she pretend to have forgotten me ? "

" Allow me to recall myself to your recollection," he responded aloud, in a very fairly easy and matter-of-fact tone. " You were kind enough, some weeks ago, to call several times at the Hôtel de Paris to enquire for my friend Travers, who was then in a bad way. On two of those occasions I had the pleasure of answering your enquiries myself."

"Ah, yes!" she interrupted him; at the same time exchanging her puzzled expression for one of gracious recognition. "I remember now, of course I remember perfectly! How stupid of me not to have known you again at once! Won't you sit down? No, don't choose that horrid little low chair; it's desperately uncomfortable. Take this one instead. And how is your poor friend now?"

"Getting well fast, I am glad to say."

"Thanks"—with a brilliant glance and smile—"to your admirable nursing, no doubt."

Mrs. M'Allan's voice, if too high-pitched to be altogether delightful to the ear, rang not unpleasantly; her American accent was just sufficiently marked to give a certain piquant unfamiliarity to her tones, but it never degenerated into a twang or a drawl. Lyon found the mixture of simplicity and ease with which she spoke highly engaging, and replied in a much less formal tone than he had hitherto employed:

"I'm afraid I can't flatter myself that I've had much to do with his recovery. In fact, as long as I had sole charge of him he made very little way. It was only after Mrs. Travers displaced me that the real improvement in his condition showed itself—which was rather humiliating for me."

"Mrs. Travers is with her husband now, then?" Mrs. M'Allan responded carelessly. Nothing could be more indifferent than her manner of putting the question. But Lyon fancied he had caught a passing look of dismay at his casual mention of Dorothy's arrival, and watched her carefully as he answered:

"Oh, yes; she is with him."

Mrs. M'Allan put one slender, beringed hand thoughtfully to her forehead. "Now, how gratuitously ill-natured people are. Would you believe it? someone assured me—I wish I could remember who the person was—assured me positively that Mrs. Travers had no idea of joining her husband here at all; that she objected to leaving those charming children of hers, even for a single night. Of course we all know what a devoted mother she is. Still, under the circumstances, it seemed a little strange that she could bring herself to stay away so long."

"It was hardly a matter of choice with her," Lyon returned calmly. "Her little boy was dangerously ill; for a fortnight after Travers' accident no one knew if the child would live or die. As soon as he seemed fairly out of danger, she of course came over here."

"Ah, well! it isn't always 'of course,' unfortunately, where married people are concerned, you know," retorted Mrs. M'Allan, with a little laugh. Lyon found himself beginning to like her less well than he had done two minutes earlier. "I am delighted to hear you think it was so, in this instance. You really are a most valuable apologist. Mrs. Travers should be grateful to you."

"Mrs. Travers needs no apologies made for her—either by myself or anyone else," said Lyon bluntly.

"I am sure she is a most admirable person in every way. A good nurse, you say?"

"An excellent one,"

"Delightful! Such a gift! to be able to make one's self useful in sickness." Mrs. M'Allan spoke somewhat absently, fingering the Indian charms which hung at her *châtelaine* in a preoccupied manner. Possibly she was thinking of a note she had despatched to the Hôtel de Paris that morning, and speculating on the probability of Dorothy's having been at Travers' elbow when he opened it.

"It is—a great gift," Lyon assented. "But I am detaining you—unwarrantably, it must seem to you, I fear," he added, with an uncomfortable sensation of starting to walk up to the cannon's mouth. "I ought to have explained why I am here."

"Before you proceed to explain, let me say that I am very glad to see you, whatever your errand," put in his hostess, smiling.

"Thank you"—heavily.

"And, as to the errand; perhaps I, or my sister, can be of some use to—your friends? If so, pray command us. In a foreign place, I know it's often difficult to get all things needful for an invalid. I trust Mrs. Travers won't hesitate to send here for anything she may require. Mrs. Warrener would be delighted, I'm certain."

"You are extremely kind. But, as it happens, Travers has everything he can possibly want. And the hotel people have shown themselves most attentive throughout. No; my excuse for calling upon you is of a different kind. I should say at once that

I don't come in the character of a messenger," he added abruptly. "Kindly understand that I have no claim to represent anybody. I am acting solely in my own behalf."

"Indeed?" Mrs. M'Allan's smile had faded, and her eyes held a look of watchful enquiry.

"Yes. My business is, in a great measure, purely personal to myself. Circumstances have compelled me, during the last few weeks, to pursue a course of conduct for which I feel that I owe you an apology, and of which I am bound to offer you a full explanation."

Mrs. M'Allan inclined her pretty head, and the watchful look deepened in her eyes.

"I will make my explanation as brief as I can. I believe you know that for some weeks after his accident Travers was in considerable danger?"

"So I was told."

"In view of his condition, the doctor gave strict orders that he was to be kept as quiet as possible. Among other things, I was expressly forbidden to allow him to read any letters. All letters that arrived for him, therefore, I put aside until he should be pronounced fit to look at them."

"How wise of you!" Mrs. M'Allan had turned remarkably pale while Lyon was speaking, but her manner still retained its former graceful self-possession. "I know, from experience, that nothing is more exhausting, when one is ill, than attempting to decipher letters. Everybody writes so badly nowadays! I think you acted most judiciously in keeping back Mr. Travers' correspondence from him for a while. Besides, you have provided his convalescence with an amusement. No doubt he will enjoy *now* reading the letters that have been waiting for him so long."

Lyon cleared his throat. "It's—it's in regard to that part of the business that I have ventured to intrude upon you."

"Really? I hardly see where I come in, just there."

"I think you easily will see, in a moment. During the weeks I spoke of, the weeks when Travers was at his worst, you were kind enough to write to him several times. Your letters, consequently, came into my hands with the rest."

Mrs. M'Allan drew a quick breath before replying, with some sharpness of tone, "Why, certainly I wrote to Mr. Travers once or twice. More than once, I know; as to the exact number of times, I can't charge my memory. Still, I am at a loss, Mr.——"

" Lyon."

" Mr. Lyon, to know how you learned the fact of my having written at all. I wasn't aware that you were acquainted with my handwriting."

" Neither was I. Had your letters come by post I should not have been able to identify them. It was the circumstance of your sending them by your maid, of their being delivered into my hands as *letters from you*, which alone gave me any knowledge of the writer. But for this circumstance I should not be able to offer them to you this morning."

With a quaking heart, but a commendably steady hand, Lyon drew a packet, containing some half dozen letters neatly tied up with red tape, from his pocket, and held it politely toward his companion.

" I felt it only right," he added, " that you should yourself decide whether you still wished these letters, now several weeks old, to be delivered."

The color had flashed into Mrs. M'Allan's face at first sight of the packet. " Your offer is a very singular one, Mr. Lyon. Why on earth did you suppose it likely that I should wish to withdraw the letters I wrote only three weeks ago, or less—seeing that one's object in writing a letter at all is that it may be sent to a certain destination ? "

" These letters have never reached their destination."

" No ; there was a special providence in the way, as I understand." In her anger she was forgetting her prudence. " I do not see, however, why you should presume that I must necessarily be grateful to that special providence, by whose action I have been made, in appearance at least, to play the part of a thoroughly unfeeling and unneighborly acquaintance. I—we have not known Mr. Travers long ; but we have known him long enough for him to expect a decent amount of sympathy from us in his misfortune. As matters stand, those letters you hold in your hand are the only proofs we can ever offer him that he has not been altogether forgotten by us. Why should I desire to prevent their reaching him ? "

" You might have desired it." Lyon had foreseen something like this challenge ; he was, consequently, prepared with his answer. "At least, so it seemed to me. Pardon me, if I argued too much from my own prejudices to yours. I have, personally, an insurmountable prejudice to sending, or receiving, a letter which has in any way become out of date; which deals with a set of circumstances no longer existing. Such a letter has always appeared to me worse than valueless—irritating to sender and recipient alike. I fancied," he added slowly, "that you might share my feeling."

"And you came here to-day to find out whether I did share it?"

"Just so."

"I ought to be very much obliged to you, I am sure! But—our acquaintance is so slight—you must really excuse me for thinking it hardly probable you would trouble yourself to take so long a walk—on such a very hot morning, too!—just to save me from the humiliation of having my letters found tedious by Mr. Travers. Come, Mr. Lyon, be candid! Hadn't you some other reason, some weightier reason, for this curious proceeding of yours? Because it is a little curious, you know."

Mrs. M'Allan launched her question with a smile, and an air of undisguised triumph. Clearly she flattered herself that she had driven her enemy into a corner.

"I was afraid it might appear so," Lyon responded imperturbably. "But I am quite willing to be candid—if to confess that I had more reasons than one for coming here to-day is to be candid. I'll not deny that I am considering Travers himself a good deal in this affair. He is much better, but he is only half recovered as yet, and he is exceedingly nervous about himself. Judge yourself whether your letters, addressed to him when he was supposed to be lying at the point of death, are likely to be wholesome reading for him in his present weak condition. It's been our endeavor, from the first, to keep him absolutely free from excitement—to tell him nothing that might agitate him in any way."

Mrs. M'Allan got up suddenly from her chair. "Does that mean," she demanded, with sparkling eyes, "that in addition to suppressing my letters to Mr. Travers you have taken upon yourself to keep him in ignorance of my visits of enquiry?"

Lyon got up also. "I judged it my duty to do so, Mrs. M'Allan. You must remember I was responsible for Travers' safety——"

"To Mrs. Travers?"—with a shrill laugh. "It is for her you hold your brief, then? *She* sent you here to-day. Ah, well! I might have guessed that sooner. Only a man who was acting as the obedient mouth-piece of a jealous woman would have dared to insult another woman as you have insulted me to-day!"

Lyon flushed darkly. But he kept his head. "I am sorry you should put an insulting interpretation on my conduct, Mrs. M'Allan. You are mistaken in so doing. I desired, and desire, to behave with all possible respect toward you. I was under the impression that you accepted what I have done as, at least, done in good faith. But, in any case, all responsibility for my action rests with myself. The lady you allude to, whose commission you suppose me to be holding, is ignorant of the very existence of these letters. She knew nothing of my purpose in coming here, nor of my intention to come. Your name, so far as I am concerned, has never been once mentioned in her presence."

"Really! That is singular. How am I to interpret such—what shall I call it ?—such delicate reserve on your part ? Did you practise it out of consideration for Mrs. Travers' susceptibilities—or mine ?" cried Mrs. M'Allan scornfully. The garment of a superficial refinement was fairly slipping from her shoulders now, and she no longer made any great effort to arrest its escape. "I need hardly enquire. Whatever else you deny, you don't dare to deny that you are acting in her interest !"

"Why should I care to deny it ? I am acting in her interest—if you choose to put it in that way," returned Lyon coolly. "Just as I am acting in her husband's interest—and in yours, too, if you would believe it. Mrs. M'Allan," he continued, slightly changing his tone, "perhaps it's time we were absolutely frank with one another. I've tried, with very poor success, I fear, to approach you diplomatically, when I suspect I should have done better by speaking my mind straight out. At any rate, let me drop all disguises *now*. Let me put the matter to you in blunt terms. Do you really think that, in a year or two's time, the remembrance of having won a petty victory over a woman much less beautiful and gifted than yourself—a woman whom the world would unhesitatingly pronounce your inferior in a hundred points—and gained some passing influence over a man for whom you don't care two straws, will compensate you for the knowledge that you have made that man and that woman alike wretched for life ?"

Mrs. M'Allan affected to laugh. "Really, Mr. Lyon, you take too heroic a tone. We are not on the boards of a theatre; please remember that ! I must protest against being held responsible for the domestic happiness or misery of every married man who chooses to find my society agreeable. It is not my business to dive into the secrets of Mr. Travers' home life. To me he is simply an acquaintance; a pleasant but—how shall I put it?—quite unimportant acquaintance."

"Pray understand," Lyon interrupted eagerly, "that I never for an instant supposed him to possess any importance in your eyes. An insignificant unit in the crowd of your admirers, with whom you perhaps felt inclined to amuse yourself a little; that was the kind of position I guessed him to occupy with you. I was right, it seems. All the same, I would ask you to remember that he has some claims upon your consideration. What is mere play to you may so easily turn out death to him."

"Or to his interesting wife?" mockingly. "Well, I'm sure I've no wish to destroy the poor little lady's peace of mind. What is it you want me to do for her?"

If only the speaker had been a man instead of a woman! A thoroughly angry man is moved by the most primitive impulses; and, had Mrs. M'Allan belonged to his own sex, Lyon would hardly have refrained himself from meeting her insolence with a rougher retort than can be conveyed by mere words. Unfortunately, such retorts are inadmissible where a lady is concerned. Poor Lyon, therefore, was obliged to smother his climbing elemental passions, and reply, with such civility as he could assume:

"I have but one suggestion to make—the suggestion I have already made in the interests of—of everybody concerned: Will you allow me to return these letters to your own keeping?"

"Is that all? Don't you wish me to promise that I will destroy them, and never, never write any more?"

"That is precisely what I do wish." Lyon perceived that nothing was now to be gained by attempting to mince matters. Affairs had reached a stage at which the plainest speaking alone was likely to prove effective.

"And supposing I refuse to gratify your wishes?" with a quick, defiant toss of the golden head backward, and a flash of the magnificent gray eyes full into his. "Supposing I decline absolutely to take back my letters? What then?"

"Why, then, of course, I shall be compelled, however unwillingly, to deliver them."

"To whom?"

"To the person to whom they are addressed, naturally."

"But, equally naturally, in the presence of some other person, I suppose? Of Mrs. Travers, for instance?"

" You must excuse me from answering that question, Mrs. M'Allan. The point is one which I have not, as yet, considered."

If ever hatred looked out of human eyes, it looked out of Mrs. M'Allan's, as, with a sudden vehement gesture of command, she stretched out her hand toward Lyon. "Give those things to me!" she said, with a sort of breathless violence.

Lyon obeyed.

She pulled off the tape which bound the packet together, roughly, without untying it, and, taking each letter separately, tore it hastily across and across. Finally, she flung the torn pieces *pêle-mêle* into the empty grate by which she stood.

" I trust you are satisfied," was her comment, as she turned once more to her visitor, speaking now with an outward show of composure, a composure by which, however, she did not altogether succeed in veiling a suggestion of suppressed rage.

" I think you have acted very wisely," was the cautious reply.

" Thanks for your good opinion," and this time she executed a smile. ("Executed" is really the only word correctly describing her performance ; the smile was so evidently made to order.) " As to my wisdom—why should I not act wisely in such a case ? There's not much merit in showing one's self wise where there is no temptation to folly. I'll own that your request staggered me a little at first. But then, you see, it was so unusual. However, I am sure you did not *mean* to take any unwarrantable liberty. And I can only say that if, by tearing up that rubbish,"—she waved her hand gracefully toward the littered grate,—" I have afforded you real relief from your anxieties, and done Mrs. Travers a service, I am delighted, truly delighted, that you should have thought of appealing to me. Good-morning, Mr. Lyon."

Lyon went back to the Paris a little intoxicated by his triumph. The triumph was unmarred by any touch of pity for his fallen foe —since he had made up his mind that Mrs. M'Allan's affections, supposing her to possess any, were in no wise engaged in this affair. A conclusion which showed that, professed student of human nature though he was, he had yet a good deal to learn where the feminine variety of the species was concerned. " A mere question of vanity," he assured himself comfortably. " No woman who really *cared* would have given in so easily."

A day or two later, Brian making all the while hourly strides toward complete recovery, Dorothy announced that the doctor had authorized her taking him to England in a week's time. She followed up this announcement—one not at all surprising to Lyon, who had been for some time in daily expectation of it—by a request which did surprise him very much. Would he add to his many kindnesses yet one more ? Would he travel with them to England, and bear Brian company for a few weeks after their arrival?

"It would be an immense pleasure to my husband," she said. "Of course," she added quickly, seeing that he did not immediately reply, "if you have other engagements, you must not think of giving them up. Malton Barnard—the place we are going to—is in the depths of the country, quiet and humdrum to the last degree; and you must have many other friends, with far greater claims upon you than ourselves."

"Well, they haven't shown any great anxiety to advance their claims, so far," returned Lyon, smiling slightly. "I have absolutely no engagements in England, Mrs. Travers; honor bright ! I am quite free to accept your kind invitation; and I accept it, gladly."

"Thank you ; you are very good. You don't know how grateful I am to you. Grateful not for this only "—Dorothy turned very pale all at once, and her voice trembled— "but for—all the rest. For one thing above all—which I can't talk about ! Don't imagine that because I never speak of that day at San Remo I have forgotten it. I shall never forget it as long as I live !" .

With that she escaped from the room, leaving Lyon, for once in his life, in a delightful glow of self-esteem. The consciousness that one has been the active means of leading a fellow-creature—hitherto frankly acknowledged one's moral superior—back from the byways of error into the strait path of righteousness, is one of the most agreeable in the world. Equally gratifying is the conviction that one has behaved admirably under extremely trying circumstances. This consciousness and this conviction were both Lyon's ; and his enjoyment of their pleasant flavor was enhanced by a touch of pride in the dexterity with which he had so lately succeeded in routing the formidable Mrs. M'Allan. Small blame to him if, for a moment, he were inclined to boast himself a little.

Unfortunately, so weak is average human nature that it can ill bear the dazzling revelation of a great moral beauty residing in itself. Thus it not infrequently happens that the ordinary man, having fallen for a while to admiring gaze before some striking manifestation of his own superior wisdom and virtue, turns from the pleasing image only to commit an act remarkable either for its

16

folly or its wickedness, or for both combined.   Lyon was not
ignorant of the proneness of mankind to give itself the lie in this
manner.   He had seen the tendency exhibited a score of times—in
the persons of other people.   Need one add that it never occurred
to him, in the present instance, to argue from other people to himself, from his neighbor's case to his own ?

CHAPTER VIII

MALTON BARNARD

" No man measures in advance
His strength with untried circumstance."

A FORTNIGHT, a month, six weeks passed away without anything
occurring to disturb the atmosphere of self-satisfaction in which
Lyon drew unusually serene breath.   Every day added something
to the strength of his conviction that his part at San Remo and
Monte Carlo had been played with credit to himself and profit to
his friends.   Fortified by this conviction, he found it easy to dismiss from his mind the misgivings which might otherwise have
found lodgment there, and to strangle any incipient stirring of
self-distrust before it could become unpleasantly articulate.   He
had no hesitation in extending his stay at Malton Barnard from
day to day, and week to week.   Indeed, he occasionally went so
far as to consider his compliance with Brian's solicitations in this
matter a new and striking proof of virtue.   Malton Barnard was
undeniably dull ; and he could easily have found elsewhere company more congenial than that of his host.   However, since his
continued presence was undoubtedly useful to Dorothy, serving to
amuse her husband, and to allay a little Brian's discontent with
his surroundings, he was magnanimously willing to remain.   He
felt himself in some sort responsible for her happiness ; if, by a
slight sacrifice of his inclinations, he could do much to make her
happy, he were surely worse than a brute to shrink back, because
of the personal discomfort the sacrifice involved !

The *rôle* of guardian angel was new to Lyon.   Possibly its very
novelty made it the more attractive to him, and caused him to
throw himself into the character with greater zeal.

It must be acknowledged that Brian's unequal moods often tried his slender stock of angelic qualities to the uttermost. Malton Barnard, which from the first he had uncivilly designated "a deadly hole," became every day a more distasteful place of residence to Travers ; and his railings at the hard fate which kept him imprisoned in so uncongenial a spot increased continually in frequency and bitterness. This temper did not tend to make him a pleasant companion, as Lyon found to his cost.

He was not long in learning the reason why Travers, hating Malton Barnard, yet remained in it. Brian, who loved to talk of his own affairs, soon gave him to understand that it was a purely financial one. His resources, at a low ebb when Lyon first met him, for he had always lived up to the limit of his handsome salary as engineer of the Bussana line, and, indeed, a little beyond it, had been further reduced by the heavy expenses incident to Robin's illness and his own ; and when his brother-in-law—husband of the whilom "advanced" Isabel, who had long since exchanged the exciting career of a Radical lecturer for the more humdrum existence of wife to a small country gentleman of strict Tory principles—had good-naturedly proffered his house in Norfolk, rent-free, for the period of his own absence in America, where he was making a twelve months' tour, Brian, it was clear, had been only too glad to close with the offer. Nevertheless, he was now vaguely persuaded that he might have found some more agreeable way out of the pecuniary embarrassments besetting him at the moment of his return to England.

His confidences did not stop here. They extended to his relations with his late employers in Italy. Out of a mass of accusations and complaints Lyon soon disentangled the fact that if directors and engineer had not parted on the best possible terms, the latter had only himself to thank for that undesirable state of affairs. Not that Brian admitted any fault on his own side ; quite the reverse. But it was clear to Lyon, nevertheless, that his congenital instability of purpose had cropped out again—to his partial undoing at least, since by his own confession the field of employment in Italy was henceforth closed against him—long before his five years' engagement came to an end. While the business under his charge remained in the exciting initial stage, he had labored at it heart and soul. But when it became question of mere mechanical execution of plans already fixed, his interest had begun to flag, and, along with this, his vigilance and his industry ; a decline which had not gone unnoted, evidently, by the keen vision of his foreign superiors.

"He is perfectly impossible!" Such was Lyon's private reflection one day, after Brian had been giving himself away rather more recklessly than usual in the matter of the wrongs he had suffered at the hands of "that rascally Italian Government." "He *can't* see the facts of any case in which he happens to be concerned himself, except in a distorted light. The idea that he might be to blame, personally, for his own failures is simply inconceivable to him. What is to become of him Heaven only knows! And yet he is clever enough! Some of his notions have a touch of genius in them. Unfortunately, he'll never take the trouble of working them out, so there's no prospect for him in that direction. A lectureship would be, perhaps, his best chance. Put him on a platform, where he could be perpetually showing off, and he might feel reluctant to come down from it. Of course, he has about as much chance of a well-endowed appointment of that kind, one on which he could live, and keep his family in decent comfort, as I have of being made President of the Royal Society."

A few days later Lyon's reflections concerning his host began to take a different turn. "It is quite time that he should be up and doing, making some effort after fresh work. If all he tells me of his pecuniary position is true, he hasn't a moment to lose. And he is perfectly well now; strong as a horse, and fit for anything."

Unluckily, with Brian, physical fitness for work did not manifest itself in any eager desire to put his strength to the test. Its chief outward signs were confined to a growing impatience of the monotony of Malton Barnard, and a growing inclination to diversify this monotony by flying visits to livelier places. At first his expeditions did not extend farther than Norwich or Cambridge and involved only a few hours' absence. After a time, however, he began to turn longing eyes in the direction of London. And, one fine morning at breakfast, he announced that he had made up his mind to take a run to town; adding carelessly, "I shall have to stay the night, of course."

"It's such a pity Brian hasn't taken more kindly to this place," Dorothy remarked wistfully to Lyon half an hour later, as they stood together under the deep porch which formed the entrance to her brother-in-law's house. The old anxious, half-fearful look was in her eyes as she spoke. "I hoped he would have liked it, while the fine weather lasted, at least. It's not amusing, I know. But then it is so pretty ! "

" It certainly is pretty enough," Lyon allowed, looking thoughtfully before him. " But—no, I don't think anyone would be found to call it amusing. Over-solitary, I should fancy, for most people's taste. The present generation has no fancy for lodges in the wilderness, let the wilderness itself be ever so fair to view."

Of the solitary situation of Malton Barnard there could be little question. The house—a rambling combination of old and new brick, built after the Elizabethan style ; many-gabled, mullion-windowed, mantled to its very chimney-tops with ivy, clematis, and Virginia creeper—stood in the midst of a deep depression among the hills, at least two miles distant from any other human habitation. Immediately surrounding it was an expanse of flat green meadows, surrounded, in its turn, on three sides by the hill-rampart, clothed from top to bottom with a mingled growth of firs and larch, mountain-ash and weeping birch, and curving gently to a point toward the east. On the fourth and western side—the house fronted west—there was a greater effect of space : here the valley opened out a little, the hills receding to form a kind of ascending gorge, in which the heather grew knee, and the bracken breast, high, while the banks on either hand were crowned with pines. But even in this direction the outlook was an extremely circumscribed one, the gorge, as it rose higher, soon losing itself in an impenetrable mass of woodland which completely barred the western horizon from view. The only hint of any wider world outside this sequestered dell was conveyed to its inhabitants by a mere glimpse, to be caught through a narrow cleft in the hill-barrier on the northeast, of a deep blue haze, impenetrable and illimitable ; offering rather a subtle suggestion of the sea's near presence than any actual vision of its tossing waters.

" For myself," Lyon continued, the pause following his last remark remaining unbroken by his companion, " I find this sort of thing"—with a comprehensive wave of the hand—"wholly delightful. To me the solitude is part of the charms. But then, you must remember that I am horribly indolent by nature, and savagely unsociable besides. Your husband is cast in a different mould. There is nothing either of the lotos-eater or the barbarian in his composition."

" No," Dorothy assented. " I am glad," she added rather abruptly, " to hear that you find Malton pleasant. I have sometimes been afraid that you, too, felt bored by such monotonous quiet, day after day."

"I? Hardly!" Lyon's glance ranged once more over the surrounding scene, and returned to the woman at his side. "I believe," he observed in an unusually subdued tone, "that these last six weeks have been about the happiest of my wandering existence."

A strange look, swift and bright as a flash of lightning, passed over Dorothy's face. But Lyon did not see its passage. Speaking, he had turned a little aside from his companion, pulling reflectively at a spray of clematis which hung down from the lintel above his head.

"After seven years of India, you can hardly imagine, perhaps, how I revel in all this. Still less can you guess how a man feels when he has been without a home for nearly twenty years, and——"

A deep booming stroke from the grandfather's clock in the hall behind him interrupted the speaker. Dorothy started slightly.

"Half-past nine!" she ejaculated. "I must go and see that Brian's packing is done at once—else he may miss the train."

She went indoors with nervous haste. But she did not immediately go upstairs; she turned first into the gun-room, where she felt pretty certain of finding her husband. There, sure enough, she found him, extremely busy with a book of salmon flies.

"I was just getting these into some sort of order," he explained, looking up from his employment as she paused behind his chair; "in case Johnson should ask me up to Scotland in September, you know. He *ought* to ask me; I've done him plenty of good turns in the past. But he always was a selfish brute; I dare say he'll never think of it."

"You might not be free to go in September—that's one consolation," Dorothy suggested rather timidly. "Supposing you get a new berth before then——"

"Oh, it's very unlikely I shall step into anything so quickly! New berths, more especially good ones, are not so easy to come at."

"I know. For that very reason oughtn't you to be making some effort now?"

"There's no hurry. We are free to stay in this deadly-lively hole till next spring; that gives me nine months."

"But—the expenses of living during those nine months! And

servants and clothes—— I don't want to bother you unnecessarily, dear, but you know one must think of these things. A
house isn't everything."

"It counts for a good deal, though. However, we must leave
any discussion of ways and means till to-morrow, when I come
back. I've no time to discuss anything now ; I must go and get
ready. I ordered the cob for ten o'clock."

"You have quite made up your mind to go, then ?"

"Why not ? You speak as if there were some objection to
my going."

"I was thinking of Mr. Lyon. Doesn't it seem a little—inhos-
pitable for you to go away and leave him to himself ?"

Brian laughed easily. "My dear girl, I really don't think Lyon
will find any difficulty in existing for twenty-four hours without
me. Certainly I see no need for any standing upon ceremony with
him in the matter. More particularly as he will not really be
alone ; he will have you to keep him company."

"That's just it," Dorothy struck in, with a sudden quick flush.
"Won't people think it strange ?"

"Think what strange ?" Brian paused in his occupation of
strapping the fly-book together, and looked up at his wife with a
puzzled expression on his handsome face.

"That you should go away, leaving me by myself with your
guest."

Brian's look of perplexity changed to one of contemptuous
annoyance. "Dorothy, I hope to goodness you're not going to
turn prude at this time of day ! I never heard anything so ridiculous in my life. Old Lyon ! whom I've known for five-and-twenty
years ! And 'people thinking it strange' ! What 'people' are
there in this desert, to 'think' anything about the matter ? Are
you afraid of Mrs. Grundy in the form of the weeding woman ?"

Dorothy, dumfoundered at the fashion in which her impulsive
appeal had been received, made no attempt to answer this ironical
question. She stood nervously rolling and unrolling a bit of string
which lay near her on the table, saying nothing.

"The truth is," Brian continued in a less vehemently scornful
tone, returning to his momentarily abandoned employment, "that
you are put out at my going to town, though you know quite well
it's chiefly business which takes me there, and so you raise this
absurd scruple. I have far too much respect, both for you and
Lyon, to let myself be influenced by any such nonsensical con-

sideration, I can assure you ! Why, the knowledge that Lyon
would be here while I'm away was the turning point with me in
deciding to go ! I should not have liked to leave you quite alone
in this solitary house—alone with the children and the maids,
without a man servant within call at night. But Lyon being on
the spot, I shall feel quite comfortable about you."

Certainly Dorothy's effort after independence, her ambitious
attempt to "live her own life," had been of brief duration. It
was hardly likely that this colloquy with her husband should have
conduced either to unruffled temper or high spirits on her part.
Yet when, less than half an hour after it ended, she came to the
door to see him off, she was smiling and good-humored as though
nothing whatever had occurred to annoy her.

"Take good care of my wife, Lyon," Brian commanded, as he
sprang up into his brother-in-law's dog-cart. "I leave her in your
charge, mind ! Don't let her walk too far, or wear herself to
fiddlestrings in the service of the nursery tyrants. Remember, I
rely upon you."

"I will do my best," Lyon responded gravely. His face, in
responding, was inscrutable, almost expressionless. If he felt any
pleasure in getting rid of Travers for a while, or any indignation
with Travers for going, his countenance certainly betrayed no sign
of either emotion.

"*Au revoir !*" cried Brian, gathering up his reins. "See you
again to-morrow evening."

It was not till the evening after that, however, that he actually
reappeared. Dorothy was apprised by telegram of the reason of
his prolonged absence—and this she communicated briefly to
Lyon. "His business had detained him," she said. Whereupon
Lyon remarked cynically, to himself, not to her, that he had no
doubt of that. Only, as to whether the business in question were
exclusively connected with Lincoln's Inn and the City, he suspended judgment.

This expedition to town was the forerunner of many similar
expeditions—these later journeys being, however, undertaken on
a more clearly defined plea. The deferred discussion on ways and
means having been held, much to Brian's dislike, on his return,
even that easy-going person had been brought to allow that
"something must be done." A day or two later he had taken a
further step; translating this vague and nebulous phrase into the
more practical: "I must set about getting an appointment at once."

But it is well known that appointments worthy of such talents as Brian's are only to be picked up in London. Brian showed a good deal of energy in going to look for them there ; and quite a singular amount of perseverance in continuing to pursue his quest when it did not at once prove successful.

He usually remained away a couple of nights on these occasions ; which recurred so frequently that before long Dorothy grew accustomed alike to his absences and to the *tête-à-têtes* with Lyon to which they condemned her. At first when Brian was not there a nervous inclination to hold herself slightly aloof from his guest had shown itself now and then ; but habit soon made an end of this touch of reserve, and she became natural and simple as ever— natural and simple as she had used to be in the days of her girlhood. Lyon, watching her in his observant, unobtrusive fashion, perceived that, half unconsciously to herself, these frequent absences of Brian were becoming so many brief informal holidays to his wife ; times of free breathing, during which she felt herself at liberty to move and speak and look as she pleased, without fear of disastrous ulterior consequences ; delicious seasons of rest, when the task of perpetually " climbing up the climbing wave " of a selfish man's unstable fancy could be momentarily suspended. Brian away, she could play with the children as though she were herself a child again, or pore over her favorite books, without fear, in either case, of interruption from a guilty conscience, bidding her go and " amuse " Brian—Brian, so often, unhappily, utterly unresponsive to her pathetic efforts to entertain him. Little by little, even her long-repressed enthusiasms in matters for which her husband cared nothing began to revive, to put out new, shy, tender shoots of thought ; and Lyon found her talking to him in the evenings of politics, and art, and books, with an interest which now and then rose almost to eagerness.

To him this recrudescence of her old self seemed at once a delightful and a pitiful thing to witness. A phenomenon full of charm, yes ; but one with which a large element of pathos was inextricably bound up. For, let her nature expand ever so freely, so happily, to-day, the morrow that brought back Brian, to be watched, and coaxed, and fascinated into good humor and content at any cost, would surely see it shrink again into its former narrow artificial limits. This consciousness of his, that her freedom was only for a time, invested her figure, in his eyes, with an unvarying sadness ; it is probable that he often pitied her in hours when she had altogether forgotten, for a while, to pity herself.

He no longer ventured to condemn her for the self-suppression he had once called by the harsh name of "hypocrisy." Her method was to so great an extent redeemed by its motive; her artifice had in it so much of nobleness, so much of unselfish devotion, that he doubted whether in truth that which he had scorned as a contemptible vice might not more fitly rank as an honorable virtue. That Brian's character should be one compelling the exercise of such virtues on his wife's part did not, however, make Lyon feel the more kindly toward him, or more tolerant of his society on those days when he happened to be at Malton Barnard. But for an increasing sense of his own "usefulness," Mr. Travers' guest would hardly have seen the month of June out in Norfolk.

As it was, he lingered on well into July. Indeed, the last week of that month had come without his making any decided movement to shift his quarters; and he was reading the *Times* under the porch after breakfast, as it had become his daily habit to do, with no clear notion in his mind as to the date when he should finally give up this and other pleasant habits connected with Malton Barnard, when he was surprised by the appearance of a mounted messenger from the nearest telegraph office, four miles away. He paid the two shillings demanded of him, took the yellow envelope—and discovered with some astonishment that it was addressed to himself.

The telegram it contained was not calculated to allay his first feeling of surprise. It proceeded from an Anglo-Indian acquaintance, a man some ten years his senior, who held a fairly high position in the Civil Service, and with whom he had at one time formed a passing intimacy, and requested an interview with him in town, "at his earliest convenience." He happened to know at second-hand that the sender of the telegram had lately come home on furlough, so the man's presence in London did not puzzle him; but why this request for a meeting? "Important business" was the sole reason laconically avouched for the demand. No word of explanation as to the nature of the business. Even Lyon's curiosity, usually a very languid quality, was stirred for the moment.

"I may as well run up this afternoon," he reflected, as he returned the telegram to its envelope. "The cob can very well go to the station a second time; he is getting fat for want of work. Then I can return with Travers to-morrow."

Brian was absent, as usual, having gone up to London by the first train, to prosecute his enquiries after well-paid appointments. To hear him talk, one might imagine that such things were retailed in the streets of the Metropolis like strawberries or penny ices.

Lyon did not add, even to himself, that the telegram had arrived at a peculiarly opportune moment—Dorothy having engaged to dine and sleep that night at the house of some old Hillshire friends who happened to be staying in a village on the coast for change of air. It is probable, however, that a recollection of this fact may have assisted his rapid decision.

Turning into the square, oak-panelled hall, which served as a sitting-room for the family in the earlier hours of the day, he met Dorothy coming out of the drawing-room, which opened upon it. She looked flurried and perturbed, and, on perceiving her guest, shut the drawing-room door rather sharply behind her; a movement which, however, passed unnoticed by Lyon, still a good deal preoccupied with the enigmatic matter of his telegram.

He began to tell his tale; but if he was preoccupied, so was Mrs. Travers. She lent him only a reluctant ear and a divided attention, while every now and then she would glance apprehensively at the closed door of the drawing-room, as if listening for a sound from within. Once, Lyon, following her glance for an instant, paused in the midst of a sentence and involuntarily listened too. But no sound made itself heard save the familiar "yap" of Rip, Robin's fox-terrier, who had evidently found his way into the room through an open window, and was begging to be let out.

He finished sketching out his plan of action; and she, making a visible effort to collect her wandering thoughts, asked him a needful question or two touching the hour at which he desired to start, rang the bell, and gave an order to the servant. Then, seeing him turn in the direction of the stairs, she said:

"If there's time before you go, after you have everything ready, I should be glad to speak to you again for a minute. I want you to give me your advice."

"Let me give it you at once—such as it is"—becoming suddenly alive to the anxiety written in her face. "I am quite at your service——"

"No, no!" she interrupted hurriedly. "You must not miss your train. But if you find you have a few minutes to spare, after putting up your things——"

Lyon's preparations were quickly made. In less than ten minutes he came downstairs again, valise in hand, to find Dorothy awaiting him in the hall. Rip was still giving audible tokens of his presence in the drawing-room, whining and howling alternately without intermission.

"Here I am !" Lyon said cheerfully, setting down his valise on a chair. "And I need not start for half an hour at least, so anything—— What a tremendous row that dog is kicking up ! "—interrupting himself at the sound of a fresh and peculiarly distressful howl from the imprisoned Rip. "Shall I see what's amiss with him ? He seems to be in trouble of some sort."

He was moving to the drawing-room door, but Dorothy intercepted his movement.

"Wait a moment, please. Rip isn't himself this morning ; I don't know what to make of him. He seemed so queer that I felt afraid to leave him with the children. So I brought him in and shut him up. Robin was crying just now because I refused to let him out till you had seen him. It is strange ; I never saw the dog like this before. And, it may be fancy, but his bark, his voice altogether, has an altered sound to my ears. Listen, you will hear what I mean."

Lyon listened attentively. The howling on the other side of the door suddenly ceased, and in its place came a series of short, snapping barks which caused his countenance to grow extremely grave.

"You say the dog has shown himself ' queer ' this morning," he remarked, turning to Dorothy, who stood a little behind him. "Do you mean savage ? "

"Yes ; savage, and at the same time ill. I could see the poor creature was suffering horribly when I brought him in. He has never been quite well, I believe, since that time three weeks ago, when he was lost for a couple of days—you remember ? He often seemed heavy and stupid ; and the children were dreadfully distressed because they couldn't get him to eat. But he has always been quite good-tempered till to-day, when he suddenly developed a propensity to fly at everyone who ventured to touch him. He flew at Dolly, and tore her frock, just after breakfast ; and when I picked him up in the garden afterward, he seemed to be choking with rage, and did his very best to bite me."

"He didn't succeed ? "—quickly.

"No; I had on my heavy coat, and all he could do was to tear a piece out of that—the thickness of the cloth quite baffled his intentions. Now, will you look at him, and tell me what I ought to do ? "

" Certainly—if you'll undertake, on your part, to shut this door behind me as soon as I'm fairly inside it. Until we've ascertained what is wrong with the poor beast, it would be the height of folly to let him loose into the house. Perhaps you might as well stay within call, if you don't mind ? Thanks—I may have to ask you to ring the bell. But don't come in, or open the door, unless I shout, 'All right.' Are you ready ? "

Lyon was over the threshold in the twinkling of an eye ; and before he could even catch sight of the dog in the semi-darkness of the room into which he had so rapidly precipitated himself—the windows were fitted with outside shutters, all of which Dorothy had closed—he had the satisfaction of hearing the door close sharply behind him. Peering about in the artificial twilight, he presently made out the terrier, huddled up against a leg of the grand piano, and tearing furiously at the carpet with his teeth and forepaws.

" Here, Rip ! Rip, come out, sir ! " he commanded, advancing cautiously. " Come out, good dog ! "

But Rip retreated, terrified at his approach, and fled howling under the nearest sofa. Lyon dropped on his hands and knees, searching this new entrenchment with an expression of growing anxiety.

" I don't like this," he muttered, after a moment's study of the terrier in his place of refuge. " A case of rabies, if I'm not greatly mistaken. Holloa ! "

This exclamation was the result of an unexpected move on Rip's part. Suddenly abandoning defensive for offensive tactics, the dog had flown savagely full at the man's face. Lyon had but just time to throw himself backward, so that the open jaws struck his chest, well protected by a stout tweed coat, instead of his defenceless throat.

The next moment he had his struggling, slavering enemy fast by the neck.

" This is a pretty piece of business ! " he remarked grimly aloud, looking down at the furious animal writhing in his grasp. " I can't move—and I daren't let go."

He felt a light touch on his shoulder. " Tell me what to do," said Dorothy's voice.

He looked up, profoundly startled—more startled than when Rip had flown at him. She stood behind him, pale, but without a shadow of fear in her white face. He knew instantly how it had all happened. She had followed him in. When she shut the door upon him, she had shut it upon herself also.

"You !" he exclaimed. "I thought I told you——"

"Never mind that now," she interrupted. "What can I do to help ?"

He considered an instant. "Ring, and send—— No, there's not time for that ; I mightn't be able to hold him so long. Go yourself to the gun-room. Get me Brian's rifle—the second in the rack, counting from the right. The second, mind. Bring a couple of No. 6 cartridges with you—you'll find them in the locker. Be as quick as you can."

He need not have added his final recommendation ; Dorothy scarcely touched the ground as she ran on her errand. The gun-room was hardly twenty paces off, yet the way there seemed terribly long to her. She found the rifle instantly, in the place indicated ; but no No. 6 cartridges were to be seen in the first division of the locker when she threw it open, and the lid of the second stuck fast for perhaps half a minute—oh, the long, the unutterably protracted agony of the thirty seconds which passed before she succeeded in wrenching it free ! At last, at last it is loose—and—yes, thank God ! the cartridges are there. Snatching them up in one hand, carrying the rifle in the other, she came flying back.

Not a moment too soon for Lyon. He was doing all he knew ; but it was clear that even his exceptional muscular strength would not have availed him to retain his prisoner much longer. Already the dog had so far released himself as to be able to turn his head, and his teeth were fast buried in his captor's right sleeve.

"Cartridges ?" enquired Lyon, as Dorothy swept up to him. "No. 6 ? You're sure ? Could you manage to slip one in, do you think ? You know the way ?"

Yes, thank Heaven ! she did know the way. One turn of her hand, and the thing was done.

"Full cock," ordered Lyon. "Now, lay it down beside me—on my right there—and go into the hall and shut the door."

But this time Dorothy made no movement to obey. "You will have to let go of him when you take it up," she said.

"Naturally. Please go ; time's precious."

"While you are taking it up, he will fly at you ! No !"—in

answer to an imperious motion of his head—" I will not go, or lay down the gun ; I'll shoot him myself, since it's necessary. Show me where—no, don't move your hand ; I didn't mean *show*—*tell* me where—that will be enough——"

" You can't do it," Lyon said gaspingly. Indeed, he was both physically and mentally out of breath.

" I can and will ! Where ? "

" Here, then, if you are determined—behind his ear. Put the muzzle quite close; closer still ! Don't think about my hand—you won't hurt it. Now ! "

Dorothy never had any very clear remembrance of the minutes which followed immediately upon Lyon's " Now ! " and her own resolute pulling of the trigger. A loud noise ; a little cloud of smoke gradually dispersing itself about the room ; a vision of Lyon, a good deal paler than his wont, getting up from his knees and shaking himself with—" That's well over ! "—then an irruption of the household in general upon the scene : frightened maids from the kitchen, quickly followed by a little crowd of excited stable-boys and enquiring gardeners, pushing one another through the doorway ; Robin, the centre of the assembly, weeping bitterly over the corpse of the defunct Rip, and most ineffectually consoled by the coachman; these were all fragmentary recollections having no seeming connection with one another ; dim and indistinct of outline, like the memories of a disjointed dream. She stood, as in a dream, hearing Lyon explain to the startled servants what had come to pass without really taking in a word either of his explanation, or their responsive comments thereupon.

His duty in this matter done, he turned to her. " Hadn't you better sit down ? " he suggested.

She shook her head vaguely, looking mechanically at poor little Rip—harmless enough now—lying stretched out in the middle of the carpet ; and he, interpreting her look to mean dislike of the sight, beckoned to the coachman. " Take the dog away," he said in a low voice.

Not so low, however, but that his order reached Robin's quick ear. Instantly the boy burst out into violent protest.

" He sha'n't ! he sha'n't ! Rip's mine—my very own ! I won't have him taken away ! "

Lyon gripped him sternly by the shoulder. " Look here, my man, we must have no more of this. The dog's dead—and you're upsetting your mother——"

"You had no business to kill him!" the child retorted furiously. Breaking from Lyon's hold, he flung himself upon Dorothy, where she still stood like one half dazed, holding mechanically by the back of the sofa. "Mother, mother, do see what Mr. Lyon has done! He has killed Rip! He is a wicked, cruel man, and I hate him!"

"Hush!" Dorothy's hand was on the boy's quivering lips. "Mr. Lyon did not kill Rip, Robin; *I* killed him."

"You, mummy?" Robin recoiled visibly as he uttered his ejaculation; but his tone was incredulous, nevertheless. Evidently he found it impossible to believe that an act which to his mind appeared quite monstrous in its brutality could have been committed by his mother.

"Yes; I, dear," she answered.

"Then it is you who are cruel——" Robin choked over the other word.

"I dare say it seems so—to you. But Mr. Lyon will tell you—— Oh, don't turn away, Robin, darling!"—for the boy was twisting himself angrily from her—"listen to me a moment! The poor dog was mad, quite mad; and Mr. Lyon was risking his life just to keep him from attacking us, from hurting us. Oh!" she cried, with a sudden and complete change of tone, passing all at once from persuasive entreaty to passionate impatience, "what is all this fuss about a dog? It is Mr. Lyon you should be thinking about—and thanking God that he is safe——"

Her voice died away suddenly in her throat; a quick shudder shook her from head to foot. Putting Robin from her, she sank down into the nearest seat, and lifted eyes of pathetic appeal to Lyon. "Get rid of—of all these people, will you, please?" she said, as soon as she could find strength to speak at all. "I don't think I can bear them here any longer."

Lyon had the room clear in a trice. "Yes, you too, my boy," he said firmly, giving Robin, who had broken out into a fresh agony of crying, a gentle push in the direction of the open door. "You see, your mother can't talk to you just now. She'll see you again in a little while, I dare say——"

"In a very little while, dear," Dorothy assented faintly, leaning back and shutting her eyes.

So Robin had to go. He went the less unwillingly that he could hear the coachman in the hall discussing the arrangements for Rip's funeral. The bare idea of a funeral had some consolation in it : it was a comfort to know that if his favorite were dead, there yet remained the melancholy pleasure of burying him.

Possibly Robin is not the only sincere mourner in whose case the anticipated excitement of " a burying " has done something to assuage the first bitterness of bereavement.

Robin, then, went. But his nurse lingered behind to suggest the propriety of a glass of wine for her mistress. Lyon supported the proposition with all the eloquence he could muster ; but to no avail. Dorothy remained obstinate in her refusal ; pressed hard to change her mind, she even became irritable.

" I want nothing, nothing ! " she asserted half angrily ; " except to be left quiet for a moment."

The servant accepted this rather broad hint, and departed to her nursery, closing the door as she went out with an air of offence. Lyon wondered whether he ought to go too ? On the whole, he thought, yes. She had expressed a wish to be perfectly quiet. There was nothing he could possibly do for her if he stayed. And, under the circumstances, it seemed at once the wisest and the most considerate course to leave her for a while wholly to herself. Much better that he should go.

Strange to say, having argued the question out thus sensibly, he did not go after all. He stayed.

But he was ill at ease in staying. He lingered nervously, fidgeting about the room in a restless fashion very unusual with him, and scarcely venturing to glance, now and then, under his lowered eyelids at Dorothy, where she lay back in her chair with closed eyes. She took no notice of his presence—which his continual movement must have made evident enough to her hearing —for some minutes. But at length she looked up, with a feeble apology for a smile.

" I am much better now," she observed in a would-be cheery tone. She half rose in her chair as she spoke ; but quickly sank back again, with a repetition of her former shudder.

" I believe Jane was in the right," Lyon remarked, watching her. " A glass of sherry would have done you all the good in the world."

" I'm not faint. It's the—the horror of the thing I can't get over at once," she responded, shivering again. " Seeing his teeth in your sleeve——" She sprang up suddenly, interrupting herself with a sort of cry. " How did I come to forget ? He may have bitten you. Let me see ! oh, let me see ! "

17

"He hasn't bitten me, I assure you. I didn't get so much as a scratch from him."

"Let me see for myself !" she persisted, catching eagerly at his arm. "You shall not prevent me ; I *will* see for myself !"—speaking with a passionate insistence which startled and almost horrified him.

Recognizing the uselessness of further resistance, he quickly unbuttoned his shirt-cuff and pushed back his sleeve. The upper side of the wrist thus bared bore no sign of any wound ; but on the under side—when she had twisted round his hand so as to expose it—there appeared a round, jagged abrasion of the skin, about the size of a shilling. At sight of this Dorothy's pale face became almost ghastly in its whiteness.

"He *has* bitten you, then ?" She had scarce breath left to utter the words.

"No, no, indeed ! Do believe me."

"What is the use of trying to deceive me any longer ? Your wrist is torn, bleeding——"

"Yes. But not from the dog's teeth. Look, the thing happened this way : His bite struck through my coat-sleeve on this starched cuff ; it went no farther. But he hung on so tightly and bit so hard that he forced one of my sleeve-links right into my arm ; I remember feeling it at the time. They're rather an uncommon shape, you see : perfectly round, and heavily worked—I got them in Benares—which accounts for these jagged edges. See, the button exactly fits the place. Are you satisfied ?"

She fell back from him a little, dropping his hand—on which she had unconsciously kept hold till now. "I must be, I suppose," she murmured. Suddenly, as if stung by a fresh doubt, she lifted her eyes and looked straight into his face. "It's not merely that you *fancy* this may be as you say ? You are sure of it—absolutely sure ?"

He paused an instant as his eyes met hers ; and in those few seconds of silence—the merest fragment of time, infinitesimal if measured by prosaic clock-ticks—his aims, his purposes, his very nature itself underwent a change so profound that he seemed, even to himself, to emerge from it, not an altered man merely, but another—one who had no relation whatever to the Anthony Lyon of half a minute earlier. His very voice sounded unfamiliar to his own ear as he responded, with lips which had grown white in the struggle of that strange metamorphosis :

" As sure as I am—that I love you."

The words were said. They could never be unsaid. How he had come to utter such words, what impulse, what devil had impelled him to the utterance, he did not rightly know. Two minutes earlier he would cheerfully have staked his life on the certainty that such words would never pass his lips. Nevertheless, having uttered them, though, as it seemed, almost without his will, he let them lie. He would not seek to withdraw, to qualify, to weaken them—much less to explain them away. Indeed, they could not be explained away. His only possible part was to wait silently the thunderbolt he had called down on his head.

No thunderbolt fell. Dorothy did indeed quiver through all her frame as he flung the blunt, amazing sentence at her, and a hot color flamed over her face for a moment. But her response held no anger—no surprise even.

"You are safe then—wholly safe," she said, almost in a whisper. "I am glad—thankful!" Then she put her hand over her eyes for a moment.

He stood looking down at her bent head, stupidly dumb. It is not too much to say that he simply dared not speak. As to touching her, no such wildly presumptuous thought even crossed his mind. He stood, waiting her pleasure ; understanding her not in the least, only vaguely conscious of a strength in her which, whatever her mind toward him, it would be madness in him to affront.

When she raised her face again, the color was quite gone from it ; she was pale once more and quite calm. " I think," she said, " I will go and rest a little in my room now. All this—has tired me ; and I have a long drive before me in the afternoon. Talking of drives, I wonder whether John, in his excitement, has remembered to get the cart ready ? You must not be late for your train."

"I don't think," Lyon began hesitatingly, "that, after all, I care much to go to town to-day. Any other day will do just as well."

" Oh, no !" she interposed eagerly, speaking, for the first time since that unforgettable speech of his with a touch of excited consciousness. " It would be a great pity to alter your plan now—at least so it seems to me. Your friend's business may be of the highest importance, and the arrangements are all made. I think you ought certainly to go."

" I will go," he answered with quiet emphasis, " since you wish it." He waited to see whether she would repudiate his submission of himself to her orders. But she said nothing.

He had now no choice but to start. " I shall be back again, I hope, to-morrow evening," he said.

" Yes."

He looked at her doubtingly. With those words between them, he hesitated to take her hand, though he believed—rightly—that she would not have refused it to him. He could not even draw a step nearer to her, just then. The words held them apart.

" Good-by."

" Good-by."

He turned and walked toward the door. Half-way there, he stopped.

" You are not as well as you would have other people believe," he broke out all at once, in a voice which very excess of feeling made unusually harsh. " Promise me to take care of yourself."

There was fear in her eyes now. Still, she could force herself to smile. " You need not be uneasy about me, I assure you," she responded. " I am simply a little shaken. But I shall soon recover myself, as you will see. By the time you come back the exciting events of this morning will have become things of the past——"

Lyon interrupted her before she could complete her sentence. " Not to me," he said huskily. " Never to me. I shall remember this morning as long as I live ! "

Then he went out, shutting the door behind him.

CHAPTER IX

TO LONDON

" Facilis descensus Averni."

HE had ample time, in the course of his journey, to consider the thing which had befallen him.

" Befallen him," yes, surely " befallen " was the right word to use ! His action had been wholly unpremeditated. Like Jo of immortal memory, he had most certainly not " gone for to do " this thing which he had done. The point in which he had failed was just the very point where he had long felt himself most secure. At any time during the last three months he would have readily hazarded the prediction that, whatever his follies or his crimes in the unknown future, of this folly, this crime, at least, he would never be guilty. Under no conceivable circumstances could he have pictured himself speaking to Dorothy Travers the words he had spoken to her that morning.

Unfortunately, his reckoning of circumstances had been left incomplete. He had omitted from it just the one factor capable of upsetting all his otherwise well-reasoned calculations. A very natural omission on his part. That he should ever be swept off the rock of resolution and self-control by her unguarded display of emotion seemed so unlikely a circumstance that he was justified in ranging it with the inconceivable, till it came to pass.

Well, it had come to pass ; and he could only say, " After this the Deluge." There was no getting back again now to the old high and dry position, safe, as he had vainly supposed, out of reach of dangerous storms ; he must e'en let the flood take him out to sea.

Many things besides self-control had gone down before the deluge in its first onrush. It had made short work, for instance, of his newborn self-esteem. He was very contemptuous with himself on the subject of the complacency with which of late he had come to regard his own character and conduct. The pretty fictions he had interposed between his naturally acute instincts and the perilous realities of his situation being shattered once for all, he looked that situation full in the face, after his old fearless fashion. " What a fool I've been all this summer ! " was his candid reflection. " And what a hypocrite to boot ! More hypocrite than fool, perhaps—it was to the interest of what little self-respect I had to impose upon myself as long as I could. Well, at least I've done with shams now—forever and a day. It has been borne in upon me, in an unmistakable manner, that I have nothing in common with the impossible being I fondly persuaded myself I could emulate : the virtuous hero of romance who loves his neighbor's wife—in all honor and unselfish devotion. I am forced to recognize the painful fact that I am a man like any other ; honorable and unselfish just as long as it suits my purposes to be so—or to appear so—and not a moment longer. While I felt instinctively that silence and good behavior served me best, I held my tongue and behaved myself. As soon as I saw an opportunity of employing different tactics, I employed them. If I believed for an instant that I could persuade her to leave Travers and the children for me to-morrow, I should urge her to take the step, and that without the smallest compunction."

In all this he did himself, perhaps, more—or less—than justice. Something must be allowed for the savage exaggeration of a freshly roused self-contempt.

Still, that the deluge had indeed come there could be no manner of doubt. Set adrift from all his moorings, he was in the mood to let the winds of his passion blow him whither they listed; how wide they had already blown him might be gathered from the fact that, so far from considering the advisability of not returning to Malton Barnard, or of bracing his mind to any step which should put a safe distance between himself and Dorothy Travers in the future, he fell almost immediately to enquiry how he could so order his life in time to come that nothing should intervene to separate them. From the prospect of returning to India, as he was pledged to do, only two months hence, leaving her in England, he recoiled as from·a monstrous impossibility. Some way must be found to obviate the necessity of such a parting; he, too, must stay at home.

Would she wish him to stay? Ay, there was the rub. If she were asked her wish now, she would probably pronounce in favor of his going rather than staying. In her mind, at this moment, he represented, doubtless, a newly embodied fear, of which she would feel genuinely anxious to rid herself. But let him wait a while; wait till she had come to dread his presence less, to fear his absence more; wait till the beginning of October. By the beginning of October she might well have learned to regard the whole situation with different eyes.

The deluge had come in truth when he could make Dorothy Travers the subject of speculations such as these.

One utterance of hers perplexed him the more, the more he thought upon it. She had said, "I am glad." But glad of what? Glad of his safety merely, or glad of his confession as well? Her words were capable of a double meaning. If she had intended them to convey one, then his path was clear indeed. Almost too clear, fastidiously murmured that part of him which, even in all the storm and stress of new-enfranchised passion, could not see its ideal stoop ever so little from her pedestal without a pang of instinctive regret.

He forgot that, at the moment when the words were uttered, he had not dreamed of putting a double interpretation upon them. His own self-abandonment, during his solitary journey, had quickly taught him to find things credible in her of which, before he flung loose the reins of will, he would have pronounced her incapable.

He was still turning her phrase over in his mind when his journey came to an end at the door of the Savoy Hotel. Recalling, with an effort, his business there, and the name of the person he had come to see, he enquired for Mr. Welldon.

Mr. Welldon was at home; a tall, thin, loose-limbed man of fifty, who looked older than his age, with a brown face and a frank smile. He welcomed Lyon in the warmest manner, and led him off at once to his private sitting-room.

"So delighted to see you!" he exclaimed for the third time, when this haven of refuge had been gained—proceeding, out of sheer cordiality, to shake hands over again. "I got your wire at one o'clock; very good of you to come to me so promptly. Hope my call didn't inconvenience you? Fact is"—assuming a confidential air, and rubbing his hands together after the manner of a man who has agreeably exciting news in reserve—"fact is, I've got a great responsibility on my shoulders; and I rather fancied you the man to take it off. Sit down, and I'll explain at length. By the way, I've ordered luncheon to be ready in half an hour; have a glass of sherry in the meantime? No? Well, then,"—evidently pleased to be able to plunge at once *in medias res,*—"to begin at the beginning of my story."

Mr. Welldon's story was a long one, and it is to be feared that Lyon did not hear more than half of it. He received a vague impression that his friend had a millionaire cousin somewhere in the North; that the cousin was going to found, or else had already founded, a new university somewhere in the Midlands; that in the curriculum of this university Science, and, more especially, Applied Science, was to occupy a distinguished place; that while the election of professors and lecturers would in future be left to the University Senate, the founder reserved to himself the privilege of making the first appointments—with much more to the same effect. Finally, it appeared that Welldon had been entrusted by his cousin with the task of finding fit men to fill his chairs of Architecture and Engineering.

"I believe I've lighted on an architect who can teach his business," the Anglo-Indian concluded, with a sigh of relief. "As for the other appointment"—leaning forward a little, while his smile subsided into an expression of anxiety—" it rests with you to take that load off my back—as I've said."

Seeing that Welldon waited for an answer, Lyon pulled himself together to reply. " I'm afraid I can't give you any names, off-hand," he said apologetically. " But I'll think over all the likely men I know, and write to you as soon as possible."

" As regards yourself, you put the thing by altogether, then ? " Mr. Welldon was nettled, to judge by his altered tone.

Lyon could not repress a slight start. " As regards—— Do you mean to say you are offering *me* the appointment ? "

" Certainly. To whom else should I offer it ? You are just the man for the place."

" I don't know about that. My scientific attainments are not profound. I'm a fairly good practical engineer, with rather a varied experience—that's all."

" And that's enough. A *practical* man, a man who knows the practice of his work, rather than the theory, has been John Blundell's cry all along. My thoughts turned to you at once."

" Very kind of you "—mechanically. " And Mr. Blundell's university is to be set going—when ? And where ? "

" Everything will be in working order by the commencement of next year. The local habitation is Kirklington—a grand centre, isn't it ? I'm afraid I explained myself badly ; I intended to have mentioned those facts at the outset. (His wits have certainly been wool-gathering during the last half-hour ; hope they won't play him that trick in his lecture-room," Welldon observed to himself, in a parenthetical aside.) " Perhaps I omitted to mention the income, too "—with a touch of good-humored mockery. " Eight hundred a year. Plenty of private pupils—if the professor cared to take 'em. You would have So-and-so "—he ran over a list of fairly distinguished names—" as your colleagues in the arts de-partment." A pause. " Well, will you think of it ? "

Lyon, scarcely knowing what he said, answered that he cer-tainly would think of it.

Welldon seemed immensely relieved. " I was afraid you might feel averse to the idea of settling down in England," he said.

" I am not so fond of India that I should be loath to leave it, I assure you," Lyon responded briefly. He felt half afraid of opening his mouth, lest he should give voice, in his excitement, to some fatuity.

"The East has its fascinations—for certain minds," returned Welldon, getting up as the door was thrown open behind him. "Ah, here's the waiter come to say luncheon's ready! Let us go down. By the way," he added, as Lyon preceded him into the corridor, "there is one other point I should have mentioned. You have the privilege of appointing your own demonstrator."

CHAPTER X

THROUGH THE HEATHER

"You love : no higher shall you go,
For this is true as gospel text,
Not noble then is never so,
Either in this world or the next."

LYON left London the following morning without having definitely accepted the appointment offered him. He had asked for time in which to make up his mind; a rather superfluous request, seeing that, in point of fact, his mind was fully made up already. In face of such an offer no genuine hesitation was possible. This professorship would give him everything he wanted : deliverance from the life of exile in the East which, for all his professed indifference to its disadvantages, he secretly detested; interesting professional work; leisure to fulfil his last lingering ambition—the completion of the book he had begun to despair of ever finishing in India. Above all, it set him free from the nightmare of that impending parting in October, and afforded him an opportunity of keeping Travers under his own eye, and so, perhaps, saving Dorothy's life from the total shipwreck with which it was threatened by her husband's light-minded selfishness. It is true, the demonstratorship to which, as professor, he gained the power of appointment, was but slenderly salaried. Beggars, however, cannot be choosers, and Brian's position just now was not far removed from the beggar's. Besides, once at Kirklington, he might easily find means of adding to his official stipend—by taking pupils, for instance. It would be in Lyon's power to do much for him; and with the influence of his professor uniformly exerted in his behalf, pupils were not likely to be wanting to one certain to prove a brilliant teacher. Generally speaking, Lyon was as little given as any man alive to the building of castles in the air. But his mood, during the twenty-four hours which elapsed between his quitting the Savoy Hotel and his descending from the train at Barnard St. Mary Station, was altogether exceptional; and in that short space of time he ran up a considerable number of those unsubstantial and disappointing structures. Never, since the sanguine days of his early manhood, had he suffered his imagination so to run riot in cloudland.

Arrived at Barnard St. Mary, he discovered that Travers—for whom he had not, perhaps, troubled himself to search very diligently on the crowded platform at St. Pancras—was not in the train. A telegram had come in, half an hour before, explaining that his return was deferred to the following morning.

On hearing this piece of intelligence from the station master, Lyon tossed his bag into the dog-cart which had been sent to meet the two travellers, announcing to the groom who drove it his intention of walking the three miles to Malton. It had just struck him that, while busily elaborating his plans for the distant future, he had altogether omitted to devise a *modus vivendi* for the immediate present. The necessity of devising one without delay came home to him all at once, on finding that, as things had fallen out, he was destined to meet Dorothy, for the first time after their strange parting, not in her husband's presence, but either alone, or with no other witnesses to the meeting than two little children. Under the circumstances, some sort of explanation appeared almost inevitable; the only question was, whether it were wisest to leave the initiative in the matter to her, or, boldly putting aside tentative measures, to step forward to the encounter of his own free will and motion? He wanted time to think this question out.

He was still revolving it painfully in his mind, as he walked slowly between the thick fir-plantations lining his path on either hand—his way lay from the first through lonely and silent woods, where nothing save the monotonous cooing of innumerable wood-pigeons, and the occasional rush and scamper of some frightened wild creature through the fern, broke the solemn quiet—crushing the heather, just beginning to show, here and there, a dash of purple, unthinkingly beneath his feet, when, looking straight ahead of him to where the narrow track swung suddenly round a corner, some fifty yards away, he saw Dorothy coming quickly toward him. At sight of her the prudent schemes he had half formed vanished into empty air, his nice balancings of expediency *versus* inclination abruptly ceased. A great, all-absorbing fear fell upon him, and withal an uneasy sense of shame, which weighed upon him like lead, when he would have quickened his pace, and made him half reluctant to meet her eyes.

She betrayed no sign of surprise on seeing him, but continued to walk forward swiftly and evenly. She wore a light summer dress, which showed almost white against the blackness of the fir-boles stretching away on all sides of her in long dark ranks—bright as was the day, with a cloudless sky overhead, scarce a thread of sunlight could filter between the close-serried branches down to the thick brown carpet of needles below—and a little round straw hat he had once or twice seen her wear at San Remo, and which always had the effect of making her look curiously youthful and even girlish. When he got close to her, Lyon perceived that her face was serious and rather pale. But her air was not one of displeasure ; and her greeting, if a little graver than usual, had not lost its friendliness. Of the two, he, for all his natural impassibility, was the less at ease. He found it difficult to look at her as they shook hands ; and he began to explain his own appearance in that place and Brian's defection with marked nervous haste. Dorothy replied calmly :

" Yes, I know. I met John driving home, and took the telegram from him."

Then she had known—for there was but one path to Malton from the station—she had known that, by taking this road, she could not fail to meet him ! Lyon's pulses gave a great leap. This was more than he had dared to hope for.

Yet, even in the midst of his natural elation at finding himself in actual occupation of a position he had barely ventured to dream of attaining after weeks, perhaps months, of patient investment and assault—he was conscious of having received an unpleasant shock. He strove fiercely to smother this consciousness. Had things indeed gone so far with him, he asked himself bitterly, that the analytic spirit which had been his curse for twenty years must spoil for him even such a moment as this ? But, strive as he would, he could not wholly repress his first instinctive feeling of distaste and disappointment. It had been his purpose to subdue her gradually to his will. He had not asked that she should come to lay herself voluntarily at his feet, resigning the field without a struggle.

"The old question of paying for one's whistle," he reflected. "I gain the woman; I lose the ideal. Well, since it's clear I can't have both, doubtless substance is preferable to shadow."

Dorothy had enquired as to the comfort of his journey, and remarked on the beauty of the day, while these thoughts were passing rapidly through her companion's brain; and he had returned a random answer to question and remark alike. Now he suddenly pulled himself together to say :

"I have to thank you for insisting on my making that expedition yesterday. As things have turned out, I've reason to be glad I went."

"Your friend's business was really important, then ? "

"Highly important." He was not quite sure in his own mind of the wisdom of adding " to me," which it had been on the tip of his tongue to add, but which he had just time to suppress.

"It is fortunate you did not put off your journey. Your being down here must have caused some delay, in any case. There certainly are disadvantages in living so far from a post-office," she went on, with an abrupt change of tone. "They have just been brought home to me very strongly."

"How ? "

"This letter of Brian's "—she glanced down at an envelope in her hand. "I ought to have received it yesterday. Then I should have had some time—nearly twenty-four hours, indeed—in which to think over the contents. As matters stand, all through there being no second post, I must make a most momentous decision, a decision affecting our whole lives, and the children's lives, for years and years to come, almost without stopping to reflect——"

She paused ; and Lyon struck in quickly :

"Travers has been offered an appointment ? "

"Yes."

"A promising one ? "

"In some respects. The pay is very good : not far off a thousand a year. But—it is in India ! "

"Ah ! " Lyon involuntarily drew a deep breath. One of his fairy castles lay shattered at his feet. There could be no question now of the Kirklington demonstratorship, with its modest stipend eked out by the payments of problematical private pupils. "Travers leaves it to you to decide whether he shall accept this post or not ? " he suggested interrogatively.

"N—no ; not exactly. I think his mind is pretty well made

up to accept it. But I might perhaps be able to persuade him to change his mind, if I were to try very hard. Only I must do it before to-morrow, when he has promised to give his final answer. And now, the question is, have I any business to urge him to a refusal? I don't know what to do. On the one hand, there is the parting from the children—having to give them up to the care of strangers, perhaps for ten years to come——"

Her voice would tremble there, hard as she strove to keep it steady, and Lyon interposed with :

" It would not be possible—you have not considered the alternative of remaining behind yourself with your children ? "

" No. That is an alternative I must not consider." She looked up from the letter, on which her eyes had been bent down for a moment or two, straight into his face. " *You* convinced me of that, last spring, at San Remo—do you remember ? "

His lips moved in a nearly inaudible assent. Her last speech had thrown all his newly conceived ideas into confusion—so utterly was it at variance with them. Had he quite misjudged her—reading his own baser meaning into an act of noble fearlessness? Was it possible that the crisis, which to him had issued in willing self-abandonment, had served her as a means of rising to more complete self-conquest ?

" And now, I want you to tell me," she went on, looking down again at her letter, " whether I may, with a clear conscience, ask Brian to give up this opening—which seems so good in many ways. If he lets this particular chance slip through his fingers, is he likely to have such another offered him? Is he likely to have *any* post offered him, at home, which will at all compare with it in value ? "

" That's a difficult question to answer," Lyon replied evasively.

" I know. I don't ask you to answer it positively. But you must have some idea as to the *likelihood* in such a case."

" I'm afraid I'm not a very fit adviser in the matter." Lyon's phrase asserted a truth, and held no unfriendly meaning—to say the least of it. But to Dorothy's ears it had the tone of a rebuff.

" I am sorry to have to trouble you," she returned a little proudly. " But there is no one else of whom I can ask advice ; and the time is very short—so short, that I hurried to meet you, when I heard you were walking from the station, because I was afraid you might not arrive before post-time—I must write to .

Brian by this post.   We ought to be moving homeward now, or I shall not have time for my letter, as it is.''

Suiting the action to the word, she turned and began retracing the way that she had come at a fairly brisk pace.   Lyon walked beside her, torn between shame and passion, and a hotly rebellious rage against his unkindly fate.   He could have fallen at her feet to entreat her pardon, even while he was secretly defying the destiny which seemed bent on separating them.   Because he was free to stay in England, she was in her turn to be exiled to the ends of the earth ?   He refused to accept tamely this fresh check in the game at which he had for a moment seen himself the winner.   With savage satisfaction he reflected that he was not himself as yet bound to Kirklington by so much as a promise.

Meanwhile, it was no part of his plan to attempt the circumvention of destiny with lies.

'' You must take my judgment for what it's worth,'' he began presently, switching the bracken with his stick as he strode along. '' I don't pretend to speak authoritatively.   But, as a matter of personal opinion, I should say it's highly improbable that Brian will find any such berth as you speak of at home.   The home market is over-stocked with engineers.''

'' In that case, I should do wrong if I dissuaded him ? ''

'' You might; you most likely would come to regret having done so.''

She bent her head a little as she walked, with the gesture of one making submission.   '' Then—I suppose it must be,'' she said, with a pitiful little break in her voice.

Lyon was walking at her left side.   He clenched his right hand till the nails bit the palm.

'' It's hard upon you, I know,'' he said huskily.

'' You can't know ! ''   She turned upon him almost fiercely in her passion of pain.   '' No one can know—but myself.   It's the difference between light and darkness—life and death !   And the worst is, I shall live through it !   I can live through anything ; nothing kills me, nothing makes me ill——   I don't know what I'm saying ! '' she cried, with a sudden shamed sinking of her excited tones almost to a whisper.   '' Don't let us talk of it any more, please ! ''

They walked on for a few minutes without speaking, Lyon, in a kind of agony, racking his brain for some word of hope with which to comfort her, and finding none.   For the moment, his quarrel with fate was forgotten, and every unholy plan, every selfish personal desire swallowed up in a passion of throbbing pity for her suffering, of torturing anxiety to relieve it. Think as he would, however, he could see no way of escape for her from the separation which was to her heart as a sentence of worse than death. In England Brian's prospect of employment was literally *nil*. That demonstratorship, indeed—— But he knew Brian Travers too well to dream for a moment of his consenting to choose comparative poverty in the place of comparative affluence, merely in order to save his wife from a sentimental sorrow. And, the demonstratorship apart, he could think of no expedient.

Suddenly there started up in his memory some parting words of Mr. Welldon's, spoken as they stood together in the vestibule of the Savoy. "I hope you'll go to Kirklington yourself. But if you should decide against going, remember you'll have to find me a man in your place! The responsibility of any further choice is too great for me—ignoramus as I really am in engineering matters."

Lyon was not ordinarily reckoned, certainly he had never reckoned himself, an impulsive man. But on the present occasion he passed from recollection to idea, from idea to purpose, and proceeded to put his purpose into words, without giving himself so much as a moment for reflection.

"It's just possible——" he began, and paused.

"What is possible? Have you thought of anything?" cried Dorothy, her recent prohibition quite forgotten.

"Yes," he replied, not looking at her, and catching his breath oddly between his words; "I believe I have thought of something which might possibly avert what you dread. Not a certainty, you understand—just a chance. But a good enough chance to justify Travers in putting off his decision for a day or two. You might suggest his doing that. He would not object to remaining in England, I suppose?"

"Not if—if other things were equal," she replied, coloring high —was it with shame? "He might think—I dare say he would think—we must not sacrifice income on account——"

"I see"—cutting her short. "Well, taking one thing with another, the post I have in my mind would be quite as valuable, pecuniarily, as the Indian one. It might easily be made much more valuable."

"It's a post you know something of, then?"—eagerly.

"One I have heard of—from a man who's to be trusted. I believe I'm not at liberty to go into the particulars without special permission. But I can say this much, I fancy you would like it. If you wish, I will write to—to make all enquiries to-night."

She turned on him a look of unutterable gratitude. "If I wish!" she repeated. "But—may I ask one question? The work? is it the sort of work Brian would——" She halted in embarrassment, evidently at a loss for a word.

"The sort of work he'd care for, you mean?" Lyon took some credit to himself that he had not said "condescend to." "Yes, I imagine it would suit him very well."

"I almost wonder," she began unthinkingly, "that you did not——" and stopped herself again.

"That I did not think of this sooner? It was stupid on my part, certainly," Lyon admitted. "How is Robin?" he asked abruptly, changing the subject in a fashion which seemed as though he were anxious not to pursue it further. "Has he recovered the loss of his dog yet? Or is he still vowing vengeance against me—as the original cause of the whole catastrophe?"

"I'm afraid there have been a good many fresh tears shed over Rip's grave this morning. But, as regards you—I am sure Robin has forgiven you long ago."

"I take leave to doubt that. I don't think Robin is of a forgiving disposition."

"Surely"—with nervous eagerness—"you didn't take what he said yesterday seriously? In moments of excitement a child like that is hardly responsible for his words. One would not always care to be held responsible for one's own, at such moments. When people get carried out of themselves, they may easily say much they do not really mean—they often do."

She spoke hurriedly, in quick, disjointed sentences; and, all the while she was speaking, her color came and went. When, at "they often do," she stopped abruptly, she was manifestly breathless.

"That is frequently the case, no doubt," was Lyon's rejoinder. "But I would warn you"—laying stress on his words—"against supposing your rule broad enough to include all cases. Sometimes the man who only speaks out tardily in a moment of excitement means all, and more than all, he actually says. He may have felt strongly all along ; the moment is merely responsible for his utterance of—of things perhaps better left unuttered."

Again Dorothy's color rose high. "In that case," she returned in a low voice, "one should try to understand—one would be ready to forgive."

Leaving his fencing suddenly, he went straight to the point ; he wheeled round a step in front of her, thus bringing her to a dead stop, and held out his hand. "Does that imply—may I take it to imply that *you* forgive *me?*" he demanded, looking her full in the face.

Her eyes did not fall before his. "Yes," she answered, and gave him her hand without a moment's hesitation.

"Absolutely ?"

"Absolutely."

"Your pardon is without conditions ?" He spoke harshly, almost menacingly.

A faint look of distress crossed her face. "I have no need to make conditions—have I ?" she faltered apparently, with a quivering lip.

He was silent an instant. Then "No; you have no need," he returned, in a strangely softened voice, dropping her hand.

They resumed their walk immediately, and reached the house, now no great distance off, without exchanging another word. Once within doors, Lyon murmured something about "getting that letter written before the post left," and, going upstairs, shut himself into his own room.

There he sat down to his writing-table in a curiously bewildered frame of mind. During that walk through the wood he had, almost in spite of himself, not merely gone clean contrary to every plan and purpose with which he started upon it, but flung away his last chance of success in life with no more consideration than if it had been an apple-paring ; cut himself off at a stroke from everything—ease, leisure, possible distinction, the society of the woman he loved—that could still give charm and value to existence ; and he hardly knew whether to be glad or sorry. "*She*, at least, has not changed," he assured himself, with a touch of sensible relief.

His letter to Mowbray Welldon was quickly written. Returning with it to the hall, he found Dorothy still there, busy at her desk, which stood in an angle of the fireplace. "I am in time ?" he asked, with a side glance at the clock.

"Oh, yes ! Thomson "—Thomson was the walking postman—

18

"has just sent up to say that, as he has the loan of a pony to-day, he will call for the bag half an hour later than usual. I am sorry I hurried you so unduly to write at once—you *have* written? And you really think Brian stands a good chance?"

"I do, indeed. At the lowest, the chance is worth pausing for. By the way, you did not mention what part of India. India is a big country, you know, with a great many climates; some of the hill-districts are healthy enough, even for children, all the year round. And it's in the hill-districts, chiefly, that we are railway-making just now."

The light of a new hope brightened in Dorothy's eyes. "That's a fresh idea altogether. If only this place should prove to be in the hills! Will you look at Brian's letter, and see whether you can decipher the name of the district? I can't. The name of the cantonment where we should be quartered is Kurree; I made out that much."

"Kurree?" Lyon repeated. There was an odd, indefinable change in his voice as he echoed the word. "There are half a dozen Kurrees, at least, between the Punjab and Cape Comorin." He seemed to speak to himself rather than to his companion.

Carrying Brian's letter to the window, he stood there, knitting his brows over it in silence for a minute or so. Yes, it was as he had hoped—or feared. The district was the district to which, resigning Kirklington, he must return himself in two months' time; the line, that very Mhabari line on which he held a subordinate appointment; Kurree, the cantonment in which his own new bungalow was even now building for him.

The bare sight of those three names in Brian's big, sprawling, unfinished handwriting set his imagination on fire afresh. She would live at his very doors, his close neighbor; within daily reach of his voice and hand; every morning and evening bringing them together; every week of exile drawing tighter the bonds of sympathy between them; every added month of separation from those terrible rivals, the children at home, deepening her sense of dependence on him, and him only, for love and tenderness. He foresaw for himself and her such a future as might make an earthly paradise of that dreary little cantonment in the midst of the burning flats of Oudh.

But he had forgotten. *She* was to go to Kirklington now.

Need it be so? There was yet time to re-write that letter; to transform it from an urgent tender of Brian's candidature into little more than a passing mention of his name among other names given to soften the blow of his own refusal. For her sake he had been willing to forego all the things a man naturally prizes highest ; for her sake he was willing to forego them still. Might he not claim the reward of his devotion ?

The flames of this fresh temptation were hot upon him. Under that scorching heat he felt the iron of his resolution growing soft and melting as wax.

" Can you make out his writing ? " asked Dorothy from her desk. " He always writes illegibly when he is in a hurry ; and he said he had barely time to save the post."

" The Kurree he speaks of is in Oudh," Lyon responded, clearing his throat first, for he found utterance extraordinarily difficult. " In the plains ; not far from Mahalabad."

" Oudh ? I could not take the children there, could I ? " She stopped writing as she spoke and turned her face toward the window.

" No; impossible."

" You know the place ? "

" Yes ; I know it."

She sighed. " Then all our hopes hang on that letter of yours."

He bit his lip. " Don't build too much on that affair. It's only a sort of off-chance."

" Nó more than that ? I thought you said——"

" I believe I said rather too much, on second thoughts. One may easily be over-sanguine."

His voice was husky with conflicting emotions. She heard in it only pity for her—and, perhaps, regret at his inability to help her more effectually.

" Whatever happens," she returned gently, taking up her pen, " I shall know you have done your best, your very best, for us. I am thankful to God for giving me such a friend—I shall always be thankful ! "

She bent closely over her writing once more ; and he knew, without looking at her, that she could not see it for tears.

He stood still in the window, quite unmoved outwardly—inwardly convulsed in every fibre of his nature. If her trust shamed him, roused in him a longing to meet it worthily, it taught him at the same time the extent of the power which he might wield, which he already wielded over her. Could he deliberately forbear all exertion of that power, knowing that he possessed it ?

The battle wavered to and fro. He glanced at her bent head ; at the envelope addressed to Welldon which he still carried in his hand ; back to her again—then he suddenly made a step toward the staircase.

To reach it he must pass in front of her. As he passed she looked up.

" Supposing——" she began.

" Yes ? "

He had stopped short at once, resting one hand on the ledge of the table which held her desk.

" Supposing that, by some happy fortune, your letter were successful—when would this appointment be vacant ? "

" By the beginning of the year."

" So soon ? " She drew a sigh of relief. " I asked, because I was afraid—I knew Brian would not consent to wait very long. Indeed, he could not afford to."

" That post on the Mhabari line is open to him now, I suppose ? "

" Yes. We should have to go out in October, he said. Why ! " Dorothy exclaimed impulsively ; " it's in October that you, too——" She stopped suddenly, flushing crimson.

Lyon, on his side, flushed also, and then turned extremely white.

" Yes, my leave's up the middle of November ; I shall have to sail some time in October, I suppose. If—— But let us hope you may not be under the same hard necessity." All at once he laid Brian's letter down upon the table close to her elbow, and with it his own letter to Welldon—noticing with annoyance, as he did so, that his hand shook a little. " Your husband's letter," he remarked briefly. " Perhaps you'll kindly put the other with yours into the bag before it goes."

Then he quietly took down his hat, and walked out of the open hall-door into the garden. It was dinner-time, three hours later, when he reappeared, having apparently occupied himself in the interim with meditation on current politics. For, though he was unusually talkative during the whole evening that followed, his conversation scarcely ranged beyond the limits of the Home Rule Bill.

CHAPTER XI

UNDER THE PORCH

" Wilt thou go forth into the friendless waste—
Leaving this Paradise of pleasure here ? "

IF, in war and in life, victory could be assured by the winning
of a single big battle, generals commanding-in-chief and ordinary men desirous of doing their duty would alike have a comparatively easy time of it.   Unfortunately, enemies, whether
of the carnal or spiritual sort, have an awkward habit of rallying
their forces anew after defeats which one had fondly imagined to
have crushed all fighting capabilities out of them.

Thus Lyon, even when he had seemingly put all possibility of
backsliding out of his power by quickly following his letter to
London, and there setting himself to work on Brian's behalf, found
that the era of conflict and indecision was not yet at an end for
him.   He had, not unnaturally, perhaps, reckoned on Brian's
finding the prospects, which to himself were so delightful that it
was like tearing the heart out of his body to resign them, quite
irresistibly attractive.   Brian, it need hardly be said, took a much
more impartial view of these prospects.   So far from jumping
eagerly at the Kirklington professorship, he was at first greatly
disposed to refuse the appointment altogether.   He averred that
he detested Kirklington ; he detested all manufacturing cities.
He did not believe the climate would suit his wife and children.
His whole soul rebelled against the society he should be forced to
keep : purse-proud, half-educated merchant princes, cocking their
crests in vulgar self-importance, and, from the sordid heights of
their cotton-pyramids, looking down with ignorant contempt on
every man having less than five figures to his income !   In this
fashion he raved for days, the truth being that the idea of India,
of Indian life, of distinction and fortune to be won in the East,
had taken firm hold of his imagination, and that, side by side with
these brilliant possibilities, the sober, limited certainties of Kirklington appeared drab-colored and uninteresting.   It was Lyon's
part to expound the superiority of certainties, however limited, to

possibilities, however brilliant, in the case of a married man with
two children and no capital to speak of ; Lyon's part to point out
the many advantages attaching to the position of which Travers
was inclined to think so lightly ; Lyon's part, by the use of argument, rhetoric, appeal, flattery, each in its turn, to persuade his
reluctant candidate along every step of the path of candidature to
the goal of final acceptance.

It may easily be supposed that Lyon did not find his self-
imposed task over-agreeable. Nor was it singular that he should
frequently be visited with doubts as to the wisdom of having
engaged in it at all. Often, after some conversation in which
Brian had given fresh proof, not only of incurable levity and
instability, but of utter selfishness and complete indifference to the
interests of those whose fate was bound up with his own, the
elder man felt impelled to ask himself why he should persist in
throwing away all his own prospects in favor of a man bound by
his idiosyncrasy to come to grief, under any circumstances, in the
end.   It was not really in the man's favor that he was acting, but
in favor of the man's wife. Well, did his conduct appear any
the wiser, from this fresh point of view ?   He was sacrificing
himself, not to bring peace and happiness to Dorothy Travers, but
in order that she might continue an experiment which had been
hopeless from the outset, spend a few additional months or years
in a thankless effort to keep some moral hold on a man who did
not care for her, and whom she had never really loved, until, by
means of accumulated failures, or some sudden startling catastrophe, she was forced to learn the melancholy truth that human
nature remains as it was in the days of old, that now, as then, the
Ethiopian does not change his skin nor the leopard his spots.   There
were times when, wearied and disgusted, he was on the point of
flinging up his brief in the affair altogether ; on the point, not
only of encouraging Travers to write his meditated refusal, but of
rescinding his own, of establishing himself at Kirklington and
endeavoring to banish the whole business from his mind.   There
were others when, convinced of the impracticability of such easy
forgetfulness, he fell to considering afresh the expediency of that
alternative plan which would set him side by side with Brian and
his wife in India. "Harm will come of that ? " he retorted
against himself. " Well, so be it ! What the world calls harm
may be less harmful than the constant self-suppression, the resolute
stunting of her whole nature, the life of acted lies to which my

virtuous conduct condemns her. Virtuous, forsooth ! It would be nearer the truth to call it cowardly. I may choose to make a private mock of these social conventions which the world is pleased to entitle moral laws, but it is clear that I am half afraid of them all the while. Otherwise, I should hardly be so scrupulous about overstepping them."

Here, luckily, the reflection would occur : " But to her they *are* moral laws—the laws of God Himself ! Am I such a fool as to suppose I could make her happy, breaking them ? Being what she is, she *must* go on with her hopeless experiment. To throw it up would be an act of apostasy, in her estimation."

And thus he would be himself driven back upon the sacrifice he half regretted, and the efforts he half despised himself for making.

Brian was won over at last : refused the Mhabari appointment, accepted the Kirklington one, and went down to his family in Norfolk to " begin making arrangements." This time Lyon would not yield to any entreaties in the matter of bearing him company.

" My time at home is running short, you see," he said, as the two men stood together on the platform at Liverpool Street. " There are several people I must look up before I sail. But I'll run down for a night next month, to say good-by—if it's convenient to Mrs. Travers to put me up when the time comes."

Now if Lyon had been anything of a hero, he would never have given this promise ; or, at the very least, he would have found means to evade its fulfilment. Unhappily, he was, as has already been made sufficiently plain, nothing at all of a hero, and very much indeed of an ordinary man. When the third week in October arrived, therefore, he went down to Malton Barnard.

The place was looking exceedingly lovely in the soft light of an October sun. But it was no longer summer there : the heather, just faintly aflush with bloom when he had seen it last, was now a sheet of purple ; the bracken had faded from green to a yellowish brown ; on all sides the woods were glowing with the hues of autumn—golden, and russet, and fiery red. The peculiar stillness of autumn was in the air, too ; and as the dog-cart in which he had driven from the station drew up before the porch where Robin stood, holding a new terrier by the collar, he could hear the crack of guns in the easterly covers lying between the house and the sea.

Something of the sweet serenity of the season seemed to have

fallen upon Dorothy.   All through his brief visit she preserved an
air of unruffled calm ; sometimes he told himself that it was only
his covetous fancy which would now and then think to detect a
shade of sadness in her smile.   Heaven knew he did not desire her
—whose portion of suffering would always assuredly be heavy
enough—to suffer because of him !   Still, to desire that she should
see him go with absolute indifference was a height of unselfishness
of which he frankly acknowledged himself to fall short.

Only once, during the hours he spent under her roof, did he see
her serenity disturbed.   This was when, in the course of some
desultory talk about Kirklington, and the life awaiting her there,
he asked—Brian chanced to be absent at the moment :

"Has Travers appointed his demonstrator yet ?   You know he
has the privilege of appointment ? "

"Yes.   I am not sure ; I don't think he has made any decided
arrangement."   She spoke hurriedly, with a change of countenance which betrayed Lyon into asking, without giving himself
time to reflect on the prudence of so doing :

"Did he tell you he had offered the place to me ? "   A queer
little smile curled Lyon's lip as he put his question.

"Yes; he told me."   The color rose in her cheeks as she bent
closely over her work.

"I was sorry to have. to refuse," Lyon went on slowly.   "But
—I couldn't take it."

He spoke very quietly.   It is unlikely that even she guessed
what that refusal had cost him : the long silent struggle, the days
and nights of horrible conflict which had preceded it.

"No."   She paused, caught her breath audibly, and added,
"He said he had no hope of your taking it, at any time.   It was
half in joke he asked you—though of course he would have been
very glad if you could have seen your way.   But it is so small a
thing."

"I could have lived upon it."   He paused in his turn.   "I
should like to know," he resumed after a moment, leaning a
little forward in his chair, "whether you think I did right in
declining ? "

She looked up from her work.   "I should always trust your
judgment," she said quickly.   "And in this case I do not *think*
merely—I am *sure* you did right."

"Thank you," he responded briefly.   Then he leaned back
again, and read the *Times* diligently till Brian returned to the room.

It had been arranged, on the evening of his arrival, that Brian should drive him to the station immediately after breakfast the following morning. In the middle of that meal, however, a message from the head keeper was brought in, requesting an immediate interview with Mr. Travers in the hall, and from this interview Brian returned to say :

"Lyon, do you think you'd mind walking as far as the lower wicket of the moors ? Because Coulson wants me to look at those young birds with the gapes at once—and the cart's at the door already. I could drive down with him, taking your traps along, of course, and so get ten minutes' start. Sure you don't mind ? All right, then ; I'll pick you up at the lower wicket."

In this way it came to pass that, when Lyon and Dorothy stood under the clematis-covered porch for his final leave-taking, they stood there alone.

For all the advantage they took of this accidental *tête-à-tête*, however, they might as well have been surrounded by an army of witnesses. Like all people at such moments, they said very little, and what little they did say was wholly without significance. Lyon remarked on the mildness of the morning, regretting that he had put on an overcoat ; and Dorothy responded that she was glad he had such fine weather for his journey. Then she asked the hour of his arrival in Liverpool Street ; and how early his steamer was to sail from Southampton the following day.

"I hope you will have a good passage, and companionable ship-mates," she added. "That makes so much difference, doesn't it—having pleasant people on board ? Of course, you will let us know how you get on—we shall like to hear." She turned abruptly to call to the children playing at some little distance on the lawn, clapping her hands to arrest their attention. "Robin ! Dolly ! come here ! Come and say good-by to Mr. Lyon."

They came : Robin rushing up boisterously, Dolly, a little shy, hanging behind her brother.

"Are you going for good, Mr. Lyon ? " the boy demanded.

"For good—or ill, Robin. I'm not sure which."

This enigmatic reply left Robin puzzled. He was not fond of being puzzled and drew back somewhat in dudgeon. Dolly, mean-while, had crept close to her mother, and was asking in a loud whisper :

"Isn't Mr. Lyon ever coming back, any more at all ? "

"I don't know, Dolly. We hope——" Dorothy turned half

involuntarily to the person concerned, leaving him to finish her sentence.

His answer was decided, leaving no place either for hope or fear. "No, Dolly; it's not likely that I shall ever come back."

Dolly suddenly let go her mother's hand. "Then, if you're *never* coming back, I *will* give it you!" she burst out excitedly, and, pushing past the visitor, ran into the house at the top of her speed.

"What can the child mean?" Dorothy murmured, looking after her in perplexity.

Robin nodded knowingly. "It's her china dog she's so fond of —the one she always takes to bed with her. She wants to give it to Mr. Lyon as a keepsake. Only she said she wouldn't give it to him unless he was going quite away—and never coming back."

Here Dolly reappeared, flushed and breathless. "That's for you," she panted, thrusting a small hard object into Lyon's hand. "And I'll kiss you, if you like."

"Thank you, Dolly." Lyon, a little out of breath himself, apparently, stooped and kissed the child's proffered cheek. Across her flaxen head he murmured to her mother: "It would be a shame to take it from her. Will you——"

"No, no!" she interrupted, speaking low but vehemently. "You must not give it back. She gave it to you of her own free will. Keep it—please keep it!"

"Very well; I will. It may be useful—as a reminder. One would not like to have it said one had obtained a present on false pretences." He bestowed the singular keepsake in his pocket. "Good-by, little Dolly; good-by, Robin. Good-by——"

From the front of the house the drive curved sharply downward to the right, where a heavy iron gate—none of your newfangled swing ornaments, but a solid two-winged barrier, fit to keep out the most enterprising of kine, and fastened in the middle by a massive bolt—led into the road across the meadows to Barnard St. Mary. By this gate Lyon let himself out; then, turning to refasten the bolt, he looked back.

Dorothy still stood under the porch, her figure framed in its drooping greenery, the autumn sunshine glinting down through the leaves on her bare head. Her children were beside her: Robin had dropped on his knees at her feet, and was busying himself with the buckle of his dog's collar; Dolly, looking up eagerly, was clinging to her dress. So he saw her for the last time. But, even as he turned, she stooped to Dolly, and, lifting the child in her arms, held her up between her own face and the gate to wave an eager farewell.

It may well have been that, as he leaned over the "lower wicket" of the moors, ten minutes later, listening for the wheels of Brian's dog-cart, Lyon said to himself, "Surely the bitterness of death is past!"

<hr/>

CHAPTER XII

OUT IN THE PLAINS

"For love—oh, how but, losing love, does whoso loves succeed
By the death-pang to the birth-throe—learning what is love indeed?"

AN over-hasty conclusion—as he was to find out, three years later.

These three years passed without leaving any special impress on his life. He spent them almost entirely in the duties of his profession: duties which, if generally prosaic and unexciting in their nature, nevertheless required of him such close attention and unceasing labor as left him little time either for reflection or for other than professional occupations. He continued, indeed, as far as his scanty leisure would allow, to work intermittently at the book he had planned out, cherishing a vague hope of finishing it "some day." It was odd the tenacity with which he clung to this literary project of his. Life held little charm for him that he should wish it prolonged in his own case; yet he would have welcomed an assurance that he should live to finish his book. The truth was, failure had been written so large across all the hopes and ambitions of his youth and of his manhood that he found himself, in middle life, thirsting with the unslaked thirst of a boy to taste the sweets of success just once before he died. With him, all, so far, had been shortcoming: abortive plans, unrealized projects. Let him but touch the goal of achievement this once—and so be able to die less contemptuous of himself!

And this, too, might not be. Before the three years were quite at an end he knew that he would not live to finish so much as his first volume.

He took his sentence in grim silence. When the military doctor

who had pronounced it proceeded to urge his going home before
the hot weather, he declined to pledge himself to the step.
" We'll see," was all he would say.

" Well, I tell you it's your only chance," the surgeon retorted
bluffly—somewhat irritated, maybe, by his patient's obstinate coolness. " That heart of yours is all to pieces. The hot weather
will bowl you over at once. While in England——"

" In England I may last—how long ? "

" Oh, I don't know exactly—but probably a good while if you
lead a thoroughly idle life, let your brain lie fallow, and take
decent care of yourself. The change of climate often works
wonders : you might even pick up altogether——"

" Don't perjure yourself, Mackenzie," Lyon put in good-
humoredly. " It really isn't worth while, when you know I
sha'n't believe a word you say. Come, now ! Will you stake
your professional reputation on my living a year in England, supposing I were to sail next week ? "

" I told you before that I declined making prophecies ; I object
to prophesying in connection with medical matters—more especially when it's a question of dates. Much would depend on your
own prudence, of course. But, in any case, you'd have twice as
good a chance as you have in Kurree."

" Thanks ; that 'll do." Lyon held out his hand. " I don't
think I'll go home ; much obliged ; I hate the voyage. Never
mind, Mackenzie ; you've done your duty in the matter, and
needn't disturb yourself further.

" Supposing I were to go, after all," he mused to himself, as,
having mounted his pony under the doctor's veranda, he rode
slowly away. " No need now to cling to my place here. And I
should have a fellow-voyager in Father Jem."

The occasional society of Father Jem, otherwise James Travers,
had been the brightest spot in the dull level of Lyon's existence
during the past three years. That portion of the Mhabari railway
specially under Lyon's charge chanced to run through districts
which Travers in his capacity of travelling evangelist was bound
to visit from time to time—a circumstance enabling the two men
to meet pretty frequently. Lyon always hailed these meetings ;
he liked Travers as well as he had ever done, and he was beginning
to understand him a good deal better than in the earlier years of
their curious friendship. Certain events in his own life had made
it easier for him to comprehend the motives that were the hidden

springs of Jem's. He, too, had had his eyes unsealed to see the beauty of sacrifice ; albeit, in his case, the love that had touched his eyelids awake was purely human.

Through James Travers came all the news that reached him, now, of James' brother Brian. Brian, detesting letter-writing, had soon suffered the correspondence he at first carefully maintained with Lyon to become intermittent, and then to lapse altogether. But Brian's wife wrote pretty regularly to her brother-in-law ; and James was tolerably communicative on the subject of her letters. From his reports Lyon gathered the main facts of Dorothy's life, as far as she herself imparted them to her correspondent; by the same means he learned that Brian took increasing pleasure in the work of his professorship, and was rapidly winning popularity as a lecturer, while still finding time amid his duties for lighter occupations, and even for an occasional taste of the sweets of London.

" Ah ! " James remarked on one occasion, after commenting on his brother's extraordinary good fortune as revealed in these letters of his wife's ; " that's the kind of berth you ought to have had, Lyon ! The book. would have got itself written easily enough then."

." Unluckily," Lyon answered in a somewhat dry tone, " such berths are not often to be had for the asking. However, I'm glad Brian considers his lines to have fallen in pleasant places. How are his belongings—flourishing ? . I suppose they will soon be sending that boy to school."

" Unless I take him as a private pupil for a couple of years—till he is fit for Winchester," James responded, with a mournful smile. " Seriously "—in reply to an incredulous raising of Lyon's eyebrows—" I believe I might do worse than set myself to preparing boys for the public schools. I suppose they would think me fit for that."

Father Travers' " they " referred, not to his brother and sister-in-law, but to the heads of his community. Poor James was going home—not under particularly happy circumstances. It had taken him exactly five years to discover that, of all lives, the missionary life was that one for which, alike by the feebleness of his physical and the peculiarities of his mental constitution, he was perhaps most unsuited. By slow and painful degrees he had been forced to recognize the hard fact that, where it is a question of enduring bodily hardships, devotion, however single-minded, can-

not take the place of bodily strength ; and that, in dealing with
opponents so formidable in argument as the highly educated Brah-
mans with whom he was daily called upon to cross swords, no
amount of zeal in a holy cause makes up for the lack of a powerful
dialectic.   And when his recall came to him from headquarters at
home, kindly and considerately though the missive was worded, he
read between its lines the verdict of failure writ clear.   He knew
that he must return to England in the character of a man who had
mistaken his vocation, and who—proven manifestly unfit for the
high career to which he had presumptuously aspired—must content
himself henceforward with the lowliest tasks.   The situation was
one to be faced bravely, and accepted humbly.   James Travers
was not wanting either in courage or humility, and he took the
mortification of his best hopes like a man and a Christian.   But
he was not therefore insensible to the bitterness of such mortification.

Lyon, to whom he spoke no word of his suffering, nevertheless
guessed something of the deep waters through which his friend
was passing, and sympathized with him in his silent, undemon-
strative fashion.   Perhaps Travers was conscious of this unuttered
sympathy, for he showed a tendency to draw closer to Lyon in
many ways during the weeks that followed his reception of the
summons home.

He had ample opportunity to indulge this tendency, as his duties
obliged him at this time to be much in Lyon's neighborhood.   On
the day of Lyon's momentous interview with Surgeon-Major Mackenzie, he had already been a month in Kurree, and had nearly
completed his final arrangements for delivering up the stewardship
of that district into the hands of the colleague on his way out
from England to assume charge of it in his room.   It was, therefore, no surprise to Lyon, on drawing rein before the temporary
bungalow just now serving him as a home—a kind of superior
shanty not many hundred yards distant from the rough encampment of huts occupied by the coolies working under his direction
—to see a white-cloaked, sandalled figure seated in the shade of his
little wooden veranda, quietly awaiting his arrrival.   But if the
sight caused him no surprise, it gave him, for once, no pleasure.
Not only did he feel altogether disinclined for society at the
moment, but he would gladly have avoided an interview with
Travers in particular.   He was conscious of being perturbed, and
he was nervously unwilling that Travers should divine the fact.

It was not unlikely that he would divine it, for he had a singular gift of penetration.

However, there was no help for it. Travers must be faced—and outfaced, if necessary.

"So you found yourself able to get over to-day, after all," Lyon began, as he mounted the rickety flight of steps leading up to the veranda. "Hope you haven't been waiting long. I—— Holloa, man! what's the matter? You're as white as a sheet."

Travers' face afforded sufficient excuse for Lyon's exclamation. No sunburn could conceal its ghastliness.

"You'd better go in and lie down for a bit," his host suggested, watching him struggle with evident difficulty to his feet. "I suspect you've got a touch of sunstroke."

At this point Travers, who had been oddly silent hitherto, suddenly found his tongue. "No, no, I'm all right. There's nothing the matter with me. But there's trouble at home. I had to come over—about this letter. I want your help."

"Trouble—at home?" Lyon repeated. He was nearly as white now as his visitor.

"A dreadful thing has happened. My brother—God forgive him!—has left his wife, and gone off to Australia."

"Left—— What do you mean? That he has left her secretly —*deserted* her?"

"That—and worse. It's a horrible business—as bad as it can be. He has thrown up his appointment, abandoned Dorothy and his children, gone to the ends of the earth—not alone, but with an American woman he met three years ago on the Riviera, and with whom he seems to have kept up an acquaintance in London ever since that time."

"Ah!" Lyon's exclamation was like a cry of pain. "And I thought—I flattered myself—— Never mind!"—seeing Travers' look of wonder—"all that's nothing. He is actually *gone*, do you say?"

"Yes."

"The d—— scoundrel!" Lyon turned suddenly upon Travers as if to check any word or gesture of deprecation on his part. "Yes, though you were fifty times a parson, and he a hundred times your brother, I say it again—he——"

"What's to be done?" interposed Travers, with white lips.

"Done?" echoed the other. "What should be done, in the name of Fortune? What on earth is there for anyone to do?"

"Something must be done," James persisted. "For Dorothy's sake, if not for his."

"His!" Lyon's voice was expressive enough for once. "I don't think we need concern ourselves greatly on *his* account. But—your sister-in-law—— She has written to you, of course?"

"Not as yet. This letter is from Brian himself. You had better read it. Yes, read it!" eagerly, as Lyon drew back from the proffered sheet. "You'll see from this that, at least, he doesn't glory in the thing—that he half repents already."

"I dare say," Lyon responded bitterly. "He was always given to half-repentances." But he took the letter.

It was an incoherent document : a strange mixture of self-accusation and self-excusing. In one paragraph the writer went so far as almost to justify the step he had taken ; in the next he pleaded the greatness of his temptation, the merit of his long resistance ; while in a third he overwhelmed himself with the bitterest reproaches for his weakness. Over all this Lyon passed hastily, with something like a sneer on his compressed lips. But, on arriving at the last page of the first sheet, he uttered an inarticulate exclamation of angry dismay, and when, after reading the page through, he looked up, his dark blue eyes had grown black with indignation.

"This is too much!" he ejaculated, making no attempt to smother his rage. "I—*I* am to step in at such a juncture—to act as his representative—to mediate between him and his wife ! explaining that there were excellent reasons for his playing her false, I suppose ! What does he take me for ? It's true, I acted for him *once*—and was successful, more's the pity ! I never did a worse day's work in my life, or one that I more heartily wished undone, as soon as it was beyond my power to undo it. Even in that case there was a difference of circumstances. What possible call have I to make or meddle in such an affair as this ? I could not, even if I would. I am in Oudh; Mrs. Travers in England——"

"He takes it for granted that, your three years here being up, you will be going home for a time," James explained. "I don't say for a moment that he has any right——"

"I am not going home!" Lyon asserted furiously. "I haven't the slightest intention of leaving India. And if I were leaving it to-morrow, I would not put out a finger in this business of your brother's ; I tell you so plainly at once."

Travers moved a few steps restlessly, and returned to his former position facing Lyon. "Let us waive the question of Brian altogether for the moment," he began again. "There remains Dorothy to be considered. She needs someone to act for her and her children. You must remember that she is quite alone in the world. Creighton was literally her last remaining relative, and he died six months ago. She has no one——"

"She has you," Lyon interrupted. "You are the proper person to act for her—and for your brother."

"But I am not a man of business! And—you have only read half the letter as yet. Read the other half, and you'll see that Brian has evidently left his affairs in most complicated confusion —confusion which I should be quite incompetent to unravel."

"You must get a reliable solicitor to help you, that's all. So he has left her—your sister-in-law—his embarrassments to cope with, in addition to all the rest, has he? Coward!" muttered Lyon between his teeth.

"There's another reason why you should interpose rather than I," Travers went on. "It's true, Brian knew nothing of the—the change in my life which sets me free to go home, when he wrote that letter. But if he had known of it, I doubt his putting himself into my hands as he has put himself into yours. He says, if you observe, that it is only the circumstance of his having mislaid your address which induces him to write to me instead of to you, in the first instance. The truth is, as you know, that my brother and I never hit it off very well. The mere fact of my being a parson tells against me with him. But if you, as a man of the world, were to set things before him in their true colors, something might be done, even now."

"You mean that he might be induced to return to his wife?" Lyon was speaking more calmly now, but it was easy to see that his calmness was the result of determined effort.

"I do. His returning to her is the only hope for him—morally speaking. His career is, of course, hopelessly ruined, in any case. Whatever he may do in the future, this wanton throwing-up of his appointment will never be forgiven him. His prospects are gone. But for himself there is still hope—one would like to think."

"And Mrs. Travers? I do not quite see where she comes in. Your scheme of salvation appears to take little account of her."

"On the contrary." James Travers, ordinarily quick-tempered, kept his temper admirably on the present occasion; perhaps

19

because he felt too wretched to be angry. "Surely it would be for her happiness that he should return—penitent."

"I don't know. She might not think so."

"Of course it's possible that she may be unwilling to pardon him."

"More than possible, I should say. I happen to know that this is not the first time he has returned to her—penitent, to use your own word, as far as appearances went. She may have grown distrustful of appearances in this case. She may even—it is not unlikely—welcome an opportunity of regaining her freedom."

"If she does refuse to forgive him—if she repels him altogether, and leaves him to sink to deeper depths for want of a helping hand, then I know," cried Travers, with conviction, "what the end will be. She may buoy herself up for a while with the remembrance of her wrongs; but that support will fail her, sooner or later—and then she will be the most miserable woman on God's earth." Lyon gave an odd little start at these words; his own phrase of three years ago in the mouth of James Travers struck his ear with unpleasant force. "I know my cousin Dorothy better than you do, Lyon, remember."

"No doubt. Well, you may be right. As you are so thoroughly convinced on the point, why not act up to your conviction? Why not reason out the matter with your brother and try to bring about a reconciliation?"

"I will, so help me God!" Travers answered with quiet fervor. Then he laid a hand beseechingly on the other's arm. "And you, Lyon? You'll do your best to help me? Six months at home will do you all the good in the world—to say nothing of the doctors predicting a most unhealthy hot season: cholera, and all that sort of thing. Get six months' leave, and come with me. You won't refuse me, old fellow?"

Lyon's dark face twitched nervously; he seemed to consider for a moment. Then, half turning away, he replied:

"It's no use. I can't leave India."

"Is that final?" Travers asked—in a different tone.

"Quite, I'm sorry to say."

"Of course," Travers rejoined, speaking now with a touch of contemptuous bitterness most unusual in him, "I understand the reason of your refusal, and I appreciate it."

Lyon flushed and the pupils of his eyes dilated. "*I* don't understand your reference," he said sternly. "Please explain!"

" Oh, it's well known that a man's friendships must count as nothing when they chance to come into collision with his plans for writing a book ! " Travers retorted. " As I said before, I quite appreciate your position. I must be off now, I think ; I've a hundred things to do before next week. This miserable business makes me anxious to be in England as soon as I can, so, if Elwin arrives on Monday, I shall try to get down to Bombay in time for the Thursday P. and O. Good-by."

" You'll look me up again before you leave ? "

" I shall be awfully busy—I'll see what I can manage."

Lyon stood looking after the white-cloaked figure as it moved rapidly away. Then he turned back into the veranda with a short, harsh laugh.

" The book ! Well, why not ? " he said to himself, as he dropped slowly into the long chair in which he had found James Travers.

He must have sat there some time, alone with his hard and bitter thoughts, drearily contemplating the ruinous issue of the one deed in his life he had been tempted to call good and pronounce successful, when he was roused by the utterance of his own name. James Travers was coming slowly along the veranda.

He got up quickly. " What ! you've come back ? " he exclaimed.

" Yes." Travers advanced nearer. " I felt I must see you again for half a minute. It's quite true that I may not be able to come over to say good-by—and I was afraid you might fancy—— In short," James broke off suddenly, " I know I lost my temper just now, and I wanted to ask your pardon. I spoke harshly, and I had no business to speak harshly. I hadn't the shadow of a right to expect you to undertake Brian's cause. But we've been friends now for a good many years. You'll forget what I said in haste ? "

He held out his hand, and Lyon took it. The almost boyish simplicity of Travers' apology gave an oddly touching force to the appeal with which it concluded.

After a moment Lyon said briefly, " I'm glad you came back, Travers. Our roads lie apart henceforward. It's possible they may never cross again."

" As Benedick says, ' I will not desire that,' " Travers replied, his old winning smile irradiating his plain face for an instant.

" Nor I. But one's desires have generally little to say in these matters. Well, I won't grumble in anticipation. Having you for a kind of neighbor these three years past was an extraordinary stroke of good luck for me—one that I've appreciated to the full."

"I wish I could feel sure you liked this life," Travers remarked irrelevantly.

"As to that—it does as well as any other while it lasts. And it won't last long—I mean, I am free to go elsewhere at the end of a couple of years more," Lyon added quickly, fearful lest his first phrase should have betrayed him.

"There's one thing I've been on the point of asking you for months past," Travers began afresh, his big expressive mouth working nervously.

"Well?"

"You remember—or perhaps you don't—a conversation we once held in London—walking down St. James' Street? You spoke of cocksureness, as you called it, in relation to supernatural belief. You do remember?"

"Perfectly."

"You seemed to consider such a state of mind as you described highly enviable."

"I haven't changed my opinion."

"But you have not—I hardly know how to put it——"

"Arrived at realizing it by personal experience? No; that's one of the many goals I've stopped short of." Lyon spoke with well-feigned carelessness.

"I'm sorry," Travers returned quietly. "I had hoped it might have been—otherwise."

Lyon gave one of his sudden searching looks into his companion's face. Something he descried there must have touched him, for he turned brusquely aside to say, in a totally altered voice:

"I've had glimpses, once and again, of what the thing might be, I fancy. I suppose the very soreness of a man's necessity may sometimes drive him, for the moment at least, into a kind of belief. Certainly it has been so with me. In the worst moments of my life, just those moments when I've felt most inclined to act like a brute or a devil, the old ideas have reasserted themselves in a curiously powerful way. Unluckily, the vision—or the hallucination—never remained with me long. It was essentially evanescent."

"It will not always be so. You will yet recognize it"— Travers spoke without a shadow of doubt or hesitation—"for the vision of the Truth itself."

"Maybe, and maybe not." Lyon stood looking out thoughtfully into the glaring, dazzling sunshine, across the burned grass of the compound, along the dusty red track of the road outside it, to the group of huts in the distance. "I wish such a thing were likely. One would be glad to feel certain that it was all worth while; that one had not thrown away the bone for the shadow."

"The shadow of an eternal reality," Travers responded, half under his breath. "There's nothing else worth while, believe me, Lyon. Some day you'll know that, once for all; I'm not afraid! Good-by, old fellow, and God bless you!"

"At least you are not wanting in cocksureness," Lyon mused to himself, as for the second time he watched his departing visitor plod briskly through the dust in the direction of the coolie encampment. "Happy being! 'Nothing else worth while'? I have yet to ascertain the truth of those brave words, James. If only I felt quite certain that they *were* true—why, all the rest would seem comparatively easy."

THE EPILOGUE

"All the world's coarse thumb
And finger failed to plumb,
So passed in making up the main account;
All instincts immature,
All purposes unsure,
That weighed not as his work, yet swelled the man's amount.

"Thoughts hardly to be packed
Into a narrow act,
Fancies that broke through language and escaped;
All I could never be,
All men ignored in me,
This, I was worth to God, whose wheel the pitcher shaped."

"ALL the doctors" were for once in the right. The hot season in Oudh turned out one of the most unhealthy on record; and, before it was half over, the cholera fiend was slaying his hundreds and his thousands daily in the cities and villages of the plains.

Of the coolies employed under Lyon's superintendence, a full third fell victims to the epidemic, while at least an equal number were temporarily disabled from work. Engineering operations being thus brought for the nonce to a standstill in his section, Lyon, who escaped infection throughout, found himself free to do what he could toward supplementing the scanty help available for the stricken ; and, in the face of difficulties and the midst of confusion and panic, displayed a power of organization and command which rendered his aid of considerable value.   When the disease, having apparently spent itself at his own station, passed on, after its manner in the East, to the next, where were the headquarters of a British regiment, the Colonel commanding the said regiment found his civilian neighbor one of the most useful among his little band of irregular *aides*.

He needed all the help that could be given him, for the cholera raged with even more fatal effect among the white men than it had previously done among the brown, and for several weeks the camp which had been hastily formed a couple of miles from cantonments was a veritable city of death.   During these weeks Lyon, whom the enfeebled condition of his men still debarred from a return to railway-making, found plenty of occupation in supplying the place of dead or dying regimental clerks, in superintending the bringing in of stores from a distance, and in looking after the sanitary arrangements of the camp.   Neither did the surgeons in the hospital tents despise such unskilled help as he had leisure left to give them.   There are times when a medical man cannot afford to enquire too particularly into the qualifications of a willing candidate for the office of sick-nurse.

It may be doubted whether Lyon had ever felt so much at peace with himself and the world as during those six terrible weeks, when he had neither time nor inclination to think of anything but the immediate duty of doing his best to relieve the suffering which everywhere surrounded him in so ghastly a form.   Still, it was inevitable that the stress and strain of the time should tell severely upon his physical strength ; that it was doing this with alarming effect his outward man soon began to bear witness.   The Colonel, meeting him as he left the hospital tent late one evening, was horrified by his altered appearance.

" Look here, Lyon," he began gruffly, " this won't do.   You're overdoing the thing, that's plain."   The Colonel's mustaches and his manners had alike a touch of fierceness ; but he carried a big soft heart under his padded tunic, and Lyon and he were acquaintances of old standing.   " We shall be having you go down next.   Can't afford that—you're too useful !   Now, take my advice.   Get to your quarters, and to bed, at once ; and don't stir again before eight to-morrow morning."

" My dear Colonel, the general panic is beginning to infect even

your steady judgment.   I assure you I haven't a single suspicious
symptom.''

"Never said you had," growled the old soldier.   "But it's all
one, whether a man dies of cholera or over-work.   I'll walk round
with you."

Lyon's quarters were in a hut about a quarter of a mile off.
But, short as was the distance to be traversed in order to reach
them, the Colonel soon became aware that his companion found it
difficult to cover.   He walked slowly, dragging one foot after
another, never voluntarily opening his lips, and replying only by
monosyllables to the remarks addressed to him.   Arrived at the
hut, he entered it hastily, staggering slightly as he crossed the
threshold, and rather fell into a chair than sat down upon it.

"Excuse me—I believe I *am* rather done up," he observed
apologetically to the Colonel, who had slowly followed him in.
"Won't you sit down?"

"Can't stay; wish I could!   You—— You're rather cumbered
with furniture here," the Colonel remarked, suddenly changing
his mind as to the wisdom of the ejaculation to which he had been
about to give voice, and looking round in soldierly disapprobation
of the disorderly room, with its medley of household goods, books,
mathematical instruments, and camp-bed, a table loaded with
papers, maps, and plans, and having a lighted lamp upon it,
standing in the midst—an island of neatness in a sea of confusion.

"Yes.   They were pulling everything down over at my place;
moving the camp bodily to a clean spot.   So I brought my traps
here for safety."

Lyon leaned back wearily, pushing the heavy hair from his
forehead.   His hair, though it had become most unequivocally
gray, was still thick.

The Colonel strode across the untidy floor, stepping over a pile
of books, a theodolite, and a pair of boots on his way, to the
business-table, where he stood looking down half absently at the
piles of papers.

"That book of yours," he jerked out abruptly.   "When will it
be finished?"

"Probably by the Greek Calends."

"Not much time for writing, I suppose?   Well, if you hadn't
come over to help us out here, you might have done a stroke of
work these last weeks.   I believe I've never mentioned the fact"—

here the Colonel cleared his throat and straightened his back—" but we're awfully obliged to you, one and all of us."

Lyon made a deprecating gesture. He appeared too tired to speak.

" It seems a pity about that book, though," the Colonel went on, with a vague idea of showing himself sympathizing. Somehow it had been borne in upon him that his companion stood in need of sympathy that evening. " Is it far advanced ? "

" No. Quite in the rough still—altogether shapeless It doesn't matter," Lyon added in a curiously lifeless tone.

The Colonel gave him a sharp glance. " Well, I must go, worse luck ! " he observed, moving toward the door. " As for you, consider yourself under orders to get to bed immediately, and stay there for the next nine hours at least."

" Very sorry to infringe discipline, Colonel "—Lyon made rather an unsuccessful attempt to smile here—" but I'm afraid I can't promise to obey those orders to the letter. I told Hart I would be back at the hospital tent by half-past three, and one of the orderlies is to call me at three o'clock. If I didn't go, Hart would be obliged to keep Morris up all night ; and the poor lad is worn out now."

" So are you."

" It's only ten ; there are four—five hours yet before I shall be wanted. I'll go to bed till three. Good-night, Colonel ; don't bother yourself about me."

" Well, good-night. You're an obstinate chap."

The Colonel shut the rickety door behind him, and tramped off. After a few moments Lyon heaved himself heavily out of his chair, and crossed to the table.

" I certainly feel queer," he muttered half aloud. " I won-der—— In that case, there are a few things—— I ought to have provided for such a contingency before. I did think of it, once or twice ; but this cholera business put everything else out of my head."

He drew another chair in front of the table and, sitting down in it, began to turn over some of the papers before him with uncertain fingers.

" Nothing of any consequence "— propping his head on his hand. " Notes for the unlucky book ; it would take a long time to tear them up. Besides, anyone is welcome to them, for waste paper or otherwise. No photographs ; no love-letters "—with a strange fugitive smile. "The only letter she ever wrote me—to say she was going to marry Travers—hardly comes under that denomination. Still, perhaps, I had better destroy it."

He reached across for a small leather despatch-box standing on the other side of the table. This, after a good deal of fumbling with the key, he proceeded to unlock; and, having taken out of it a square envelope, extracted from the envelope a sheet of paper which he read once through, and then tore carefully into small pieces. "The pity of it!" he said bitterly to himself, as the fragments fluttered down from his hand upon the table. "The unutterable pity of it all! How is it with her now, I wonder? James is there by now. Will James be able to effect anything? Curious to think that I shall never know."

Some of the fluttering fragments had fallen into the open box; mechanically putting in his hand to pick them out, he struck it against something hard. "What's this?" he exclaimed, lifting it to the light of the lamp.

It was the china dog that had been little Dolly's parting gift. He laid it gently down upon the table beside him, with a passing quiver of the lip.

"At least I need not trouble to destroy *that*," he said to himself. "There remains the letter to be written. I don't suppose it will do any good. At the same time, it can't do any harm."

He drew a sheet of paper toward him, dipped his pen, after knocking it two or three times awkwardly against the outer rim of the ink-bottle, and wrote, in a shaky hand which sprawled unevenly across the page:

"CAMP, KURREE, August 10, 189—.

"MY DEAR BRIAN:

"We have known each other so long that I venture to hope you won't take this letter amiss. Dying men are supposed to be privileged in various ways; you must forgive me if I make use of my privileges in a fashion that is distasteful to you."

Lyon's hand did not grow any steadier as he wrote. On the contrary, he experienced an increasing difficulty in controlling its movements. Also, each time he dipped his pen, it took him longer to find his way into the ink. Still, he struggled to write on:

"I had best be quite frank. My sole object [here his handwriting became almost illegible] in writing at all is to make an appeal to you.   Is it too late——"

And now, not only was he unable to decipher what he had written, but the very sheet on which he had written it seemed to have turned from white to black.   As for the inkstand it appeared to be yards distant from him.   He dropped his pen with a groan of despair.   "I can't," he muttered helplessly, leaning his face on his hands.   "I can't.   Not to-night, at any rate.   To-morrow, perhaps—unless this is the beginning of the end.   Ah!"

With a sharp cry, wrung from him apparently by some sudden acute pain, he fell forward across the table, his outstretched right hand clenching the little china toy lying close to it in a grasp of iron.   When, after a few minutes, the paroxysm passed, and he could lift his face again, he lifted it, not merely white and drawn, but significantly altered.   The shadow of a great change had passed upon it.

Slowly and uncertainly he got to his feet.   "There's no doubt about it," he murmured.   "The Colonel was right.   I must go to bed at once."

With the help of the furniture he dragged himself painfully across the room.   In his exhausted and only half-conscious condition it never occurred to him to put aside the object on which his fingers had closed involuntarily in his agony, and he sank down upon his camp-bed still holding fast Dolly's china dog.   The change of posture brought a blessed sense of relief.

"Only a passing attack," he told himself.   "That pain was horrible while it lasted, though; I suspect it signifies a good deal. I must get the letter written to-morrow, without fail."

.   .   .   .   .   .

It was just four o'clock on the morrow when the Colonel carried a face graver even than that he had worn since the commencement of the epidemic into the drawing-room of his bungalow, two miles distant from the cholera-camp, where his wife and sister were sitting.   So downcast was his expression that the two women were moved to ask in one breath:

"Is anything the matter?   Has there been a new outbreak?"

"No, there were fewer fresh cases during the night; and only two deaths.   But—we've had a loss."   The Colonel laid down his helmet with a shaking hand.   "Poor Lyon's gone."

" How terribly sudden ! " exclaimed the wife. And—" I saw him only yesterday morning," chimed in the sister. " Of course, when cholera is in question——"

"It wasn't cholera. Heart-disease—aggravated by over-exertion, *I* suspect. He has been working like a horse this past fortnight."

" When was it—this morning ? "

" The hospital orderly went to call him at three o'clock, and found him lying on his bed, still dressed. All had been over hours before, Mackenzie says ; he must have died quite early in the night." The Colonel gulped down something in his throat, and walked over to the window. " We buried him an hour ago."

" Are you certain he died of heart-disease ? " This question proceeded from the Colonel's wife—a strong-featured, strong-minded lady entirely devoid of sentiment. " People are so fond of killing themselves nowadays ; and he was just the kind of man likely to commit suicide : a trifle morbid, and very bad-tempered."

The Colonel interposed roughly : " You may dismiss any idea of his having killed himself from your mind altogether. Mackenzie had known for months that he was in a precarious condition, and warned him, some time ago, that his only chance of prolonging his life lay in going home. I'm ashamed to say, the same conjecture did occur to me for one moment, when Mackenzie first called me in to look at him—and I believe to some of our fellows as well. He had something tight clenched in his hand, and we very uncharitably leaped to the conclusion that it was a chloroform bottle."

" It *was* a bottle ? "

" Nothing of the kind. A ridiculous little china ornament—dog, or cat, or animal of some description ; looked like a child's toy more than anything else. How he came to have it in his hand, no one knows, of course. But his desk was open, and his papers and things were all scattered about : plainly he had been trying to make a clearance of his belongings—tearing up letters and what not—before he lay down and fainted, or fell asleep, whichever it was. He may have had associations connected with this toy."

" Not very likely, seeing the poor man had neither wife nor child." Mrs. Colonel pursed up her lips. " I am sorry to hear of his dying in this mournful way," she added, after a moment.

"Not that I ever particularly liked the man. There was something cold and hard about him. And, really, it seems that he is chiefly to blame for his own death. When Mackenzie told him to go home, he should have gone. He could easily have got leave ; and, being a man without ties, pecuniary considerations could not have stood in his way."

"One never knows," her sister-in-law put in kindly, moved by an amiable wish to defend the character of a person forever precluded henceforward from self-defence. "I dare say he lingered out here partly with a view to finishing his book. He was writing a book on India, wasn't he ?"

"I know he was supposed to be writing one. I'm not quite sure I ever believed in that book."

"No supposition about the matter," the Colonel said shortly. "I've seen some of the notes he had got together for the work."

"Just so," nodded his wife, who was not easily silenced or subdued. "The notes I don't doubt. But did you ever see anything beyond the notes ? For my part, I shouldn't fancy any work of Mr. Lyon's likely to get further than the note stage. His whole career, as far as I know it, seemed to be a history of beginnings, with no results following. People of his temperament don't write books ; or if they begin to write them, they invariably leave them unfinished. Do you know in what state he has left his papers, George ?"

George growled something, hardly intelligible, about "rough drafts," and "Lyon's not having had time to reduce his material to order."

"He never would have had time, you may be certain—not if he had lived to the age of Methuselah, take my word for it !" the lady retorted, with firmness. "How old was he, by the by ? Someone told me he was only two-and-forty, but I always thought he looked forty-eight at the least. You will have to write to his people, of course. Very painful. Who were his nearest relatives ?"

"He had no relatives that I know of—near or far. He has left a letter, just commenced, to a man called Brian, who would seem to have been an intimate friend ; Mackenzie is trying to find some clue to this man's address among the papers. I hope we may light upon it. If we don't, I shall send a line to the little padre who went home the other day—what's his name ? Travers. I know

Lyon used to see a good deal of him. It seems to make the business all the sadder, there being no one to whom one can even send the news of the poor fellow's death !"

"Really, I can't agree with you there, George. Since he is dead, it's just as well his death should not be cause of special grief to anyone. At the same time, his being so poor in friends does not speak well for him. It shows him to have been what I always pronounced him, thoroughly unsympathetic."

"Well, he wasn't over-genial, perhaps," the Colonel admitted ; his habitual awe of his self-confident and determined partner getting the better of his distaste for such outspoken criticism of a man who had only lain just an hour in his grave. "Still"—here generosity got the upper hand once more—"you mustn't be too hard on the poor chap, Bessie. He wasn't a bad sort at bottom. But he stood quite alone in the world ; I think he was rather painfully conscious of having no special place in it. And that kind of consciousness doesn't tend to make a man amiable."

"Whose fault was it, except his own, if he did stand alone ?" demanded the implacable censor, rising to her feet, as a preparation to quitting the room and the discussion. "People can always make themselves a special place in the world, if they please. All the same, I am sorry to hear your news, George ; very sorry. In a way, the death of a man who has done nothing with his life is sadder than that of one who has accomplished great things. One feels that there has been such a waste of opportunity."

With this parting shot the lady retired, shutting the door behind her. Her sister-in-law remained silent until all sound of retreating footsteps had died away ; then she timidly addressed the Colonel, who still stood at the window with his back toward her.

"George !"

"Well ?" The Colonel's voice sounded hoarse.

"George, don't think me foolish, but—but I should so much like to know what you did—with that thing you found—the toy, I mean ?"

The Colonel cleared his throat noisily. "Oh—ah ! the toy ! What did I do ? To tell you the truth, I was rather puzzled *what* to do. There might be associations, as I said ; and I knew of no one to whom to send the thing. So I considered—and—and in the end the simplest plan seemed—just to leave it where it was."

"You buried it with him ?"

The Colonel nodded assent. Then he took off his glasses, and began to polish them violently, still carefully keeping his back to the room.

"It—it was a piece of confounded idiotic sentiment, no doubt," he said, in even huskier tones than before. "I ought to be ashamed of it. But it seemed about the only thing one could do for the poor chap. You needn't mention this nonsense to Bessie," he added apprehensively, with a quick glance over his shoulder at the closed door. "Do you hear, Amabel?"

Amabel signed her acquiescence, not having any words at command just then. Like her brother, she was soft-hearted, and, at times, a trifle sentimental.

THE END

By CONSTANCE F. WOOLSON.

HORACE CHASE. A Novel. 16mo, Cloth, $1 25.

JUPITER LIGHTS. A Novel. 16mo, Cloth, $1 25.

EAST ANGELS. A Novel. 16mo, Cloth, $1 25.

ANNE. A Novel. Illustrated. 16mo, Cloth, $1 25.

FOR THE MAJOR. A Novelette. 16mo, Cloth, $1 00.

CASTLE NOWHERE. Lake - Country Sketches. 16mo, Cloth, $1 00.

RODMAN THE KEEPER. Southern Sketches. 16mo, Cloth, $1 00.

Delightful touches justify those who see many points of analogy between Miss Woolson and George Eliot.—*N. Y. Times.*

For tenderness and purity of thought, for exquisitely delicate sketching of characters, Miss Woolson is unexcelled among writers of fiction.—*New Orleans Picayune.*

Characterization is Miss Woolson's forte. Her men and women are not mere puppets, but original, breathing, and finely contrasted creations.—*Chicago Tribune.*

Miss Woolson is one of the few novelists of the day who know how to make conversation, how to individualize the speakers, how to exclude rabid realism without falling into literary formality.—*N. Y. Tribune.*

Constance Fenimore Woolson may easily become the novelist laureate.—*Boston Globe.*

Miss Woolson has a graceful fancy, a ready wit, a polished style, and conspicuous dramatic power; while her skill in the development of a story is very remarkable.—*London Life.*

Miss Woolson never once follows the beaten track of the orthodox novelist, but strikes a new and richly-loaded vein which, so far, is all her own; and thus we feel, on reading one of her works, a fresh sensation, and we put down the book with a sigh to think our pleasant task of reading it is finished. The author's lines must have fallen to her in very pleasant places; or she has, perhaps, within herself the wealth of womanly love and tenderness she pours so freely into all she writes. Such books as hers do much to elevate the moral tone of the day—a quality sadly wanting in novels of the time.— *Whitehall Review*, London.

PUBLISHED BY HARPER & BROTHERS, NEW YORK.

R. D. BLACKMORE'S NOVELS.

PERLYCROSS. A Novel. 12mo, Cloth, Ornamental, $1 75.

Told with delicate and delightful art. Its pictures of rural English scenes and characters will woo and solace the reader. . . . It is charming company in charming surroundings. Its pathos, its humor, and its array of natural incidents are all satisfying. One must feel thankful for so finished and exquisite a story. . . . Not often do we find a more impressive piece of work.—*N. Y. Sun.*

A new novel from the pen of R. D. Blackmore is as great a treat to the fastidious and discriminating novel-reader as a new and rare dish is to an epicure. . . . A story to be lingered over with delight.—*Boston Beacon.*

SPRINGHAVEN. Illustrated, 12mo, Cloth, $1 50; 4to, Paper, 25 cents.

LORNA DOONE. Illustrated. 12mo, Cloth, $1 00; 8vo, Paper, 40 cents.

KIT AND KITTY. 12mo, Cloth, $1 25; Paper, 35 cents.

CHRISTOWELL. 4to, Paper, 20 cents.

CRADOCK NOWELL. 8vo, Paper, 60 cents.

EREMA; OR, MY FATHER'S SIN. 8vo, Paper, 50 cents.

MARY ANERLEY. 16mo, Cloth, $1 00; 4to, Paper, 15 cents.

TOMMY UPMORE. 16mo, Cloth, 50 cents; Paper, 35 cents; 4to, Paper, 20 cents.

His descriptions are wonderfully vivid and natural. His pages are brightened everywhere with great humor; the quaint, dry turns of thought remind you occasionally of Fielding.—*London Times.*

His tales, all of them, are pre-eminently meritorious. They are remarkable for their careful elaboration, the conscientious finish of their workmanship, their affluence of striking dramatic and narrative incident, their close observation and general interpretation of nature, their profusion of picturesque description, and their quiet and sustained humor.—*Christian Intelligencer*, N. Y.

PUBLISHED BY HARPER & BROTHERS, NEW YORK.

☞ *The above works are for sale by all booksellers, or will be sent by the publishers, postage prepaid, to any part of the United States, Canada, or Mexico, on receipt of the price.*

WALTER BESANT'S WORKS.

We give, without hesitation, the foremost place to Mr. Besant, whose work, always so admirable and spirited, acquires double importance from the enthusiasm with which it is inspired.—*Blackwood's Magazine*, Edinburgh.

Mr. Besant wields the wand of a wizard, let him wave it in whatever direction he will. . . . The spell that dwells in this wand is formed by intense earnestness and vivid imagination.—*Spectator*, London.

There is a bluff, honest, hearty, and homely method about Mr. Besant's stories which makes them acceptable, and because he is so easily understood is another reason why he is so particularly relished by the English public.—*N. Y. Times.*

ALL IN A GARDEN FAIR. 4to, Paper, 20 cents.

ALL SORTS AND CONDITIONS OF MEN. Illustrated. 12mo, Cloth, $1 25; 8vo, Paper, 50 cents.

ARMOREL OF LYONESSE. Illustrated. 12mo, Cloth, $1 25; 8vo, Paper, 50 cents.

CHILDREN OF GIBEON. 12mo, Cloth, $1 25; 8vo, Paper, 50 cents.

DOROTHY FORSTER. 4to, Paper, 20 cents.

FIFTY YEARS AGO. Illustrated. 8vo, Cloth, $2 50.

FOR FAITH AND FREEDOM. Illustrated. 12mo, Cloth, $1 25; 8vo, Paper, 50 cents.

HERR PAULUS. 8vo, Paper, 35 cents.

KATHERINE REGINA. 4to, Paper, 15 cents.

LIFE OF COLIGNY. 32mo, Cloth, 40 cents; Paper, 25 cents.

SELF OR BEARER. 4to, Paper, 15 cents.

LONDON. Illustrated. 8vo, Cloth, Ornamental, $3 00.

ST. KATHARINE'S BY THE TOWER. Illustrated. 12mo, Cloth, $1 25; Paper, 50 cents.

THE BELL OF ST. PAUL'S. 8vo, Paper, 35 cents.

THE HOLY ROSE. 4to, Paper, 20 cents.

THE INNER HOUSE. 8vo, Paper, 30 cents.

THE IVORY GATE. 12mo, Cloth, $1 25.

THE REBEL QUEEN. Illustrated. 12mo, Cloth, $1 50.

THE WORLD WENT VERY WELL THEN. Illustr'd. 12mo, Cloth, $1 25; 4to, Paper, 25 cents.

TO CALL HER MINE. Illustrated. 4to, Paper, 20 cents.

UNCLE JACK AND OTHER STORIES. 12mo, Paper, 25 cents.

PUBLISHED BY HARPER & BROTHERS, NEW YORK.

☞ *Any of the above works will be sent by mail, postage prepaid, to any part of the United States, Canada, or Mexico, on receipt of the price.*

WILLIAM BLACK'S NOVELS.

LIBRARY EDITION.

A DAUGHTER OF HETH.
A PRINCESS OF THULE.
DONALD ROSS OF HEIMRA.
GREEN PASTURES AND PICCA-
DILLY.
IN FAR LOCHABER.
IN SILK ATTIRE.
JUDITH SHAKESPEARE. Illus-
trated by ABBEY.
KILMENY.
MACLEOD OF DARE. Illustrated.
MADCAP VIOLET.
PRINCE FORTUNATUS. Ill'd.
SABINA SEMBRA.
SHANDON BELLS. Illustrated.

STAND FAST, CRAIG-ROYSTON!
Illustrated.
SUNRISE.
THAT BEAUTIFUL WRETCH.
Illustrated.
THE MAGIC INK, AND OTHER
STORIES. Illustrated.
THE STRANGE ADVENTURES
OF A HOUSE-BOAT. Ill'd.
THE STRANGE ADVENTURES
OF A PHAETON.
THREE FEATHERS.
WHITE HEATHER.
WHITE WINGS. Illustrated.
YOLANDE. Illustrated.

12mo, Cloth, $1 25 per volume.

WOLFENBERG.—THE HANDSOME HUMES.

Illustrated. 12mo, Cloth, $1 50 per volume.

Complete Sets, 25 Volumes, Cloth, $28 50 ; Half Calf, $54 00.

CHEAP EDITION, IN PAPER COVERS:

Donald Ross of Heimra. 8vo, 50 cents.—*Sabina Zembra.* 4to, 20 cents.
—*White Heather.* 4to, 20 cents.—*Judith Shakespeare.* 4to, 20 cents.—
Yolande. Illustrated. 4to, 20 cents.—*Shandon Bells.* Illustrated. 4to,
20 cents.—*That Beautiful Wretch.* Illustrated. 4to, 20 cents.—*Sunrise.*
4to, 15 cents.—*Macleod of Dare.* Illustrated. 8vo, 60 cents. Illustrated,
4to, 15 cents.—*Green Pastures and Piccadilly.* 8vo, 50 cents.—*Madcap
Violet.* 8vo, 50 cents.—*Three Feathers.* Illustrated. 8vo, 50 cents.—
A Daughter of Heth. 8vo, 35 cents.—*An Adventure in Thule.* 4to, 10
cents.—*A Princess of Thule.* 8vo, 50 cents.—*In Silk Attire.* 8vo, 35
cents.—*Kilmeny.* 8vo, 35 cents.—*The Strange Adventures of a Phaeton.*
8vo, 50 cents.—*White Wings.* 4to, 20 cents.—*The Maid of Killeena, the
Marriage of Moira Fergus, and Other Stories.* 8vo, 40 cents.—*The Mon-
arch of Mincing-Lane.* Illustrated. 8vo, 50 cents.—*The Strange Adventures of a House-Boat.* Illustrated. 8vo, 50 cents.—*In Far Lochaber.*
8vo, 40 cents.—*Prince Fortunatus.* Illustrated. 8vo, 50 cents.

PUBLISHED BY HARPER & BROTHERS, NEW YORK.

☞ *Any of the above works will be sent by mail, postage prepaid, to any part
of the United States, Canada, or Mexico, on receipt of the price.*

www.ingramcontent.com/pod-product-compliance
Lightning Source LLC
LaVergne TN
LVHW012205040326
832903LV00003B/132